Ohx

02/04

17.99

SCOTLAND IN THE EIGHTEENTH CENTURY

SCOTLAND IN THE EIGHTEENTH CENTURY

UNION AND ENLIGHTENMENT

David Allan

An imprint of Pearson Education

Harlow, England · London · New York · Reading, Massachusetts · San Francisco
Toronto · Don Mills, Ontario · Sydney · Tokyo · Singapore · Hong Kong · Seoul
Taipei · Cape Town · Madrid · Mexico City · Amsterdam · Munich · Paris · Milan

PEARSON EDUCATION LIMITED

Head Office:
Edinburgh Gate
Harlow CM20 2JE
Tel: +44 (0)1279 623623
Fax: +44 (0)1279 431059

London Office:
128 Long Acre
London WC2E 9AN
Tel: +44 (0)20 7447 2000
Fax: +44 (0)20 7240 5771
Website: www.history-minds.com

First published in Great Britain in 2002

ISBN 0 582 38247 5

British Library Cataloguing in Publication Data
A CIP catalogue record for this book can be obtained from the British Library

10 9 8 7 6 5 4 3 2

Typeset in 11/13pt Baskerville MT by Graphicraft Limited, Hong Kong
Produced by Pearson Education Asia Pte Ltd
Printed in Singapore

The Publishers' policy is to use paper manufactured from sustainable forests.

CONTENTS

List of Maps ... vii

Acknowledgements ... viii

1. Nation ... 1
   - Convergence and crisis ... 3
   - Treating for Union ... 8
   - The machinery of post-Union politics ... 14
   - Management and patronage ... 20
   - Politics and the people ... 25
   - Patriotism and identity ... 34

2. Belief ... 40
   - A presbyterian Revolution ... 41
   - Controversy and conformity ... 45
   - Jacobitism: ideology and intrigue ... 49
   - The 'Forty-five ... 56
   - Moderatism: toleration and civility ... 63
   - Evangelicalism ... 68
   - Dissent and Popery ... 72
   - Popular superstition ... 76

3. Lives ... 81
   - Population and settlement ... 81
   - National crisis and economic change ... 85
   - Agricultural improvement ... 90
   - Commerce, trade and manufactures ... 96
   - Industrialisation ... 103
   - Social structure and social experience ... 108
   - Social institutions ... 118

4. Ideas ... 127
   - Scottish society and polite culture ... 128
   - 'Nature and nature's laws' ... 133
   - The limits of knowing ... 137
   - 'From savage to Scotchman' ... 142

Sense and sentiment 150
In the mind's eye 156

5. Empire 165
Migrants, mercenaries and the will to empire 165
North America and settlement 168
India and the East 177
An imperial Union 184

6. Endings 186

Bibliographical Essay 192

Index 205

LIST OF MAPS

Map 1 Eighteenth-century Scotland 2
Map 2 Jacobitism and northern Britain, 1689–1746 50
Map 3 North America in the eighteenth century 169
Map 4 India in the eighteenth century 178

ACKNOWLEDGEMENTS

In producing a work such as this, one inevitably accumulates debts to other people, and it is a pleasure to acknowledge their assistance here. Numerous friends and colleagues shouldered the burden of reading and commenting on my drafts, frequently (though probably not always) saving me from myself: Rab Houston, Keith Brown, Bill Knox, Bruce Lenman, Richard Saville, Robert Crawford, Nicholas Phillipson, Alexander Murdoch, Andrew Mackillop, Roger Emerson, Andrew Nicholls, Mark Spencer, Helena Thorley, Alexander Thorley, David Palmer and Katie Price (now Allan). I am grateful also to Hamish Scott for some important kindnesses, and to Andrew Maclennan and Heather McCallum at Longman for editorial support throughout the period from proposal to publication. Finally I should mention those undergraduates in the University of St Andrews to whom I have tried to explain different aspects of eighteenth-century Scotland. They may be surprised to learn that their suggestions and encouragement were important factors in the completion of this book.

CHAPTER ONE

Nation

One issue above all was made so problematical by eighteenth-century events that it continues to perplex the Scots even today: their nationhood – the need continually to ask 'Who are we?' The answer, of course, has never been entirely straightforward. A convoluted political and religious relationship with the English, the unavoidable fact of extreme geographical proximity and deeply rooted ethnic and linguistic ties have ever muddied the water. Yet the late-medieval conflicts with England, continuing sporadically into the sixteenth century, had somehow fashioned a collective identity among Scotland's disparate inhabitants, infusing them with a profound sense of their own separateness. If knowing what properly defined a Scot remained complicated – first amid intensifying hostilities between the country's Gaelic-speaking Highlanders and Scots-speaking Lowlanders and then because of the people's own violent religious differences following the Reformation – a working solution to the problem, frequently repeated and almost universally endorsed by all ranks and persuasions, gradually emerged. Whatever else they might be, the Scots, by the later seventeenth century, could at least be sure that they were not English.

The impact of the Treaty of Union, by whose ratification in 1707 the last Edinburgh Parliament agreed that Scotland should be incorporated into a newly forged British state governed from the English capital, was therefore necessarily unsettling. Deciding whether to establish these new arrangements in the first place, as well as which of several possible variant forms they might take, inevitably caused internal convulsions. All manner of other issues were also left unresolved for the Scots by the creation of a new polity. Key questions were in fact settled not in the surprisingly laconic treaty but in the slow and difficult evolution of political practice over succeeding decades: What precisely was to be the new role of Scotland's politicians and

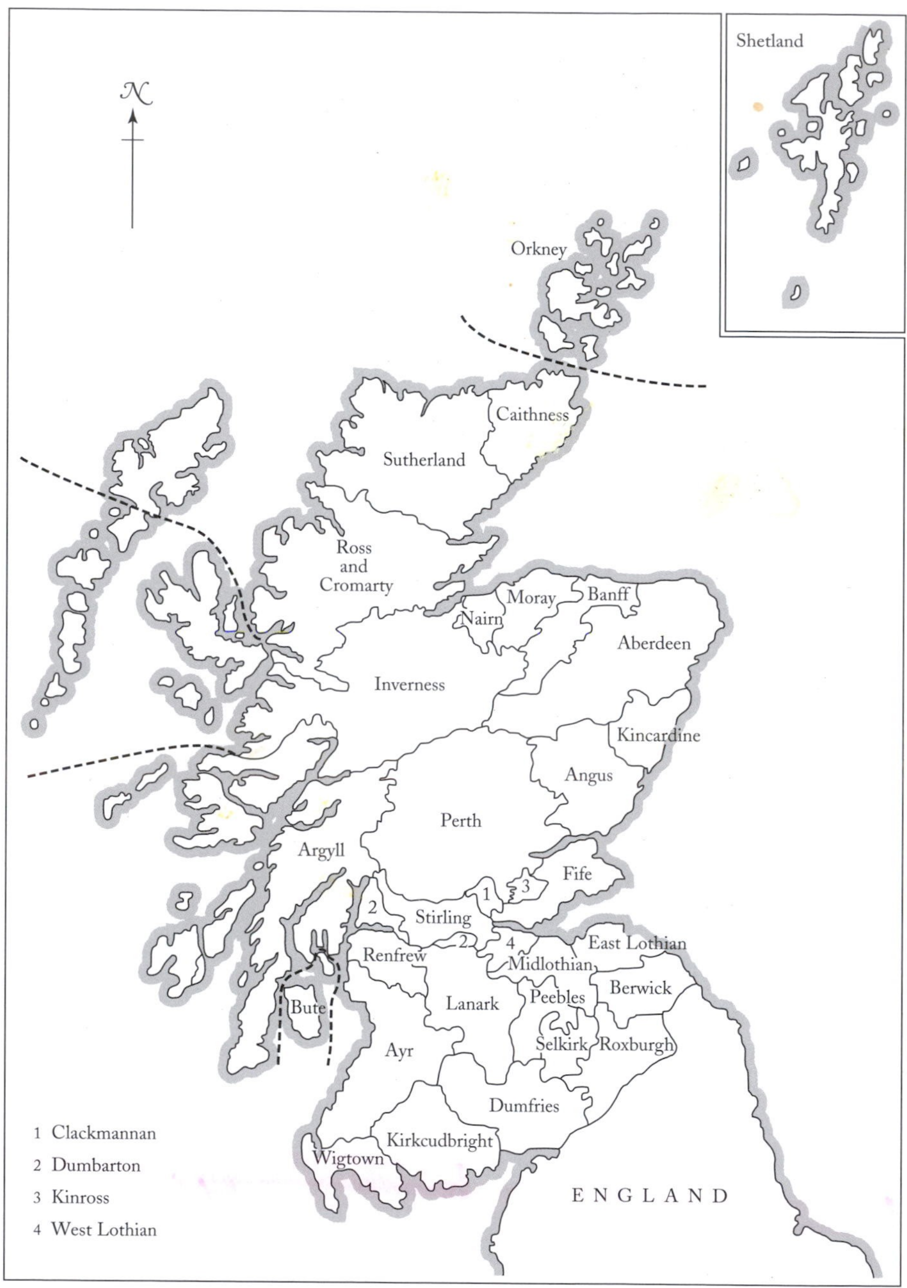
N
Shetland
Orkney
Caithness
Sutherland
Ross
and
Cromarty
Moray
Banff
Nairn
Aberdeen
Inverness
Kincardine
Angus
Perth
Argyll
Fife
1
3
2
Stirling
2
4
East Lothian
Renfrew
Midlothian
Berwick
Bute
Lanark
Peebles
Selkirk
Roxburgh
Ayr
Dumfries
Kirkcudbright
Wigtown
ENGLAND
1 Clackmannan
2 Dumbarton
3 Kinross
4 West Lothian

Map 1 Eighteenth-century Scotland

institutions? How might the Scots secure their own interests within a predominantly English state? And would Westminster seek to preserve or to erode Scotland's distinctiveness? Even less clear were the ramifications for the Scots' identity. In particular, if nationhood were ordinarily expressed through the free exercise of sovereign self-government, had Scotland itself also ceased to exist in 1707? Whatever their views, and however they preferred to answer these questions, all Scots were forced to confront the consequences of Union. It is with the background to this epochal event that we must begin.

Convergence and crisis

In 1700 the separate kingdoms of Scotland and England still had a considerable distance to travel before their slightly awkward marriage could be consummated. Mutual suspicion, at times verging on a complete breakdown in relations, marked the notably cantankerous years leading up to the treaty. Superficially it can appear that Union was the result of irresistible processes of convergence – that, if not quite inevitable, it was the product of long-term forces pressing the two neighbours ever closer to some kind of lasting political unification. While this interpretation certainly dominated between the eighteenth and mid-twentieth centuries, recent historiography, less deferential towards older pieties, has begged to differ. It is now generally agreed that, although specific trends of convergence can indeed be identified as far back as the sixteenth century (especially those arising out of both people's shared formal commitment to Protestantism), so too were deeply rooted patterns of divergence also strongly evident. These were in fact still driving the two old enemies further apart until a surprisingly advanced stage in the pre-Union proceedings.

The political developments of the seventeenth century were not the least of the hindrances to closer and happier Anglo-Scottish relations. The experience of the 'regal union' or 'union of the crowns', stemming from 1603 when James VI of Scotland had succeeded his mother's childless cousin Elizabeth, Queen of England, thus beginning an often unhappy arrangement by which two historically antagonistic kingdoms shared the same monarch, lay at the root of the strained relationship. Pro-unionists ever since 1603 have pointedly interpreted this royal connection as a milestone on the road to greater intimacy; and the Treaty of Union was indeed, as we shall see, in many ways a solution to the constitutional and diplomatic tensions which were James VI and I's peculiar legacy to his successors (though it was not, it should be added, the only possible solution: elsewhere in seventeenth-century Europe, the Habsburgs' awkward tenure of both the Bohemian monarchy and the German emperorship did not result in a unified state). But the intrinsic problems of multiple monarchy, especially when it is remembered that a third throne – that of Ireland – came along with James's English inheritance, led many Scots to even greater resentment of England's pre-eminence within the British Isles. It also prepared them to resist any suggestion that their own future might lie with absorption in what would inevitably be an anglocentric polity.

Historians have lately grown fond of interpreting seventeenth-century British history in terms of this so-called 'three kingdoms' perspective. Yet the tangled relationships between the separate polities ruled over by the Stuarts after 1603 do seem to provide the key to understanding many of the age's major events. The political and military crisis of the late 1630s and 1640s, for example, which lost James's son Charles I not only his three crowns but his head, might convincingly be explained as a disastrous manifestation of the problems latent in Britain's haphazardly arranged multiple monarchy, the patchwork product not of coherent planning or rational strategy but of the biological accident of James's inheritance. In this context Charles's catastrophic attempt to import essentially English religious forms into a very different Scottish environment, so compelling his irate Scottish subjects to apply pressure to their shared king by successfully invading northern England in the so-called 'Bishops' Wars', was the immediate trigger which ignited the combustible materials which had accumulated in the south by 1642.

Attempts by successive Stuarts to consolidate the narrowly personal union of 1603, and to make the multiple monarchy more congruent and more manageable, also met with little success. James himself had tried in vain to persuade his English and Scots subjects to form a unitary state. His grandson Charles II likewise failed to convince the sceptical statesmen of London and Edinburgh that royal proposals for economic union (1668) and parliamentary union (1670) were in their mutual interests. Indeed, it says something not only about the obvious administrative attractions but also about the formidable obstacles in the way of Anglo-Scottish union that between 1652 and 1660 it was Cromwell's all-conquering revolutionary regime, the only real military dictatorship in British history, which briefly boasted this unique achievement among its dubious accolades.

The fundamental contradiction of multiple monarchy – a compelling pragmatic case for institutional integration so as to make possible its more effective management, yet also continuous resistance from each kingdom arising out of distinctive identities and traditions – runs throughout the entire seventeenth century, afflicting all who shared, or aspired to share, a wider British vision. The difficulties of tripartite government, however, were not only those of Stuart ministers or Cromwellian administrators struggling from London to rule three incorrigibly divergent peoples. Seen from the perspective of the Scottish people or the Edinburgh Parliament, multiple monarchy was not that much more satisfactory. Even discounting the ill-advised attempts by both Charles I and Charles II to impose an Anglican model on the Scots' distinctive religious institutions, always regarded as the *locus classicus* of the threat posed to Scotland by a monarch whose own ideas and inclinations were disproportionately shaped by English experiences, the decades prior to the Treaty of Union offered abundant further evidence against the regal union. In particular, this period had underlined the fact that the convoluted inheritance of James VI and I would tend more often than not to work to the disadvantage of the smaller, weaker and more distant of the two main Stuart kingdoms.

Not only had a reigning King of Scotland deigned to visit his subjects just twice since ascending the English throne (James VI in 1617 and Charles I in 1633). To the obvious problem of absentee monarchy was also added the grave constitutional risk that decisions affecting Scotland's crown – and indeed other vital aspects of her national life – would effectively be dictated by the English Parliament. On this point the seventeenth-century evidence was distinctly discouraging. It was mainly agreements between Westminster and Charles II that had brought about that king's unexpected return to his late father's three British thrones in 1660. Again in 1688–89 it was a narrow conspiracy among English parliamentarians which engineered William and Mary's successful invasion and James VII and II's consequent loss of his predecessors' British patrimony. In both cases Edinburgh was left to grapple with the results of unforeseen English decisions which nevertheless had the most drastic implications for Scotland's own government. Finding itself negotiating the conditions on which these monarchs might govern in Scotland long after their general suitability had already been determined by London, the Scots Parliament was more than once forced to accept that, precisely because they were not the concern of an exclusively English parliament at Westminster, Scotland's vital interests were being compromised by a fundamental asymmetry in the geo-political architecture of seventeenth-century Britain. Thus when William after 1689 had once more raised the possibility of parliamentary union, it is not surprising that many Scots, including some who would later oppose the 1707 treaty, favoured it. Indeed, the proposal eventually foundered more on English apathy than on Scottish resistance.

This assessment of Scotland's chronic weakness in its relations with its own sovereign, which had attained widespread credibility throughout the political community at the turn of the eighteenth century, had most recently been borne out by the events of the 1690s. England's preponderance in national wealth, military and naval power and political ambition was becoming ever more obvious. Under William's firm hand the Westminster Parliament was emerging at the helm of a fiscal–military state of considerable authority, leading a Continental coalition at war with the France of Louis XIV between 1689 and 1697 and engaged in confident imperial and commercial extension as far afield as the Indian subcontinent and North America's eastern seaboard: small wonder that the views and advice of the king's Edinburgh parliamentarians, especially if unwelcome or contrary, were ignored. To compound insult with injury, William's wars also badly hit Scotland's export trade. Although they closed many northern European ports to all British vessels, the Scots' exclusion from England's Atlantic trade and consequent over-dependence upon North Sea commerce in particular meant that they suffered disproportionately. Worst of all, with armies still substantially controlled by kings rather than parliaments, Scottish soldiers and officers, as part of the royal army, were routinely used by William, alongside those of his regiments raised south of the Border, to pursue the crown's strategic objectives on the Continent.

By far the most dramatic recent case of English priorities overriding Scottish interests, however, was the infamous Darien scheme in which the Scots Parliament had lent its full support to an attempt to establish a trading colony on the coast of Central America. Inspired by a desire to emulate English and Dutch colonial successes, the first expedition set sail in July 1698 with orders 'to proceed to the Bay of Darien . . . and there make a settlement on the mainland as well as the said island, if proper (as we believe) and unpossessed by an European nation or state in amity with his Majesty'. Although a second voyage was made in 1699, the venture was an unmitigated disaster. The territory in question was claimed by Spain. William, whose peaceable relations with Madrid were an integral part of his strategy against Louis XIV, declined to employ his diplomatic or military resources to protect his ill-advised Scottish subjects from Iberian wrath: the king's refusal to intervene may have greatly pleased rival English trading interests (particularly the powerful East India Company) but it caused predictable fury in Scotland. It remains true that tropical disease and inept planning were also factors in a financial catastrophe which lost investors huge sums. Yet the wider constitutional lessons were no less evident to politically literate Scots. Labouring under a form of multiple monarchy which granted the peripheral kingdom little leverage over its own sovereign and no say at all in the parliamentary deliberations of the dominant nation, Scotland was in crying need of some kind of re-working of the British systems of government.

Just as these painful examples of Scotland's progressive marginalisation were accumulating, contemporary events also offered further evidence that the country's existing political apparatus was becoming less and less effective. Indeed, even eventual opponents of the 1707 treaty seem to have become convinced that the status quo – a kingless kingdom within a multiple monarchy whose centre of gravity lay elsewhere – was no longer a viable option. The ensuing debate about Scotland's destiny, however, was strongly coloured by the economic crisis which afflicted the country throughout the 1690s. Partly this was the product of the Continental wars disrupting Scottish trade; but it was also the result of a succession of dreadful harvests across Scotland through the second half of that blighted decade. Starvation, famine and unemployment occurred on an alarming scale, all the more worrying against the backdrop of the deepening disaster in Darien, and ever greater awareness of England's contrasting plenty and prosperity, which clouded the last years of the old century.

Most Scottish politicians by 1700 were therefore agreed that fundamental change was needed to guarantee national survival. For some, like Andrew Fletcher of Saltoun, with his fiery temperament and lairdly prejudices but also his brilliantly original mind, the solution lay in a linked series of measures which he recommended as commissioner (i.e. parliamentary representative) for East Lothian and as the author of several topical pamphlets, most notably *Two Discourses Concerning the Affairs of Scotland* (1698). These included draconian measures to bind the poor to the soil and deport vagrants to the Venetian galleys; the establishment of a militia subject to ferocious discipline; a prohibition on the charging of interest; a programme of concerted agricultural development; some equalisation of personal wealth; and, most intriguingly, a speculative scheme reorganising Britain and Europe into roughly equal states under the public-spirited control of their propertied elites. Fletcher's latter-day admirers understandably gloss over the illiberal elements in this extraordinary package. But the consistent preference for devices which would check the growth of central authority also betrays his sense that Scottish liberties and Scottish interests were coming increasingly under threat from an Anglo-Dutch commercial and military superpower. This perception, leading him strongly to oppose the Treaty of Union in due course (even though he had earlier supported William's union proposals), has naturally made Fletcher an icon for modern anti-unionists. Yet the far-fetched nature of his constitutional proposals, at least to his unconvinced contemporary opponents, also spoke volumes about the state of the country. In essence, they confirmed that Scotland, unquestionably a nation in crisis, was rapidly running out of credible alternatives.

Treating for Union

This was the variegated longer-term background to the making of the treaty: a confusion of centrifugal and centripetal forces pulling England and Scotland apart while simultaneously pushing them together, all of them at work in an environment in which informed Scottish opinion was becoming more and more convinced that the nation's condition required drastic improvement. The first years of the new century were not much different, except that, just as the reasons for seeking an Anglo-Scottish union became even more cogent, so resistance to it also grew more intense. England's burgeoning wealth and power were unarguable facts which still bewitched most Scottish observers. Yet it was actually a new problem which was to prove decisive. Crucially, it was this that finally convinced English politicians, long at least as sceptical as their Scottish counterparts, that union with the king's much smaller and poorer northern kingdom was in their own interests. Typically, however, this issue also generated even greater tension in Anglo-Scottish relations in the short term, at first making any kind of voluntary union between the kingdoms appear only a remote possibility.

The new factor was the royal succession, an issue rendered peculiarly fraught by William's childlessness and the growing awareness that Mary's younger sister Anne, whose only surviving child died in that year, was likewise unable to supply a living heir. Given the very real possibility (actually borne out in 1715) that the exiled James VII and II or his son might exploit these failings by attempting a Catholic restoration by force of arms, aided by their protector and co-religionist Louis XIV, who strongly backed their claim, Westminster once again decided to take matters into its own hands. In 1701 the Act of Settlement was passed in London, specifically excluding Catholics from the English throne. It settled the destination of the crown after Anne's death on a distant but impeccably Protestant candidate: Sophia, Electoress of Hanover and the German grand-daughter of James VI and I.

This was in one sense an understandable precaution given contemporary paranoia about the twin evils of Popery and tyranny supposedly associated with the deposed Catholic line of the Stuarts. Yet the Act was greeted with horror in Edinburgh. As a unilateral English decision, it flagrantly ignored legitimate Scottish interest in the identity of future British monarchs: just as in 1660 and 1688, Westminster, concerned solely with English interests, had pre-empted any decisions by the Scots Parliament and effectively presented Scotland with a fait accompli. This realisation produced two important reactions. First, an extensive and thought-provoking debate developed among the parliamentarians as they sought to arrive at an appropriate Scottish response: encouraged by Fletcher, they considered both the succession and, more widely, the need to secure greater control over their monarch. These discussions culminated in Scotland's own Act of Security, which explicitly restated the country's prerogatives with regard to the Scottish crown and contained thinly veiled threats that they might yet prefer a non-Hanoverian candidate unless specific restraints (particularly strengthening the powers of the Edinburgh Parliament) were placed on the government. An accompanying piece of legislation, the Act Anent Peace and War, pointedly asserted Scotland's right to pursue an independent foreign policy after Anne's death. By the time she reluctantly gave the royal assent in 1704 in return for the Scots' grant of supply (i.e. taxes), the former statute had been watered down, but the limitations proposed on royal power, strongly influenced by Fletcher's florid denunciations of executive excess, remained prominent.

The second and no less inevitable consequence of Westminster's undiplomatic Act of Settlement was a pronounced chilling in Anglo-Scottish relations. Coming on top of centuries of intermittent mistrust and with Darien and the economic consequences of renewed English wars against France adding fuel to the fire, it is not surprising that the Scots responded aggressively. For the English, however, Scotland's Act of Security was itself both an affront and a threat, seemingly blackmailing their own future monarch so as to obtain concessions for Scottish interests and, what was worse, leaving open the possibility of a rival, perhaps even a Catholic, candidate securing the throne of Scotland as a likely precursor to an attempt also to claim the English crown. London duly responded to what it perceived as an ultimatum with one of its own.

The Alien Act of 1705 gave the Scots just ten months to repeal the Act of Security and either formally endorse the Hanoverian succession or enter into meaningful negotiations about a political union between the kingdoms. If Scotland refused, then the rights of English citizenship enjoyed by Scots since James VI's time would be revoked and their duty-free imports of cattle, coal, sheep, wool and linen into England terminated. This was a crude but effective ploy, striking directly at the Scots' most vulnerable points: in the words of Sir John Clerk of Penicuik, who, significantly, gravitated from early scepticism to eventual support for union, it was simply an unavoidable truth that 'our country's fortunes depend on England; the only wealth we have comes from the horses and cattle we sell there'. Following this English move, jeopardising key economic activities about which the Scots were acutely sensitive, one of the most notorious incidents in Anglo-Scottish relations occurred: anti-English rioting in Edinburgh was accompanied by the execution of the unfortunate Captain Thomas Green and two crewmen of the English merchantman *Worcester* – one of them ironically a Scot himself – on Leith sands in 1705, on a trumped-up charge of piracy.

As will be clear, the forces impelling the Scots and English to consider union in the first five years of the century were once again simultaneously stirring up the most determined opposition. Yet this time, after much soul-searching and not a little arm-twisting, the critical new departure which was England's willingness to embrace Scotland, together with deepening fears among the Scots about the diminishing range of sensible alternatives, eventually settled the issue. Thus it was that in the summer of 1705 the Scots Parliament finally nominated its commissioners to treat for union with their English counterparts. This was in fact to be the crucial part of the whole process, for on the composition of the negotiating team depended the nature of the treaty which would subsequently be presented for ratification in both Edinburgh and London.

An earnest debate heard all the familiar arguments rehearsed. Opponents of the government, the 'Country' party, initially appeared to have a majority. But the sense that Scotland lacked other options, and indeed the inability of the crown's miscellaneous opponents actually to produce a coherent rival solution to the intractable political and economic difficulties confronting Scotland, gradually undercut resistance. When the government finally won over James Hamilton, 4th Duke of Hamilton, previously an opposition leader (and later rewarded for his timely conversion with the English dukedom of Brandon), it was agreed that Anne, in her capacity as Queen of Scotland, should choose the commissioners herself. This, of course, ensured that they would largely be pragmatists willing to work constructively with the English delegation.

The proposals hammered out were predictably a series of compromises, between Scottish and English interests but also between a coherent programme for a mutually acceptable union and a variety of more disparate provisions designed to win the support of key interest groups and to buy off potential opponents. The latter, a necessary feature of contentious legislation in all ages, explains several striking clauses in the draft treaty. These included guarantees of the preservation of the Scots law and legal system (of obvious interest to the powerful legal lobby in Scotland), as well as compensation for the Scots acquiring a partial share in England's accumulated National Debt and reimbursement for the Darien investors (represented by a sum known as the 'Equivalent'). It was also agreed, by a separate Act of Security, that Scotland's presbyterian church would remain forever separate from the Church of England: this, as Clerk observed, 'did something to calm the outcries of the mob and the fears of the clergy'.

But the most important question of principle was resolved only by implacable opposition from England to anything other than a fully incorporating union. It had been possible to imagine other scenarios emerging, especially a federal British union not unlike that previous proposed by

Fletcher and perhaps initially favoured by most other Scottish politicians. But the scope for continued independent Scottish action which that would entail was anathema to London's commissioners, obsessed by the need to guarantee a united British front over the succession, war and international relations. Lockhart of Carnwath, the treaty's implacable enemy (and indeed the only Scottish commissioner consistently to oppose the project), justly complained to a friend that, despite all of his colleagues' apparent enthusiasm for advancing federal solutions to their national predicament, 'upon the English declaring they'r aversion to it, they let it drop'.

It was for this reason that the draft treaty eventually brought before the Scots Parliament envisaged something quite remarkable in European history: the voluntary absorption of two kingdoms into a unitary state called Great Britain, with one sovereign (Hanoverian after Anne), one legislature (at Westminster), one executive, one flag and one citizenship. In other words, in return for sacrificing their independence, the Scots were granted a small but vital say in London, where unilateral decisions, based exclusively on English interests, had increasingly cast a pall over Scotland's own internal affairs. Furthermore, the treaty stipulated that Great Britain should have a single currency and economic regime. This too was crucial to the Scots, opening up not just England but England's vast overseas markets to unrestricted trade. Indeed, given the Scots' profound anxieties in the wake of agricultural failure and amid deepening commercial gloom, this prized concession might appear to have made the complete package almost irresistible.

The ensuing debate was a credit to the last crop of Scots parliamentarians, a series of set-piece confrontations over the separate articles of the bill to ratify the treaty. Several gave rise to such eloquent effusions and so many insightful meditations on fundamental political principle that they have achieved almost legendary status in the Scottish pantheon. Second only to Fletcher, the leading light of the anti-union cause was John Hamilton, 2nd Lord Belhaven, a landowner and disgruntled Darien subscriber who had switched from early support of William's regime to bitter hostility towards an unaccountable court and its latest brain-child. Some saccharine sentiments evoking the doleful countenance of 'our Ancient Mother Caledonia' prettify one of the most memorably emotive speeches ever delivered by a Scot. But his perceptive analysis of the constitutional problems disguised by the sheer brevity of the proposals, anticipating in particular the dangers of Scotland's relatively weak voice being continually drowned out by a deafening chorus of English interests, is what really deserves to be better known. Belhaven should rather be seen as initiating a tradition of intelligent Scottish criticism of an inevitably unequal union between a budding London-based superpower whose 'Circumstances are Great and Glorious' and what he soberly described (in a phrase which explodes the myth that anti-unionism necessarily rested on a favourable assessment of Scotland's own position) as 'an Obscure poor People'.

Belhaven's most skilful sparring partner was Sir William Seton of Pitmedden, son of another old enemy of James VII and one of Anne's chosen commissioners. Seton rehearsed the potent counter-argument for embracing a full incorporating union as a pious national duty, seeing it as absolutely essential for Scotland's political, religious and economic salvation. He insisted that

> by this Union, we'll have Access to all the Advantages in Commerce, the English enjoy; we'll be capable, by a good Government, to improve our National Product, for the benefit of the whole Island; and we'll have our Liberty, Property, and Religion, secured under the Protection of one Sovereign, and one Parliament of Great-Britain.

These observations too were a pointer to the future. They demonstrated that Scottish patriotism and British unionism would be compatible rather than mutually contradictory for those able and willing to make the necessary leap of political imagination.

It would be nice to record that these high-minded salvoes of classical rhetoric were the key to the Scots Parliament's decision between November 1706 and January 1707 to endorse the treaty. Unfortunately it would also be mistaken. For grubby politicking – 'management' as it was customarily described by apologists – also helped bind together the shaky and short-lived alliance of pro-unionists which eventually delivered an impressive-looking majority of 110 to 67 in the final division. Crucial people had in fact been detached by the 'Court' party from the oppositional 'Country' grouping: in effect, habitual enemies of royal policy were by one means or another converted into supporters, however temporarily. John Kerr, 5th Earl of Roxburghe, surprised many by changing horses in mid-race. The comparatively independent and sceptical 'Squadrone Volante' (or 'Flying Squad') faction, led by the widely respected John Hay, 2nd Marquis of Tweeddale, proved especially important when they switched en bloc under encouragement from Anne's representatives John Campbell, 2nd Duke of Argyll (one of the crown's leading generals in the Continental wars, known by the impressive Gaelic soubriquet 'Red John of the Battles'), and James Douglas, 2nd Duke of Queensberry ('The Union Duke'). Roxburghe's musings in 1705, repeatedly quoted but apt nonetheless, best encapsulate the diversity of concerns which gave this hetereogeneous assemblage sufficient reason to ratify the treaty: 'The motives will be, Trade with most, Hanover with some, ease and security with others, together with a general aversion at civil discords, intolerable poverty, and the constant oppression of a bad ministry.'

Yet both money and other inducements were also clearly implicated: a peerage here (notably Roxburghe's dukedom, which followed by a suspicious coincidence of timing in 1707) and payments there (including £1,750 back-pay for Tweeddale), not to mention the Equivalent (barefaced bribery or rightful compensation, depending upon how one looks at it). White-hot controversy surrounds such transactions to this day, with scholarly partisans engaged in essentially unresolvable disputes over their exact scale and consequences for individuals' behaviour. It is clear that such dealings – which is to say, the trading of gifts, opportunities, office and rewards in return for favour and support – were the normal currency of political life, not just in Scotland but also across Europe. Though falling far short of the standards expected of later British statesmen, the manoeuvres of 1703–7 were unremarkable three hundred years ago and need to be judged accordingly by the historian. But it would also be naive to think that the tempting rewards offered were not sometimes decisive in winning friends and influencing people. Several politicians performed spectacular somersaults over relatively short timescales, and it is difficult not to think ill of their reasons for doing so, however mixed their motives may actually have been: in a popular refrain that Burns later adapted to powerful effect, from some angles it did indeed appear as though the country had simply been 'bought and sold for English gold'.

Most Scots played no part in the unfolding drama, though the townspeople of Edinburgh did supply a seething chorus of discontent, roughly menacing the nervous politicians who scurried through Parliament Close. The populace also staged riots, as did the citizens of Glasgow; hostile petitions flooded in from burgh corporations and church congregations. Because of this the charge is frequently heard that the Union was, and therefore by implication must still be, illegitimate. This is, of course, a convincing riposte to any suggestion that a more democratic age should feel bound by its specific provisions. But with respect simply to the historical interpretation of an episode in early eighteenth-century politics, it is patently anachronistic. After all, accusations of unaccountability could with equal justice be levelled at the Declaration of Arbroath of 1320 – not the settled will of the wider Scottish people but the partisan rhetoric of the Bruce's chancery propagandists – or even at the seventeenth-century National Covenant, itself scarcely the product of a free and fair ballot. Not surprisingly, such objections are much more likely to be heard in relation to the events of 1706–7. Yet it is difficult to believe that the inevitably unrepresentative political processes of earlier times, when the views of the population at large were neither sought nor even considered remotely relevant, can be judged solely by whether they yielded results of which several centuries later we ourselves happen to approve.

The making of the Union – tortuous, convoluted and profoundly undemocratic as it necessarily was – was the result of the coming together of several different factors in specific historical circumstances: it was to some extent fortuitous though not remotely accidental; unsurprising rather than strictly inevitable. The problem of the succession and the need for a consistent foreign policy finally aroused England, long the most reluctant of spouses, into a state of unquenched ardour. Declining trade, arrested economic development and a recognition of growing national impotence were also understood by articulate opinion in Scotland to be matters requiring fundamental and urgent change: to do nothing was the counsel only of fools. Increasing numbers of Scottish politicians therefore persuaded themselves, or allowed themselves to be persuaded, that what this undoubtedly eligible suitor was now offering, a union bringing a generous dowry and a promise of future good behaviour, was quite simply the best (and almost certainly the only) catch available. It was this calculation, and not the play of great historical forces, which brought about something which the wildest dreams of crown propagandists and the practical needs of successive monarchs had failed to achieve: the Treaty of Union was a marriage of convenience, the two partners having different but largely complementary reasons for entering into what they both hoped would be an advantageous new relationship. The consequences of this decision marked Scotland's political life forever.

The machinery of post-Union politics

In an important sense Union savagely culled Scotland's active politicians. The eighty-eight county and sixty-seven royal burgh representatives in the last Scots Parliament were replaced by just thirty and fifteen MPs respectively in the new Parliament of Great Britain. Scotland received fewer seats in the re-fashioned House of Commons than its probable share of Britain's then-population might have suggested (though such considerations were, strictly speaking, irrelevant to contemporaries lacking not only our democratic assumptions but also our demographic data). Offsetting this, the country also received rather more Commons representation than its tiny contribution to total British state revenues would initially have justified. Similar numerical shrinkage befell the Scottish noblemen who sought admission to the reconstructed House of Lords: the seventy-seven peers in the final Edinburgh Parliament were in fact whittled down to just sixteen elected representatives at Westminster (though to these must be added those Scottish aristocrats whose English titles or admission to the new Great Britain peerage conferred automatic membership of the Lords). Lockhart characteristically denounced this as 'the depriving our nobility of their birthright', and it certainly excluded from direct participation many previously active noble politicians. As a result, the century saw incessant jostling among the ermined classes, even after the crown secured effective control over the nomination of Scotland's representative peers.

If the opportunities for continued parliamentary participation were thus in one sense clearly truncated by the Union, then in other ways a surprising amount of Scotland's old representative system survived, either unaltered or only slightly modified, under the new dispensation. Both the post-1707 electoral system and the sharing out of the forty-five Commons seats were determined not within the treaty but in decisions taken by the last Scots Parliament. The Scottish royal burghs were grouped into fifteen districts of four or five: for example, Ayr, Irvine, Rothesay, Campbeltown and Inveraray sent a single MP to Westminster. As the capital, Edinburgh alone now returned its own parliamentary representative. Similarly twenty-six Scottish counties were awarded an MP each, while Orkney and Shetland were treated as one and the six smallest (like Nairn and Cromartyshire, the latter a bizarre patchwork of estates associated with the eponymous earldom actually scattered across the larger county of Ross-shire) were paired and given representation in alternate parliaments.

In other respects, too, pre-Union Scottish conventions were followed religiously when integrating the counties and burghs into the Westminster system. Above all, since the Scottish elite, like their new English partners, still assumed that seats in parliament needed to be identified with local political communities rather than with equal subdivisions of the wider national population, no attempt was made to reflect changing demographic realities. Populous and economically important counties like Aberdeenshire and Perthshire returned a single MP. But so did the far smaller shires of Banff and Kirkcudbright. The historical accidents which had given no fewer than fourteen of Fife's royal burghs a voice in the old Scots Parliament also continued after 1707 – even though this meant that only three of Aberdeenshire's towns, and in Perthshire the county town alone, were represented. Rapid population growth soon made these traditional imbalances even more striking. Booming industrial settlements like Motherwell and Coatbridge, which, demographically speaking, emerged virtually from nowhere after 1750, remained unrepresented at Westminster until the next century, except for their marginal influence over the Lanarkshire county elections. Even Glasgow, Scotland's largest town by the 1780s, enjoyed only a quarter-share in a district MP until the 1832 Reform Act, while Dornoch, Pittenweem and Cullen, each with populations barely in hundreds, received identical representation.

The terms on which Scottish electors participated also did not change after the Union: the old County Franchise Acts of 1661 and 1681 simply continued in force for Westminster elections after 1707. Shire voters had either to own the feudal superiority of land valued at 40 shillings under the Old Extent (a thirteenth-century tax survey), or, where that valuation could not be determined, to hold the same rights to property worth £400 Scots per annum. Not surprisingly this severely limited the size of electorates: even as late as 1788, when a group of opposition politicians commissioned a private survey of the political lie-of-the-land, they discovered that there were still only 2,668 registered voters throughout all of the Scottish counties. This narrow qualification also ensured the replication among electors of the dramatic inequalities in county representation: Bute's MP was returned by a mere twelve voters while candidates for Aberdeenshire faced a comparatively competitive electorate of 178. The agreeable convention that the newly returned member for Kincardineshire entertained his electors over dinner at the Mill Inn in Stonehaven says more about a limited franchise than it does about unusual wealth or conviviality.

Burgh representation was even more limited. Before 1707 Scotland's urban franchise had merely been extremely narrow. Afterwards, and again because the British political system simply adapted traditional Scottish practices, it was often little short of farcical. As before, votes remained the preserve of the bailies (the magistrates) and ordinary councillors. Commonly these comprised an incestuous clique, nominated annually by their own predecessors rather than chosen freely by the members of the merchant and craft guilds – let alone by the swelling population of urban-dwellers at large. The post-Union districts effectively tightened these restrictions still further through an electoral college arrangement by which each council was required to send a delegate to a district election meeting. Astonishingly, therefore, the thirty-three councillors who directly elected Edinburgh's own MP represented by far Scotland's largest urban electorate. Elsewhere the fifteen or twenty members of a typical Scottish royal burgh council merely chose a delegate, four or five of whom would together actually elect the district's MP.

Not least because the Parliament of Great Britain was essentially seen as representing a constellation of local interests throughout the two kingdoms, it is worth looking more closely at the other political structures which existed across eighteenth-century Scotland. For here too the post-Union period overwhelmingly saw the continuation of existing practice. Participation in local government remained a privilege, and was usually accorded only to those with a significant investment in the community. Typically this meant that, even in the burghs, heredity and property were the twin determinants of personal status and political power. When John Learmonth, a Stirlingshire merchant and landowner with business interests in the port of Leith, became a burgess of Edinburgh in 1793, he was admitted specifically because his father and grandfather (Alexanders both) had previously enjoyed this coveted rank. Yet even wealthy and well-connected men like Learmonth, who never became a magistrate or a councillor in the burgh, actually had no vote in Edinburgh's parliamentary elections: 'omnipotent, corrupt, impenetrable' was the short but devastating analysis of the capital's political machinery by Lord Cockburn, an early nineteenth-century critic.

A Scottish royal burgh's internal government was still largely prescribed by custom as enshrined in its particular 'sett' (constitution). Commonly, however, its primary duty was to protect the interests of the burgesses enrolled as members of the merchant guild. The corporation, presided over by a provost or lord provost, frequently exploited the opportunities which the restricted franchise afforded for factional entrenchment: the fact that the corporation of Annan in Dumfries-shire through the 1750s was comprised entirely of the relations of two local landowners was merely an extreme illustration of what was possible under a system of literal self-perpetuation. By 1800 these closed fraternities were gradually being discredited: councillors diverted funds into their own pockets; they profited from mortgages secured on public property; they sold the common assets; and they failed to keep competent accounts (as was spectacularly found to be the case in Edinburgh itself in 1799). Conversely the council's legitimate functions were strictly limited. It upheld the burgh's regulations in respect of markets, prices, buildings, customs and other dues, particularly through the court of the dean of guild; it enforced law and order through a town guard or constables, usually the council's principal employees; and the bailies in particular had responsibility for dispensing justice in civil and petty criminal cases – though in practice their business was dominated by small debts and property disputes.

Peculiarly Scottish forms of burgh incorporation also survived the Union intact. Sixty-six royal burghs (though, in a characteristic exception, excluding traditionally non-functioning examples such as Newburgh, Falkland and Auchtermuchty in Fife) shared district representation at Westminster: major communities like Cupar, Dingwall and Jedburgh were naturally intensely proud of the foothold this gave them in national politics. The same towns also had a collective voice in the Convention of Royal Burghs, which organised their share of 'stent' (i.e. national taxation) and adjudicated when the inevitable disputes arose. By contrast, the hundreds of burghs of barony, often tiny like Livingston in West Lothian, founded by the Earls of Linlithgow, or Pitlessie in Fife, established by the Lords Lindsay of the Byres, were usually much less exalted. Essentially the creations of local noblemen and lairds, their privileges were mostly limited to the right to hold markets and fairs and to exercise certain judicial powers. Yet there remained points in common. Royal or baronial, large or small, wealthy or impoverished, the political machinery of the burghs was everywhere both antiquated and unrepresentative. Moreover, with Westminster reluctant to interfere in the unfamiliar minutiae of Scottish local government, they would continue so for more than a century after the Union.

Like the burghs, the shires' formal governmental functions also remained limited in this period, and largely confined to the provision of justice and the collection of taxes. Theoretically the sheriff, as the crown's representative, was still the most important officer. Yet in twenty counties and stewartries (the latter being districts like Kirkcudbrightshire, traditionally associated with royal proprietorship), this had long since been converted into a hereditary sinecure for a local nobleman. Moreover, despite some success in relation to certain kinds of problem – such as cases of debt, 'spuilzie' (borrowing without the owner's consent) and 'bloodwite' (brawling) – the sheriffs continued after 1707 to be only one part of the effective judicial system. Crucially, the Union had not curbed the ancient powers of the landowners. The influence of the latter continued to be felt through a confusing network of courts of barony and regality which exercised wide criminal powers across much of the country. At best these traditional structures offered a useful forum for communal self-regulation; at worst they were a crude device giving Scotland's lairds and aristocrats a hold over local affairs of which their English counterparts could only have dreamed. The distinctive flavour of Scottish franchise jurisdiction into the eighteenth century is perfectly captured in the surviving records of the Barclay family's barony of Urie near Stonehaven, a litany of petty indictments such as 'the keeping and useing of a gun and shooting of hares and fowls contrair to law', 'throwing doun and grapling with the said Alexander Keith, they being both inebriat', and 'beatting and whipeing of James Laurie'.

Only in the aftermath of the last great rising of 1745–46 on behalf of the exiled Stuarts, which convinced London (wrongly, as it happens) that disaffected Scottish landowners had exploited their private judicial powers to raise a rebel army from among an abused and fearful tenantry, were most of these structures finally swept away. But even then, as the notorious Appin Murder showed in 1752, feudal power could still matter greatly in rural Scotland: the dubious conviction of James Stewart for complicity in the shooting of a government factor owed much to the Duke of Argyll's ability to pack an Inveraray jury with reliable Campbell kinsmen. More positively, the later 1740s saw the reinvigoration of Scotland's hitherto underdeveloped sheriff court system: a cadre of professional sheriffs-depute, assisted by sheriffs-substitute, now finally supplanted the old hereditary sheriffs. By the end of the century these well-trained and usually assiduous officials – 1799, for instance, found the young lawyer and man of letters Walter Scott serving diligently as sheriff-depute of Selkirkshire – were unchallenged as the government's principal representatives in the shires, notwithstanding the eventual introduction in 1794 of patrician Lords Lieutenant on the English model.

The eighteenth century also saw efforts to re-energise another Scottish county institution, previously ineffectual following its undistinguished Jacobean transplantation from England. This was the commission of the peace – the bench of JPs – who, shortly after the Union, were finally endowed with equivalent responsibilities to their southern counterparts. They were required to convene variously in petty, quarter, general and special sessions held at regular intervals. They were also much involved in key areas of local economic regulation such as wage-determination and the fixing of grain prices. Yet their practical importance in matters criminal – not unlike the sheriffs – was constrained first by the survival for several decades of franchise jurisdictions and at all times by the enduring legal peculiarity which in Scotland reserved the 'four pleas of the crown' (murder, rape, robbery and arson) for Edinburgh's High Court of Justiciary or for its peripatetic circuit judges sitting on 'ayre', the latter also being regularised after 1707. As a consequence, eighteenth-century Scottish JPs chiefly imitated English practice in their social exclusivity, with leading patricians dominating throughout: in Lanarkshire, for example, the commission of the peace was chaired after 1707 by John Carmichael, 1st Earl of Hyndford, a former Secretary of State, and included two other members of his immediate family.

Much more important in local government across Scotland was the commission of supply, first established in the 1660s. This met several times each year in the county town or one of the other principal burghs. It was charged mainly with overseeing the collection of the cess (i.e. the Scottish land tax) and raising revenues for the county's roads, bridges and ferries. Crucially, the peers were invariably outnumbered on the commission by the lairds and other landowners: larger than the number of parliamentary voters because qualification was less stringent (Aberdeenshire, for example, had 260 eligible in 1805, as against the 178 electors identified seventeen years earlier), it very much articulated the views and interests of Scottish landed society as a whole. The executive office of collector of supply might therefore be vigorously contested between competing factions in the same way as any other representative position. But at the same time, the commission, whose assessment of property ownership and valuations for tax purposes also had obvious implications for the determination of electoral qualification, usually resisted the inevitable efforts of individual noblemen, and especially of forces external to the county's landed community itself, to exert undue influence. Indeed, as a potent organisational tool firmly in the hands of local interests, the commission of supply was in many ways the embodiment of the traditional self-government which so often survived in Scotland in the century after 1707.

Management and patronage

Because rather than in spite of its peculiar systems of parliamentary representation and local government, active political competition continued in post-Union Scotland. The electorate was, of course, small enough positively to invite attempts at direct manipulation. Moreover, not only were relations between candidates and voters often highly personalised. Local rivalries were also exacerbated by national tensions which divided people into supporters or critics of a particular government or into nominal members of the very loose proto-parties which since the 1680s had been emerging at Westminster – the Tories (supposedly but not always defined by staunch support for royal supremacy in church and state) and the Whigs (who notionally shared a commitment to parliamentary sovereignty and religious pluralism but in reality were scattered confusingly across the entire spectrum, ranging from the establishmentarian 'Court' through the less predictable 'Squadrone' grouping to dissident 'Country' radicalism). Given such polarisation and fragmentation within Britain's wider political community, keen and colourful competition for control of a locality was always likely. Yet the scope for 'management' in practice varied greatly, depending very largely upon the electorate in question.

Scotland's royal burghs posed particular difficulties in this regard. As might be expected, local proprietors could directly influence individual towns: the Roses of Kilravock, for example, traditionally controlled nearby Nairn. But the complexities of the district system, with constituent towns not necessarily even in the same county (in the Northern Burghs, Kirkwall was in Orkney, Wick in Caithness, Dornoch in Sutherland and Tain and Dingwall in Ross), frequently thwarted attempts at monopolisation by a single landowner. In one crucial respect, however, urban elections were still more susceptible to interference. For, untroubled by the proud ideal of 'independence' which frequently inhibited status-conscious country gentlemen from responding to something so patently ignoble as a financial inducement, the fewer and typically more venal electors in the commercialised social milieu of the towns often proved rather more easily swayed. George Dempster's success in the Dundee Burghs in 1768 actually turned on the lavish disbursement of cash to Cupar's councillors, an expedient for which he was later unsuccessfully pursued in the High Court of Justiciary: 'Cupar in Fife rivals Gomorrah', Dempster memorably observed of his electors' moral standards. Sir Lawrence Dundas, too, a financier and government contractor (a 'comely, jovial, Scotch gentleman, of good address but not bright parts', gossiped Boswell), first became MP for the Linlithgow Burghs in 1747 – though the Commons immediately unseated him on appeal – by purchasing the votes of the councillors of Selkirk.

The likelihood of genuine political competition in a particular Scottish county, and both the need and the scope for direct manipulation, was more commonly a function of the traditional electoral legislation as it interacted with local social and economic patterns. Fife, for example, with 187 qualified voters in 1788, lacked the overbearing influence of any dominant aristocrats. It therefore seemed propitious territory for Henry Erskine, Dean of the Faculty of Advocates, leader of Scotland's opposition and the man for whom that year's confidential survey of the county electorates was actually prepared. Perthshire, whose 277 voters were strongly polarised between two camps, the administration's Duke of Atholl and the opposition's Earl of Breadalbane, was more typical in its exposure to competitive magnate influence. But the epitome of proprietorial control was Sutherland. Here Elizabeth Leveson-Gower, eponymous countess, continued to exercise her family's traditional vice-like grip. Her crushing influence over the tiny qualified electorate of just thirty-four meant that Sutherland's parliamentary seat was effectively in her gift. In 1790, for example, she was able to return a pro-government candidate without any actual contest being forced, the opposition's researcher having accurately judged her position 'almost insurmountable' and any challenge to it as 'entirely fruitless'.

A practice which emerged precisely because of political competition was the barefaced manufacture of county votes. As we have seen, electoral qualification was predicated not on the occupation or even on the actual ownership of a given quantity of land but on formal possession of the legal right of feudal superiority. Ever-obliging lawyers duly invented conveyances bestowing upon dependent voters the requisite title to appropriate-sized subdivisions of their clients' vast estates. These 'liferent' or 'faggot' votes, and the phalanx of so-called 'parchment barons' wielding them in the service of the larger landowners, could easily prove decisive in view of the limited size of real electorates. A notorious case in point is Lanarkshire, by no means the smallest Scottish county: here in 1788 the genuine voters (of whom there were just sixty-six) were comfortably outnumbered by the ninety-five essentially fictitious voters created either by the opposition-minded Duke of Hamilton or by his rivals working in the government interest.

Such deft sleight-of-hand, of course, illustrates very starkly the practical advantages of legal expertise in the post-Union management of Scotland. After all, career politicians themselves now spent much of their time in the south. The Scottish Privy Council, which had formerly helped a Whitehall-based crown monitor developments and formulate its policies, had also been dissolved – in 1708, at the behest of the Whiggish 'Squadrone', who feared its malign electoral influence on behalf of the government. It was in the resulting administrative vacuum that the professional lawyers, who had themselves survived the Union unscathed, came into their own. They possessed unrivalled specialist knowledge of the major traditional institutions rooted in Scots law: almost alone they fully understood the arcane rules and practices which governed Scotland's electoral system, heritable property and the established church. They also inhabited a nationwide hierarchy of courts, uniquely placing them to gather information from across the country and then to disseminate instructions and ensure strict enforcement in return. Already by as early as the 1720s, the lawyers and judges had therefore become so indispensable to the major political players that, had they not existed, they would surely have had to be invented.

During those immediate post-Union decades, when the 2nd Duke of Argyll and his brother and successor Archibald, Earl of Ilay (sometimes rendered 'Islay'), dominated Scotland's affairs, it was their allies among the law officers who in practice ran the country. Duncan Forbes of Culloden, who rose to the commanding heights of Lord Advocate (the crown's chief prosecutor and legal advisor) and then Lord President (head of the judiciary), was a figure of immense political authority on behalf of the so-called 'Argathelians' – the formidable interest maintained by the two Argylls. Forbes was in turn succeeded in 1747 by Ilay's long-time associate Lord Milton: with supreme irony, this formidable epitome of Hanoverian management, mere Andrew Fletcher beneath the courtesy title, was the nephew of the Union's most famous original opponent. Milton thereafter served the 3rd Duke of Argyll as Lord Justice Clerk, the office technically responsible for Scotland's criminal law. Dispensing valuable patronage, massaging a demanding electorate, alternately fending off and mollifying opponents, reporting discreetly on local developments and offering expert advice on Scottish policies and legislation, such men, sitting unchallenged atop the country's traditional legal pyramid, were the embodiment of Scotland's semi-autonomous government under the first two Georges.

The practice of mediating power and patronage through law officers acting as *sous-ministres* (under-ministers), and of receiving a constant flow of information and advice in return, was so effective that it easily survived the final eclipse of the Argathelian interest early in the reign of George III. It continued through their short-term replacement by James Stuart Mackenzie, Argyll's nephew and the brother of the first Scottish Prime Minister, John Stuart, 3rd Earl of Bute: indeed, during this transitional phase, in the early 1760s, Milton's tried-and-trusted services were prudently retained.

The power and expertise of such figures was, if anything, an even more important factor in Scottish administration by this time, with the final abandonment of yet another formal political office, the Secretaryship of State. The failure of the last incumbent, John Hay, 4th Marquis of Tweeddale, to combat the 1745–46 rebellion, together with the obvious fact that the ruthless Argathelians had managed increasingly to bypass this ineffectual relic of aristocratic government through the use of skilled and dependable professional lawyers, merely confirmed just how far politicians had in practice come to rely upon the good offices of Scotland's legal bureaucracy.

By the 1770s matters had moved so far that an ambitious lawyer could even aspire to manage Scotland for himself rather than on behalf of a blue-blooded patrician. Henry Dundas, son of a Lord President and himself Solicitor-General (the crown's agent in civil actions) and sometime Lord Advocate, dominated the country during the governments of North and, into the next century, William Pitt. Successively MP for Midlothian and for Edinburgh, he held cabinet office as Home Secretary, First Lord of the Admiralty, Treasurer of the Navy, Secretary for War and President of the Board of Control for India. His power, however, rested always on an awesome capacity to control Scottish elections through mutually advantageous deals struck with regional power-brokers like his friend Henry Scott, 3rd Duke of Buccleuch. At the height of his colossian powers in the 1790s, 'Harry the Ninth' or 'The Uncrowned King of Scotland', as Dundas was variously known, could deliver thirty-four of the forty-five Scottish MPs to his Westminster allies. Even Erskine, his great nemesis (and, inevitably, yet another lawyer and erstwhile Lord Advocate), was unable to compete with a professional lawyer who had either neutralised or co-opted most of the country's leading electoral interests and fixed himself at the very hub of the British political system.

To a great extent the political leverage enjoyed by the lawyers, and especially by Scotland's great legal office-holders, also reflected the attractiveness of well-paid employment to eighteenth-century voters. For the granting or promise of rewards was what ultimately allowed the construction of a viable political interest, cementing ties between obliging politicians and grateful electors. A Lord President or Lord Advocate, for example, was potent not least because he could attract a father's support by finding a lucrative but not necessarily very demanding appointment for a modestly talented younger son. In the Courts of Session, Justiciary and Exchequer in Edinburgh, or in one of the numerous other public jurisdictions across Scotland, the number of positions was growing steadily under the impact of post-Union commercialisation, economic diversification and legal reform. But other openings were also available to aspiring brokers of patronage, similarly proliferating in volume and variety as the century progressed.

An increasing and very attractive source of patronage – and clearly only possible because of the Union – lay in England's, now Britain's, overseas possessions. A doctor, administrator or soldier in the East India Company might acquire not only legendary rich pickings but, for men of talent and ambition, the chance to wield great power and responsibility while still relatively young. Well-placed Scots, such as Henry Dundas himself, George Dempster (a Company director) and David Scott (MP for Angus, then the Dundee Burghs, and chairman of the Company), could oblige supporters with privileged access to a glittering world of excitement and enrichment. In effect, this granted Scotland's politicians, in Adam Smith's sardonic aside, a share 'if not in the plunder, yet in the appointment of the plunderers'.

More prosaic but no less useful were positions on the British crown's own payroll. Excise appointments and army and naval commissions proved valuable currency indeed amid expanding trade and regular eighteenth-century warfare. Many a young Scot consequently found himself an ensign aboard one of His Majesty's frigates in the Mediterranean or Caribbean on the understanding (rarely, of course, made tastelessly explicit) that his father's vote would go with a particular candidate. It was, for example, through a constant trickle of plum naval appointments that the 1st Baron Keith, ensconced at the Admiralty at the close of the century, helped preserve the Elphinstone family's influence in Stirlingshire (largely exercised, it might be noted, in steadfast independence from Dundas and the government). Small wonder that, as the Scottish novelist Tobias Smollett observed during Bute's dominance in the early 1760s, English hostility towards his countrymen appeared to have been provoked above all by the 'great numbers of those Northern adventurers who had wriggled themselves into all the different departments of civil and military institution'.

Patronage, then, was crucial to all Scots with aspirations to active participation in government. It was the essential lubricant for the smooth working of their rudimentary political machinery. It was also by far the best way, at least in an age before coherent party identities and organisational discipline had evolved, of exerting some measure of control over the progress both of elections across Britain and of legislation through Parliament – then as now, the principal occupational hazards facing politicians in any system where power ultimately depends upon being able to win sufficient votes. Used adroitly, as by Dundas's namesake and *bête noire* Sir Thomas, the son of Sir Lawrence, who for thirty years secured himself in the affections of Stirlingshire's voters, patronage could sustain an enduring political presence. Used incompetently, as by Sir James Campbell of Ardkinglas, Sir Thomas's predecessor in the 1750s, whose attempts to install an unpopular clergyman in a local parish sorely tested the patience of previously loyal Argathelian voters, it could seriously damage an interest's electoral health.

The occasional implosion of a longstanding interest, like Berwickshire's loss by the Earls of Marchmont, in 1779–80, or indeed the Argathelians' initial relinquishing of Stirlingshire to Sir Thomas in 1768, was a salutary reminder to politicians and managers alike of just how fickle dissatisfied voters might be.

Starry-eyed foreign commentators like Voltaire and Montesquieu, who pronounced the Hanoverian constitution the quintessence of liberty, were clearly guilty of exaggeration. But they were perceptive enough about one feature of Britain's representative system of government which was highly unusual by contemporary standards: the dependence of the monarch's ministers upon a majority in the Commons, and thus on the continuing indulgence of a shifting constellation of local interests from Cornwall to Shetland. The behaviour of MPs in the lobbies was, of course, often supine. The power of the managers was certainly formidable. The electoral franchise was self-evidently exclusive. Yet those who sat in the Commons were still, both formally and often in practice, the representatives of others. This inescapable truth established a complex relationship between politicians and voters, maintained, according to universally understood social conventions, by the acknowledgement of common interests and the reciprocal exchange of favours.

Politics and the people

Management, skilfully deployed within the framework of a restrictive franchise, meant that the outcome in most Scottish parliamentary seats was usually determined prior to election time: active competition occurred in just sixteen out of forty-five in 1790 because of Dundas's iron grip; in the event, it proved impossible even for Erskine to contest Fife. Yet the course of politics by no means always ran smooth. The best-laid plans of statesmen and managers continued to be confounded by events, and, more especially, by the unexpected tenacity of views and interests of which they had failed to take proper account. This was particularly likely in relation to Scotland. Few British ministers had first-hand knowledge of its distinctive character. Scottish society, moreover, was reasonably literate: an emerging popular press (by 1800 more than thirty towns had a newspaper) kept an interested public abreast of topical controversies and policy developments. Not only voters and politicians but also the wider public were therefore able to come into conflict – with each other, with other groups within Scotland and even with governments at Westminster. In short, and despite what is sometimes assumed, there is no good reason to believe that the Union marked the end of Scottish politics.

The 1734 parliamentary election in the Dunfermline Burghs affords a striking instance of how distinctively Scottish enmities and opinions could still be articulated within the seemingly inflexible architecture of the existing representative system. For it was here, strongly supported by the Marquis of Tweeddale and the Erskines of Mar, oppositional Squadrone Whigs with territorial influence in the district, that James Erskine of Grange (later infamous for secretly imprisoning his supposedly deceased wife for seven years on St Kilda, lest she betray his treasonable plotting) attempted to secure his return to Parliament. To Grange's advantage were a set of political views calculated to win over local hearts and minds. He even took the unusual step of advertising them in print, a stratagem clearly presupposing some benefit from an appeal to the wider community. He vigorously denounced the Excise Bill, much disliked by most Scots; he praised the opposition's proposal for a triennial parliament (intended to shorten the seven-year interval between parliamentary elections); and he indicated his sympathy for the well-respected local clergyman Ebenezer Erskine, recently suspended from the Church of Scotland. Peter Halkett of Pitfirrane, an army officer and the government's man, was still eventually returned following sharp practice by a key elector, the provost of Inverkeithing. But the majority of burgh opinion seems to have been successfully mobilised behind the opposition candidate by an appeal to specific issues and concerns – some local in focus, some with a Scottish dimension, all powerfully in his favour. Even with such seemingly irresistible forces behind him, however, it proved impossible to dislodge the virtually immovable object of the Argyll interest. Grange had to console himself for the moment as MP for Clackmannanshire.

Another striking instance of authentically Scottish concerns revealing themselves in a political context, this time not among local people but at Westminster itself, occurred in the aftermath of the 1745–46 rebellion. Government, as we have seen, had determined to abolish most of Scotland's private courts. But in this situation a British government found itself falling foul of the familiar herd instinct of Scotland's politicians when faced with an issue on which their own national identity and traditions, as well as their own personal interests, seemed in jeopardy. Just as after the 1715 rebellion, when Forbes had led Argathelian attempts to moderate the government's retribution, so again was much of Scottish opinion, normally squarely behind the administrations of Henry Pelham and the Duke of Newcastle, actively mobilised in opposition. Led by the 3rd Duke of Argyll, backed also by most Scottish peers and MPs, and bolstered by a thundering chorus from Edinburgh's legal establishment, the bill's opponents pointed out that the proposals contravened the Treaty of Union; that they threatened the maintenance of law and order; that they vitiated the sacred rights of property; and, of course, that extensive compensation would be owing to those whose incomes would be reduced by what amounted to the nationalisation of a lucrative private sector within Scotland's judicial system.

In the event the Heritable Jurisdictions Act still passed in 1747, a reminder that British governments, overwhelmingly beholden to English MPs, could on occasion choose to ignore even the most keenly felt Scottish sensitivities. But the collective will of Scotland's normally divided politicians in opposing the legislation, and the fact that even the Whiggish Argathelians' support of a Whig administration was shown to be conditional upon approval of its policies, confirms that Scottish opinion had survived as an identifiable force in British politics. This interpretation is underlined by the way in which the same interests sought to temper the government's retaliation against suspected rebel sympathisers in the Highlands. And it was seen again nearly forty years later when Dundas severed his connections with the waning Fox–North coalition and hitched himself to the rising star of Pitt, thereby keeping Scotland's main political interest usefully positioned in London. Scottish backing for government was to this extent contingent, whether upon continuing access to patronage or upon specific policy considerations. The fabled dependability of Scotland's over-managed parliamentarians for a Walpole, a Pelham or a Pitt – and, in the main, that reputation was justified – did not make it impossible for a Scottish interest to strike out on an independent course if it seemed appropriate or advantageous to do so.

Distinctively Scottish passions, however, found their most dynamic expression by means other than focused electoral or parliamentary opposition to the government of the day. More diffuse processes revealed not only the tensions between nascent British statehood and continuing Scottish semi-autonomy but also those between a narrow governing elite and the unenfranchised population 'out of doors'. Such strains could produce complex political phenomena with both orthodox and extra-parliamentary dimensions. They might begin, like the controversy over the heritable jurisdictions, with a hostile Scottish reaction to a government policy or decision. But, having a popular aspect which threatened the civil order, they would accelerate when an equivocal response was offered by ambivalent members of the Scottish elite, torn between their native sympathies and their statutory responsibilities as upholders of the crown's authority. They would achieve final resolution only when a new accommodation was hammered out between leading Scottish interests and the government itself. These tangled relationships between popular opinion, the Scottish political classes and Westminster are clearly seen in two of the most famous crises of the first half of the century, the Shawfield Riots and the Porteous Riot.

The former were explosions of popular fury in June 1725 following Walpole's imposition of the malt tax. Amid general rioting in the west, a

Glasgow mob attacked the home of Daniel Campbell of Shawfield, the local MP, an Argathelian whose government affiliations made him an obvious target. The official response in Scotland, however, was initially hamstrung. Roxburghe, as Secretary of State, justified the Squadrone's reputation for political unreliability by declining to act. Robert Dundas, Lord Advocate, was similarly unhelpful, for he sympathised with the rioters, regarding the tax as a flagrant breach of the Union: he was duly dismissed. Responsibility eventually fell upon the shoulders of Forbes of Culloden, Ilay's choice as Dundas's replacement. Forbes simply called in General George Wade, the Commander-in-Chief in Scotland, whose soldiers quickly restored order. Several rioters were subsequently transported. Significantly, however, Forbes also fined Glasgow corporation to compensate Campbell: the burgh's failure to prevent the disorder, and the evidence that some of the rioters had been respectable members of the citizenry, hinted at municipal complicity in a politically motivated crime. Ilay, because of what Forbes had ultimately turned into an impressive piece of internal housekeeping, was able to use the affair to consolidate the Argathelians' growing reputation for competent management of Scotland. But the episode also served as a useful warning at Westminster that unenfranchised opinion, backed by dissident native politicians, could still vent a peculiarly Scottish sense of alienation with violent articulacy.

The other case, only partly similar in structure and with very different consequences, centred on Edinburgh in 1736, where Andrew Wilson and George Robertson, two smugglers from Pittenweem in Fife, arrested during an attempted robbery of an excise officer (and thus popularly regarded as martyrs to a hated tax), faced hanging. Robertson was helped to escape; but after Wilson's sentence had been carried out, an angry mob confronted Captain John Porteous of the town guard, who ordered his men to open fire. Several people were killed or wounded. Tried by Lord Milton and condemned for murder, Porteous was immured in the Tolbooth. But, after Queen Caroline in London had granted him clemency, another carefully organised mob broke into the prison and lynched him – 'a figure wavering and struggling as it hung suspended above the heads of the multitude', as Scott immortalised the moment in *Heart of Midlothian*. The town council had proved itself suspiciously impotent, and the affair, like the Glaswegian case, rapidly developed into a trial of strength with a Westminster administration which believed that not only the populace but even Scottish local government was bent on humiliating the crown and its ministers. But this time there was a twist. Walpole demanded punitive legislation removing the historic privileges of Edinburgh's corporation; and this helped destroy the often tense relationship between the elderly 2nd Duke of Argyll and the Prime Minister of Great Britain.

Argyll, rehearsing his brother's role in the mid-1740s as Scotland's defender, successfully thwarted Walpole's more extreme proposals. But the experience rent the Argathelian interest asunder, also further dividing Scotland's wider political community. Ilay, whose relations with his elder brother were frequently strained, stood by the ministry, continuing to disburse its Scottish patronage. By 1739, however, Argyll had recoiled into opposition alongside a motley assortment of frustrated Tories and embittered Squadrone Whigs: in the 1741 election this unlikely alliance captured many government seats (Erskine of Grange, for example, finally secured the Dunfermline Burghs), an important factor in Walpole's epochal resignation and the collapse of the fabled 'Robinocracy'. The lessons again were clear. Scotland's sensitivities needed the most delicate handling by British ministers, especially in relation to its precious semi-autonomy in law and public administration. Furthermore, not even the most apparently loyal of political allies north of the Border could be taken completely for granted by English politicians.

Including even the admittedly colourful instance of Jacobitism (which, as an ideological phenomenon rooted in the ecclesiastical and doctrinal controversies of the previous century, is considered in the next chapter), the longest-running Scottish political concern in the first century of Union was simply the system of government itself. For intrinsically, the cause of parliamentary reform was neither radical nor unrespectable. Indeed, the conclusion that Scotland's county and burgh franchises required modification was scarcely unlikely among those smaller landowners and opposition politicians who manipulated the system less successfully than the government and the great proprietors. Even Parliament itself, with acts of 1714 and 1743, and the Court of Session, notably following the 1768 debacle when the temporary lack of a recognised government manager in Scotland produced a particularly chaotic poll, made periodic forays into the mire, attempting with limited success to stamp out the gravest abuses. David Steuart Erskine, 11th Earl of Buchan and elder brother of Henry, also began in 1768 a successful campaign for reform of the procedures by which the crown packed the Lords with compliant Scottish peers.

None of these movements, however, was remotely democratic, either in composition or in aspiration. All were self-serving to some degree. Typical were the fruitless endeavours by the commissioners of supply in Inverness-shire, Moray and Caithness after 1782 to have the subdivision of feudal superiorities outlawed: the aristocratic multiplication of fictitious votes was, of course, mainly unacceptable to the complainants because it devalued the electoral currency of their own. Campaigns for burgh reform were no more impressive. Led by Thomas McGrugar, an Edinburgh burgess, and involving Erskine and other familiar opposition politicians, a committee was set up in 1783 to demand voting rights in corporation and parliamentary burgh elections for all resident burgesses – 'men in the middle ranks of life', as it was put. Blocked at Westminster by Dundas and hamstrung by their own lack of coherence and determination, the disgruntled merchants were still denied a share in the narrow domination of their own communities. It would take more radical intentions, less well-heeled organisations and the disorienting impact of external events to make Scottish reformism begin seriously to worry the establishment.

In some ways Scottish responses to the French Revolution merely mirrored those in England. Initial and widespread admiration for the Estates-General in 1789 was followed by growing controversy and embitterment: the increasing alarm of the educated and the propertied everywhere contrasted with the greater vestigial fervour of the less respectable as political conditions in France during the early 1790s steadily deteriorated. The recantation of George Dempster, long-standing opposition MP and former sympathiser with a project which had at first seemed to promise 'the happiness of mankind', was typical of so many erstwhile Scottish reformers: 'alas', he complained to a friend about the violent turn of French events, 'our philosophers only open'd the gates of the police to let in a band of ruffians to cut their throats . . .'.

Even so, progressive political instincts always remained more visible – and perhaps more common – in Scotland. The raw egalitarian experience of national poverty in the recent past may well have encouraged greater Scottish susceptibility to French arguments for equality and fraternity. This tendency was doubtless reinforced by the populist suspicion of hierarchical authority which was such a cherished part of the Scots' religious heritage. The liberal Whig politics of some influential university teachers may also have promoted the same sympathies: John Millar at Glasgow (of whom Erskine, for example, had been a favourite student) eagerly taught the crucial importance of socio-economic status in determining access to political power; William Ogilvie of King's College, Aberdeen, even advocated common ownership of the land. Ardour for France, perhaps especially of this more cerebral and educated kind, was certainly encountered in Scotland at a later stage than in the south. It is no surprise that it was a young Inverness-shire lawyer, Sir James Mackintosh, 'the Whig Cicero', a student of arts at Aberdeen and of medicine at Edinburgh, who in *Vindiciae Gallicae* (1791) offered the definitive rebuttal of Edmund Burke's famous attack on the French experiment – although, like most, Mackintosh eventually changed his mind about the Revolution before pursuing a highly successful career in India.

The stronger Scottish support for the Revolution also exacerbated domestic political divisions. France became, as Cockburn recollected, 'the all in all. Everything, not this or that thing, but literally everything, was soaked in this one event.' In newspapers, among academics, in burgh councils and among the lawyers, businessmen and landowners, respectable opinion, broadly sympathetic to the French experiment in 1789, became not only bitterly split but also, on balance, increasingly hostile. Every word of deepening radicalism across the Channel ensured that the well-heeled in Scotland grew more nervous about domestic reform. This in turn ensured that the relative influence of other groups on Scottish reformism grew proportionately, further encouraged by comparatively high levels of popular literacy (contemporaries noted how the country's lower orders devoured Paine's *Rights of Man* in particular). In July 1792 the Scottish Association of the Friends of the People was founded in Edinburgh's Fortune's Tavern. This earnest organisation avowed constitutional activity but also aimed openly to promote the democratic ideals of the French: discernibly less gentrified than its English counterpart, the Scottish organisation was much more obviously the creature of shopkeepers, weavers and other skilled craftsmen. Loyalist organisations, like the Goldsmiths' Hall Association in Edinburgh, also emerged in the increasingly polarised atmosphere. Sympathisers with the French Jacobins vented their feelings on the king's birthday, 4 June 1792, burning an effigy of Dundas and rioting through the streets of the capital.

A prominent Friend at the movement's first Edinburgh convention, the advocate Thomas Muir of Huntershill, previously rusticated from the University of Glasgow for his irascible conduct, defended one of the rioters, Alex Lochie, who was transported. Against a background of economic stringency (the harvest of 1792 was poor), a willingness to challenge the governmental structures of Scotland and Britain grew, again particularly among groups, such as the skilled craftworkers, not hitherto much involved in active politics. Muir attempted unsuccessfully to ally the Friends with the leading burgh reformers and the parliamentary Whigs: both shied away from an inflammatory demagogue and from people whose motives and ideas they mistrusted, judgements which further reveal a lack of cohesion among Scotland's disparate reformers. By January 1793, with events in France demonstrably spiralling out of control (Louis XVI was executed that month and France declared war on Britain shortly afterwards), moderate opinion was shying away from reformist politics, exposing and isolating those who remained.

Even Erskine and many other leading Whigs now backed off, arguing that agitation for domestic reform was unwise given the perilous international situation. Muir himself was arrested for seditious words spoken at a Friends' convention. After a lengthy delay, during which time he actually visited France, he found himself before Robert MacQueen, Lord Braxfield and Lord Justice Clerk. Muir's conduct of his own defence was neither calm nor competent (he had rashly rejected Erskine's offer of assistance), but the result, with the martinet Braxfield able to pack the jury and construe his own definition of sedition, was inevitable: Muir was convicted and sentenced to fourteen years' transportation to Botany Bay. Other radicals, like the dissenting clergyman Thomas Fyshe Palmer of Dundee, prominent in the Friends' second convention, were similarly condemned. In both cases it had been expected that the convicts would request clemency, which could then be granted with a show of ostentatious official mercy; but both Muir and Palmer preferred political martyrdom and they were duly despatched to Australia. After a third convention in Edinburgh in November 1793, at which the much-reduced band of disproportionately extremist Friends talked bombastically about armed resistance, further arrests were inevitable.

Dundas not only by these means removed the handful of leading Scottish radicals. He also secured the suspension of the Act Anent Wrangous Imprisonment of 1701, which had prohibited detention without trial. Times were desperate, and desperate measures seemed justified. In France, respectable moderation had descended inexorably into violent revolution; any signs of a similar trajectory in Scotland were now regarded with the utmost seriousness, increasingly by former liberals as well as by hardened reactionaries. Thus when a cache of arms was discovered in Edinburgh in 1794, a full-blown conspiracy, the 'Pike Plot', was soon unravelled, the government claiming that it stretched all the way from the Friends in the capital to the poor labouring districts around Glasgow. Robert Watt, a former government spy, was executed for treason, though most historians remain sceptical about the scheme's wider extent. Another shadowy movement also emerges indistinctly at around this time: the United Scotsmen, a covert insurrectionary grouping of artisans and weavers. Strong throughout central Scotland in towns like Glasgow, Perth and Dundee, they were inspired by the contemporary United Irishmen, who organised the great Irish rising of 1798. The Scots' leader, George Mealmaker, a Dundee weaver, was transported for sedition in 1797. Committed to universal male suffrage – still a strange notion from the far end of the contemporary radical spectrum – the movement was effectively suppressed within two years.

In the same year the government's decision to form a Scottish militia by parish ballot provoked rioting in the mining community of Tranent in East Lothian: eleven died when dragoons were called in. Similar outbursts occurred elsewhere, notably among the colliers of Bathgate in West Lothian in 1799. Yet it is significant that recruitment to the newly formed Volunteers met with much less hostility. Indeed the Scots flocked to the colours rather more enthusiastically than the English: 4 per cent of the eligible male population (against just 2 per cent in England) volunteered initially; by 1804 the proportion of Scottish males who were either serving or had indicated their preparedness to do so had reached impressive levels, especially in traditional rural counties (91 per cent in Argyllshire and 71 per cent in Ross-shire). Eulogies like that on James Grant, minister of Liberton near Edinburgh from 1789, who 'in the period of social and political danger which followed the French Revolution . . . was strongly and actively loyal, and chiefly instrumental in raising a local volunteer corps, in which he held a commission as lieutenant', well reflect the passionately conservative affiliations of very many forgotten Scots from this period. In particular they caution against regarding understandable hostility to the then-innovative practice of military conscription as convincing evidence of near-universal popular political radicalism.

As British commerce and liberty were imperilled by an imminently expected French invasion, patriotism was in fact the preponderant public posture in Scotland at the end of the eighteenth century, the accompanying language of king and country instinctively aped and echoed by the clear majority of the articulate. With the country already the personal fiefdom of Henry Dundas, the internal situation and the external threat together ensured almost complete quiescence: calls even for the most modest reforms now seemed not just untimely but positively dangerous. Yet a satisfactory explanation for this outcome, and so for the failure of late eighteenth-century radicalism, must take full measure not only of events after 1789. It must also consider the wider character of post-Union Scotland and its governmental arrangements. For, despite glaring faults that in easier times had attracted well-merited criticism, the existing order possessed crucial advantages in the estimation of very many politically active contemporaries.

Above all, Scotland was a largely self-governing country within a successful British polity which, by prevailing standards, was also relatively permissive of divergent views and normally respectful of the rule of law: the very fact that the madcap Watt, caught in possession of revolutionary weaponry in wartime, was the sole Scottish radical to be executed emphatically sets apart the mundane reality of the so-called 'Dundas despotism' from those far less pragmatic regimes, from revolutionary France to twentieth-century Europe, under whom the sacrificial victims of an unbending ideology would literally prove numberless. Nor is it coincidental that Scotland's traditional elites of the 1790s, like those in England, successfully avoided the grisly fate of their French counterparts. They retained strong instincts in favour of paternalistic flexibility. They also, as we shall see, co-opted the most ambitious members of other social groups, thereby further enriching and dynamising rather than undermining their own social and political system. The obvious next question, however, is whether the Scots' distinctive politics, which survived the Union and then successfully absorbed the more immediate shocks of domestic radicalism during the 1790s and of a threatened

French invasion around 1800, also sustained a continuing sense of identity: in short, did patriotic Scots still believe that they were a nation?

Patriotism and identity

By his retirement as a major in the Royal Marines, Thomas Arnot of Chapel had served the British state for thirty years. Beginning his career in 1755, before the Seven Years War, in which Britain's amphibious forces launched successful attacks on the French coast and on Louisbourg, Guadeloupe and Cuba, Arnot served through to the end of the American war in the early 1780s, in which George III's maritime forces once again were prominently involved. By 1788, however, Arnot was comfortably installed back at his family home on the hill above Kingskettle in the Howe of Fife. There, on the same estate which his ancestors had held for more than two hundred years, he lived the distinctive life of a traditional Scottish proprietor, a veritable pillar of the community. A 'heritor' in his parish (that is, an owner of inherited property who shared legal responsibility for the church, school and minister's manse), he also held a county vote in the next Westminster election, tactically allied with the larger interest of his cousin and neighbour Balfour of Balbirnie. Such varied ties affected growing numbers of eighteenth-century Scots, within the elite but often far beyond; and they complicated the previously straightforward patriotic identities of people on whom not just traditional Scottish but also strongly British and even global experiences and loyalties were exerting an increasingly powerful pull. For the sake of convenience, three broad positions on national identity might be delineated in these dramatically altered circumstances of the first post-Union century: retaining older notions of exclusive Scottishness; abandoning that Scottishness for full immersion in a new British identity; and hovering ambivalently somewhere between these two extremes.

The first form, traditional in nature and reliably signalled by forceful expressions of antipathy towards the English and all their works, had its heyday in the first decades after 1707. This is hardly surprising. For most people who lived through the immediate post-Union years recognised that, if the promised benefits of the treaty had not yet materialised, the drawbacks certainly had. The imposition of England's treason laws in 1709, controversial measures affecting the Church of Scotland in 1712, and various government proposals for a Scottish malt tax – each of these did violence to the letter or spirit of the treaty. Such grievances not only amply vindicated the continuing doubts and fears of the Union's original opponents. They also strengthened the reservations of those less committed (or, among the politicians, biddable) Scots who had initially persuaded themselves of its merits.

From the outset, however, clear-cut anti-Unionism of this sort, based on the constitutional and economic cases for revoking the treaty, co-existed with other attitudes less exclusively defined by a desire for renewed Scottish political independence. Above all in the early decades, expressions of intense hostility towards the Union came to be associated with support for the return to his British thrones of the son of the deposed James VII, the self-proclaimed 'James VIII', who was astute enough to promise solemnly (if, given the Stuarts' congenital unionism, somewhat implausibly) to annul the treaty once reinstated. In individuals like Lockhart of Carnwath, the Lanarkshire laird who opposed the Union into the 1730s, or Thomas Ruddiman, the Edinburgh scholar–publisher who as late as the 1740s was still engaged in patriotic polemic against perceived English slights, conventional expressions of Scottish patriotism intermingled naturally with pro-Stuart sentiments: 'Is it commendable in a Scotsman to write against the ancient constitution of his own Nation', Ruddiman demanded of one of his countrymen during a protracted wrangle over the traditional autonomy of the crown of Scotland, 'and run down the Antiquity and Independency of it?'

Other early eighteenth-century Scots, though certainly willing to argue for independence, were also transparently motivated more by a festering mass of personal and factional resentments than by straightforward political nationalism. In June 1713, for example, the most unlikely temporary alliance coalesced at Westminster to engineer the repeal of the treaty. It included men as different as the previously pro-Unionist Earl of Mar and the unreconstructed anti-Unionist George Baillie of Jerviswood. According to Lockhart, who was inevitably a participant in the plan, it also embraced Ilay, subsequently the bulwark of the Hanoverian monarchy, as well as his equally Whiggish brother Argyll, one of the Union's original architects. But even this seemingly definitive outbreak of traditional hostility to English dominance of Scottish affairs, which eventually failed by just four votes in the Lords, scarcely represented the re-awakening of the political elite's collective commitment to the ideal of an independent Scotland. Rather, their utterly contradictory motives, ranging from anti-government pique and covert Stuart dynasticism to a partisan desire to maintain the presbyterian clergy's grip on the Scottish church, indicates that their opposition to the treaty, and articulation of the conventional patriotic affinities which invariably went along with it, was essentially opportunistic – merely a useful means by which a set of individuals pursued a wide variety of mutually exclusive ends.

Some Scots in the early post-Union years, of course, did retain a more straightforward relationship with traditional patriotism, readily harking back to the loss of ancient liberties, conceived here simply as Scotland's age-old freedom from English domination. Even the symbols of Gaelic-speaking Scotland, which in other circumstances signified only the superstition and backwardness of their estranged Highland relations, might for some Lowland Scots after 1707 increasingly appear preferable to embracing the Union flag. Such thoughts were certainly entertained by some hardline presbyterians, particularly following the rash of unwelcome Scottish ecclesiastical legislation imposed by Westminster in the first years after the Union. For example, William Wright, minister of Kilmarnock, claimed in 1717 that, despite the substantial economic sweeteners offered with the treaty, the political losses suffered by the Scottish nation remained the more important consideration: 'Liberty is the best of all Things', he insisted, 'I'd rather have a Highland Plaid with Liberty, than the greatest Dainties, with a Hook in the Heart of it.'

Yet as the years passed, exclusively Scottish patriotism of this older kind faded, perhaps tainted by its association with the Stuart cause and certainly undercut by the accumulating evidence of the treaty's substantial benefits. Anti-Unionism and a hankering after renewed Scottish independence became less and less common by mid-century. Indeed, by the 1770s, strong expressions of Scottishness had begun to serve new and quite different political purposes. No longer was militant Scottish patriotism the preserve of unreconstructed conservatives who wished simply to turn the clock back to 1707, reconstituting Scotland as a self-governing state. Emphatic Scottishness was now more often expressed by forward-looking critics of the British state's antiquated representative apparatus. Robert Burns is the best-known mouthpiece: 'Scots, Wha Hae', for example, with its recollection of the victories of medieval patriots over the presumptuous English ('Lay the proud usurpers low!/Tyrants fall in every foe!/Liberty's in every blow!/Let us do, or die!'), skilfully transformed the ancient rhetoric of national independence into powerful buttressing for the poet's plea for modern constitutional change. The 11th Earl of Buchan, Henry Erskine's elder brother, was similarly adept at putting this traditional Scottish patriotism to new purposes: a progressive peer most comfortable when wallowing in his country's martial heritage (and who sponsored the re-publication of Wallace's biography), in 1784 he told his friends that 'as a Friend to Peace, to Liberty & to Science . . . I considered myself as an inhabitant of an United Kingdom; but as a Citizen I could not help remembering that I was a Scot'.

Nevertheless the evidence for an increasingly radical tinge to Scottish patriotism can also be pushed too far. Certainly it does not support any rigid equation of progressive politics with specifically Scottish national consciousness. For in other instances, such as the 'national' conventions of the Friends of the People (which actually referred to the British, not Scottish, nation), the key roles of Irish and English campaigners in Scotland (notably

Palmer of Dundee, who was actually a Bedfordshire clergyman) and, above all, the widespread tendency of articulate Scottish reformers to hanker loudly and vacuously after a return to a mythical golden age of pan-British constititional liberty (commonly utilising not very well-disguised adaptations of the hallowed 'rights of free-born Englishmen' or 'Magna Carta' traditionally evoked in the south), even the radicals of the 1790s as often embraced a British as a Scottish identity. Indeed, this facility was doubtless encouraged by the fact that Scottish and English politics were in certain respects demonstrably converging: for example, between 1754 and 1790, no fewer than sixty Scots managed to secure English constituencies; and by the 1780s Scots like William Murray, 1st Earl of Mansfield (Lord Chief Justice), and Alexander Wedderburn, Lord Loughborough (Lord Chancellor), had reached the very apex of England's own supposedly separate legal system. Such convergence inevitably served to moderate exclusively Scottish patriotic idioms – which were implicitly if not explicitly anti-Union in import – in respectable public discourse.

At the same time, it is important to recognise that the second form of patriotic identity available, the kind where Britishness simply supplanted any remaining attachment to Scotland, was even less common than the long-term survival of militant anti-Unionism. John Belfour, writing at a time of heightened British military and commercial self-confidence, did use his *History of Scotland* (1770) to issue a most striking request: 'may the disagreeable distinction of Englishman and Scotchman be for ever lost', he pleaded, 'in the common, in the glorious, and in the envied name of – BRITON'. Yet this desire entirely to replace Scottish with British identity was extremely rare. Indeed, the necessary preconception that nationhoods must by nature be exclusive – that, in other words, a commitment to Britishness is incompatible with the retention of Scottishness – appears to have been unfamiliar to most Scots after the mid-eighteenth century who cared to vent their patriotic feelings. Certainly such clear-cut demarcations would not help at all in making sense of the accumulated experiences of increasing numbers of contemporaries, people like Thomas Arnot himself, whose personal affiliations elicited loyalties simultaneously as immediate as the parish church and as distant as the North American colonies.

Alexander 'Jupiter' Carlyle, the famous minister of Inveresk near Edinburgh, is an instructive example of how the ambiguities inherent in being a Scottish Briton in the post-Union age not only established tensions with which contemporaries were forced to grapple but, more often than not, also allowed them to arrive at a practical resolution. Carlyle's vigorous arguments in support of the campaign to allow Scotland to raise a militia for coastal defence, long resisted by untrusting London governments still wary of Scots bearing arms, skilfully interweaved the two patriotisms, British and

Scottish. On the one hand Carlyle argued in 1760 that the proposal would reinforce, as any English pamphleteer might have put it, the 'liberty, strength, and security of Great Britain'. In other words, extending to the Scots the same rights of active military participation as the English already enjoyed was essential to the proper functioning and survival of the Anglo-Scottish state. But on the other hand, Carlyle also drew upon the familiar resources of distinctively Scottish libertarianism, conjuring up the spirit of the Wars of Independence to suggest that, if not permitted to defend themselves, the Scots would become 'silent and spiritless, like the effeminate inhabitants of a conquered nation'. Union, he insisted, had inaugurated a partnership of equals. Not the subjugation of the Scots and the sublimation of Scottishness but rather the successful mobilisation and incorporation of Scotland's traditional martial libertarianism within a British framework was what would allow both peoples' political destiny to be fulfilled.

Such appeals to Scotland's distinctive heritage in fact occurred even in the staunchest supporters of Union, particularly when English indifference or hostility was suspected. William Robertson, Carlyle's associate and the leader of the established church, confronted English insouciance in his *History of Scotland* (actually published in London in 1759) with some tart reminders of 'the reputation for military virtue, which has always been the characteristick of the Scotch Nation'. The Edinburgh schoolmaster John Lawrie, no anglophobe but still nervous lest Scotland's peculiar value to the British state be underestimated in the south, expatiated at length upon 'that glorious undaunted military courage, for which [the Scots] have always been accounted famous, both at home and abroad'. Even John Belfour, despite his express wish to see the two nations' identities subsumed within a new British consciousness, felt a twinge of traditional pride sufficient to recall at the same time 'those brave and warlike people the Scots – who, of old, struggled in the cause of liberty, with the most amazing fortitude'.

These conscious and usually fruitful ambiguities of allegiance, particularly significant in later eighteenth-century discussions of political relations within Britain, also had frequent parallels in relation to the Scots' broader sense of identity from 1750 onwards. David Hume's frantic self-purging of so-called 'Scotticisms' from his language is well-known; though elsewhere, as we shall see, he could flourish Scotland's achievements with considerable patriotic emphasis. Equally curious are the endeavours by James Beattie to help his fellow countrymen overcome their supposed linguistic disabilities (famously his *Scoticisms, Arranged in Alphabetical Order, Designed to Correct Improprieties of Speech and Writing* (1779)), as well as the enthusiastic reception accorded in Edinburgh in 1761 to Thomas Sheridan's – that is, an Irishman's – public lectures on correct English usage. In neither of these cases, of course, did a sense of linguistic inferiority prevent enthusiastic acknowledgement of a continuing Scottish identity. Indeed, resolute pride in Scotland continued to be expressed forcefully through vehicles such as the militia campaign (actually led by some of those who cheerfully submitted themselves to Sheridan's hectoring), or through the celebration of the country's distinctive intellectual culture (again, even those who wished to expunge their own native dialect had little patience with English jibes about the Scots' alleged ignorance or superstition). It was, however, where politics, history and national culture most problematically intersected, in the domain of religious faith and its accompanying institutional structures, that Scotland's distinctiveness from England – and to a considerable extent the continued separate identity of the Scots as a people – was to be most influentially maintained in the century after Union. It is to this crucial aspect of contemporary Scottish life that we must now turn.

CHAPTER TWO

Belief

The painful history of the national church in the years prior to 1700 held an inescapable grip on Scottish life in the succeeding decades. Under both Charles II after 1660 and his younger brother the Catholic convert James VII and II from 1685, a church governed by 'prelates' (that is, by bishops and archbishops) was formally re-imposed on the Scots. This episcopalian dispensation granted the Stuart monarchs considerable control over the Church of Scotland – a vital necessity in royal eyes because of Scotland's recent experiences of radical theology, militant clerical independence and popular participation in religious affairs which, under the Covenanters, had actually been a primary cause of Charles I's ejection from his British thrones in 1649. There was, however, deep-rooted opposition to the return of episcopacy. Many Scots still demanded a national church reflecting what they saw as the true heritage of their national Reformation: that is, a presbyterian settlement based on the strict Calvinist doctrine of the separation of church and state. In this view the Scottish church would be governed not by the crown's appointees but by an ascending hierarchy of committees, stretching all the way from nine hundred parish kirk sessions through more than sixty local presbyteries and several regional synods to an annual General Assembly in Edinburgh.

In the early 1680s, when still Duke of York, James had actually resided in Edinburgh, effectively governing Scotland on behalf of his brother. It was during this period that he had achieved particular infamy in presbyterian circles for his attempts to suppress the 'conventicling' movement – unlicensed gatherings of Covenanting preachers and their followers who utterly rejected the crown's prelatical church. The penal legislation and judicial harassment that James oversaw became known to his victims as the 'Killing Times', and this recent experience of persecution at the hands of a Catholic

Stuart prince goes a very long way towards explaining the consistent hostility of many Scots in the succeeding generations to any suggestion that James's rightful heirs (the 'Jacobites', from *Jacobus*, the Latin for James) might yet be restored to the British thrones from which he himself was deposed in 1689. But before we consider the career of Jacobitism and the potent intermingling of religious and political commitments which it represented, we need first to appreciate the fundamental importance of presbyterianism in the making of eighteenth-century Scotland.

A presbyterian Revolution

The means by which presbyterianism came to be re-established in the Church of Scotland in 1689–90 were in fact by no means straightforward. For the principal cause of this change lay neither in Scotland itself nor even in the benevolent intervention of God's Providence (despite predictable claims to this effect by later presbyterian propagandists). In truth, the dramatic removal of James and his replacement jointly by his Dutch son-in-law William of Orange and his own Protestant daughter Mary was in its origins essentially an Anglo-Dutch affair. An opposition alliance of Whig and Tory grandees at Westminster had emerged by 1688, determined to put an end to the king's increasing usurpation of parliamentary privileges and to thwart his suspected plans for a full-blown Catholic revival. It was these English noblemen who had invited William and Mary to invade Devon in early November 1688, accompanied by 15,000 mainly Dutch soldiers. The English Parliament, on William's arrival, was pleasantly surprised at the haste with which James obligingly fled to France and disgruntled exile. What became known to admiring eighteenth-century historians as the 'Glorious Revolution' was glorious not least in that scarcely any English blood had had to be shed in ridding the English political elite of an unwanted king.

The Scots therefore patently did not set the pace in these epochal events. Yet nor did their own Revolution slavishly follow the southern precedent. Chiefly this was because of the deeper loyalties which still existed in Scotland both to the Stuarts (a royal dynasty, of course, with strong Scottish roots) and to the principle of indefeasible hereditary right on which their British thrones rested. James VII retained deep wells of sympathy in many parts of the country. This was particularly true in the north-east and in the Highlands: the Catholic and episcopalian clans, who largely shared his religious and political instincts, had been since the 1640s a reliable reservoir of support for troubled Stuart kings in their vicious spats with Lowland presbyterians and truculent English parliamentarians. The attitudes of many

Scots towards James were also shaped by the familiar aphorism 'No bishops, no king'. This implied that divine-right monarchy was inextricably bound up with the absolute right of the king's bishops to govern the nation's church on his behalf. James's personal Catholicism, though a grave misfortune in the eyes of virtually all Protestants, was in the final analysis tolerable to most Scottish episcopalians, as to many orthodox Anglicans south of the Border, if his legitimacy as a God-given secular prince would at least continue to underwrite the God-given ecclesiastical authority of the episcopacy and the national church.

With politics and religion so completely intertwined, it was probably inevitable that the Scottish Revolution would take its own distinctive form. One difference with the situation in England was that Scotland actually possessed in its presbyterian community a coherent and already radicalised grouping determined to make themselves the lasting beneficiaries of William's unexpected arrival. This factor helps explain the militant stance adopted by the assembled Scottish parliamentarians in the so-called 'Convention' which met in Edinburgh on 4 April 1689. Explicitly condemning James for his tyranny, they declared that he had forfeited any right to the throne of Scotland. Westminster, by contrast, soon began to embroider a manifestly ridiculous but much less problematical version of events. James, it was claimed, had abdicated the English throne; his departure had been willing; the kingdom had not been invaded; the Dutch soldiers accompanying William and Mary had only been bodyguards. In short, the apparently revolutionary abrogation of the hereditary principle of kingship by England's parliamentarians was not really a revolution at all but merely a felicitous response to an unforeseen vacancy.

Yet despite the Scots' very much more forthright approach to the removal of James, their freedom of manoeuvre in replacing him was both more extensive and less real than that enjoyed by London's politicians. Their power was greater in the sense that, in so boldly forfeiting James, Edinburgh's politicians had re-engaged directly with the explosive argument, periodically deployed by Scottish presbyterians since the Reformation, that an ungodly king might legitimately be removed by Parliament acting on behalf of the people: thus in theory the crown of Scotland really *was* theirs to bestow. But in practice the options available in Edinburgh were more restricted than it might appear. For unless they were prepared unilaterally to terminate the regal union with England, a drastic step with uncertain but potentially disastrous consequences, Westminster's prior acceptance of William and Mary as James's lawful successors had presented the Convention with a fait accompli.

A second crucial deviation from the curiously bland English pattern of revolution, again determined largely by the greater religious polarisation in

Scotland, was the emergence of an active resistance movement committed to defending James's right to the throne. Led by the charismatic John Graham of Claverhouse, 1st Viscount Dundee, earlier prominent in James's attacks on the Covenanters, this body of loyalists, chiefly comprising Highland clansmen and Lowland episcopalians, undertook what was effectively the first of the Jacobite risings. This even achieved a spectacular but hard-fought victory over Williamite forces under Hugh Mackay of Scourie in the pass at Killiecrankie north of Pitlochry on 27 July 1689. But Dundee, in a stroke of catastrophic misfortune that was also to become something of a Jacobite tradition, was mortally wounded. The following month, the disparate supporters of the ousted king, having lost their talismanic leader, fought a less decisive encounter against a force of Covenanters at nearby Dunkeld. In the spring of 1690 they were finally routed by Williamite cavalry at the Haughs of Cromdale on Speyside. At least as an immediate military threat in Scotland, Jacobitism had been contained.

Again in contrast with England, the key political events of the Scottish Revolution might usefully be thought of as a protracted presbyterian coup d'état. For, not least in the absence of Jacobite loyalists from Edinburgh and with Covenanting militants in the ascendant in southern Scotland, a strongly presbyterian accent was given to the hammering out of what became known as 'the Revolution Settlement'. This was a remarkable development in ecclesiastical terms. William and Mary, no less than Charles and James, would have preferred an episcopalian church along Anglican lines that would be susceptible to royal control. But the episcopalians, ideologically committed to divine-right kingship, were resistant to the Revolution itself. Such stubborn loyalty to the old regime destroyed the political viability of Scottish episcopacy in the eyes of the new. Meanwhile, in hijacking the Revolution for their own ends, the presbyterians had already presented James's successors with a severely limited range of ecclesiological options in Scotland. In due course William and Mary reluctantly endorsed a presbyterian establishment in accordance with the wishes of their own declared supporters in Edinburgh.

The presbyterians' strength and disproportionate influence, personified by the formidable William Carstares (jocularly known as 'Cardinal Carstares'), post-Revolution Principal of the University of Edinburgh, is well seen in the Articles of Grievances and the Claim of Right issued by Scotland's parliamentarians. In these trenchant documents James's unpardonable sins were enumerated at predictable length: above all, it was declared that he did 'by the advice of wicked and evil counsellors, invade the fundamental constitution of this Kingdom, and altered it from a legal limited monarchy, to an arbitrary despotic power'. Catholics were also expressly debarred from holding public office. In June 1690, in the aftermath of the Jacobites' final military defeat, the Scots Parliament abolished episcopacy, reinstating presbyterianism in the national church in a statute to which the crown prudently gave its assent. Around two hundred ministers of episcopalian convictions, especially in the strongly Covenanting south, were 'rabbled' (that is, hounded from their parish posts). A process of 'visiting' (in other words, purging) the universities was also initiated. Not surprisingly, in the coming years and decades, most Scots, though they had played little part in bringing about the Revolution, wisely conformed to the new presbyterian order.

Some ordained episcopalians nevertheless still refused to accept this triumphant regime in church and state. These 'non-jurors', for whom swearing the required oath to William and Mary, and thus abandoning their previous loyalty to James as God's anointed king, seemed an unconscionable act of betrayal, were removed. The magnitude of the decision to refuse to break a solemn undertaking is easily underestimated by an age accustomed to ostentatious but risk-free political gestures. But it should be borne in mind that James's defenders not only faced automatic marginalisation. For men who were bishops, ministers and academics, non-juring also meant the loss of employment, income and home, together with exposure to judicial harassment and persecution. In central Fife alone, the incumbent ministers of Kettle, Auchtermuchty, Logie and Strathmiglo knowingly embraced this fate, losing their livelihoods in August 1689 rather than commit what they saw as unforgivable perjury. However difficult it may now be to sympathise with a conscientious belief in indefeasible hereditary right as the foundation of a society's political arrangements, their courage in following their deepest convictions at great personal cost, just like that of James's presbyterian victims during the 'Killing Times', is undeniably impressive.

This resentful and excluded strand within Scotland's Protestant community long remained an irritating thorn in the side of the Williamite state, and of its successor, the united Anglo-Scottish polity ruled over after 1714 by the House of Hanover. Natural wastage only to some extent moderated their small but disproportionate influence: the last pre-Revolution archbishop, Arthur Ross of St Andrews, survived until 1704; the last original bishop, Alexander Rose of Edinburgh, until 1720. To the end they declined to abjure their primary allegiance to James and his lawful heirs and successors. But still and thereafter, ministering to a dedicated flock especially strong north of the Tay and among the aristocracy and landed elite in particular, the episcopalian clergy survived, with each new generation trained and ordained by its predecessors. And above all, their very existence in presbyterian Scotland remained an uncomfortable reminder of the political chicanery of 1688–89 which had unseated the rightful Stuart king and brought Dutch and ultimately German usurpers to rule over his three British kingdoms.

Controversy and conformity

The presbyterians who emerged so comprehensively victorious by 1690 inevitably dictated the pattern of Scottish life long into the new century. Not least, the clergy of the established church responded in a way that is psychologically characteristic of successful revolutionaries who have been granted sudden and decisive triumph: they indulged in a bout of doctrinal introspection and mutual recrimination lasting for roughly forty years. In practice this involved attempting to release the latent spiritual enthusiasm of the faithful, as well as resisting what seemed to them a series of renewed threats to their own cause. This tendency to find counter-revolutionary activity everywhere they looked was certainly encouraged by the worrying knowledge that, until James's unexpected removal, the majority of Scots had simply conformed to the prescribed episcopalian dispensation. Added to the instinctive suspicion of presbyterianism on the part of both the crown and England's churchmen and politicians, and taken together with the very real threat to Britain's Protestant kingdoms during the continuing wars against Catholic France, it is not difficult to understand the distinct edginess of many of Scotland's presbyterian churchmen in the generation after the Revolution.

Their defensiveness was further encouraged by what seemed to be the tenacity, perhaps even the proliferation, of heterodoxy within Scotland itself. Newtonian science was forcing its way into the Scottish universities by the 1690s, with consequences for a view of the universe and of man's place within it which had yet to be determined. Deism (that is, a belief in a Creator-God) was at the same time beginning to find Scottish exponents like Archibald Pitcairn, the Edinburgh doctor who took aim at the parochial absurdities of the presbyterian church in several satirical plays. Quakerism, a most un-presbyterian approach to Christianity, had also travelled from England to infect more than a few people in Aberdeenshire, where its adherents had been persecuted since at least the 1670s. Most perplexing of all, the orthodox Calvinist Scot, rather than wallowing contentedly in the warm afterglow of the Revolution, was instead forced nervously to ponder the inexplicable survival of significant episcopalian and Catholic minorities in a supposedly godly kingdom.

With what Robert Fleming of Cambuslang, a member of an old presbyterian family, insisted in 1709 were 'atheism, deism, Socinianism, irreligion, profaneness, scepticism, formality, hatred of godliness, and a bitter persecuting spirit' all multiplying in Scotland by the day, there seemed to be ample grounds for the post-Revolution church to deal harshly with the merest hint of deviancy. The most famous victim of this mood was probably Thomas Aikenhead. The son of an Edinburgh apothecary and an undergraduate at the university, he had unwisely described the doctrine of the Trinity as 'a rhapsodie of faigned and ill-invented nonsense'. Prosecuted under a statute against blasphemy recently re-affirmed by the zealously presbyterian Parliament, Aikenhead was publicly hanged in the city's Grassmarket in 1696.

Acute sensitivity to doctrinal error remained an important characteristic of Scotland's national church for at least two generations. John Simson, professor of divinity at Glasgow, was undoubtedly the most eminent offender, twice finding himself before an inquisitorial committee of his fellow clergymen. Between 1714 and 1717 he was investigated for Arminianism in his lectures (in other words, for emphasising the benefits of good works at the expense of the trademark Calvinist insistence upon predestined salvation). Obscurity and inconsistency in Simson's arguments eventually led to the case being dropped by the General Assembly. But between 1726 and 1729 his frustrated enemies tried again, this time accusing him of promoting the Arian heresy (that is, of denying the Trinity – in effect, of questioning the divinity of Christ). This second charge, probably because of his inflammatory tactics in the face of persecutors for whose scholarly credentials the professor had little respect, was eventually upheld. Simson was duly suspended from teaching, a celebrated if unattractive martyr to the cause of intellectual freedom in presbyterian Scotland.

The same earnest desire to keep the nation within the bounds of theological orthodoxy, however defined, also gave rise to the once-famous 'Marrow' controversy. This revolved around the re-publication in Scotland in 1718 of an old English text, Edward Fisher's *The Marrow of Modern Divinity*, believed by many evangelical Calvinists to offer much-needed clarification on the central Christian doctines of justification and redemption. Yet the work's supporters, including Thomas Boston, minister of Simprim in Berwickshire, and James Hogg, minister of Carnock in Fife, were condemned by the General Assembly of 1720: the allegation against the 'Marrowmen', that the text was in fact antinomian – that is, that it encouraged lax behaviour by emphasising too strongly the guarantee of predestined salvation – was patently absurd, given that Fisher's work argued explicitly against such teachings. The real significance of this cause célèbre was that it revealed the profound tensions not just between the strictly orthodox and the unambiguously heretical but even among the orthodox themselves. In effect it confirmed that only marginally different interpretations of Calvinist doctrine could still give rise in Scotland to violent clerical disagreement.

Yet even as the presbyterian church was gripped by uncertainty over how to maintain and exploit its new-found dominance, the old problem of relations with a mistrustful and unsympathetic state continued to fester.

Reluctantly forced to accept the presbyterian settlement in 1690, an assertive London-based monarchy inevitably experienced periodic difficulties with a strictly Calvinist and fiercely independent Church of Scotland, even though William had eventually conceded that it was ultimately not subject to the state. As early as 1694 there was major disagreement, only Carstares's formidable diplomatic skills defusing the king's anger at the refusal of many ministers to subscribe the new Oath of Assurance. Tensions continued into the new century as first the Treaty of Union and then two pieces of Westminster legislation in 1712 threatened to drive a wedge between the crown and its subjects (and, at least in terms of the continuing polarisation between Jacobite and Williamite sentiment, still nominally its principal allies) among the established clergy.

Curiously, Union proved easier to finesse. Kirk sessions and individual ministers freely voiced their doubts about what they perceived as the threat to Scotland's distinctive religious heritage posed by the doctrinal laxity and episcopalian structures of the Church of England: Robert Wodrow, for instance, a loquaciously orthodox minister of Eastwood near Glasgow, feared greatly that creeping anglicisation would 'bind up our hands from asserting our religiouse and civil libertys, and menteaning a work of Reformation'. But with the passage of an Act of Security in 1707 explicitly guaranteeing the integrity of the Church of Scotland, institutional resistance withered. Relations between church and state, however, worsened rather than improved in the early post-Union years, precisely because of the difficulties English politicians encountered in adjusting to their new role in the government of Scotland. With the abolition of the Scottish Privy Council, there was at best only a very limited appreciation at Westminster of religious conditions north of the Border. It is thus not entirely surprising that two pieces of Scottish church legislation were soon enacted, neither of which could have been better calculated to offend delicate presbyterian sensitivities.

The first was the Toleration Act of 1712, effectively the unwanted Scottish offspring of the political ascendancy of the English Tories under Queen Anne. The measure was the ill-considered Westminster response to a successful appeal to the House of Lords by James Greenshields, an Edinburgh episcopalian minister whose use of the Anglican liturgy before a Scottish congregation had brought him the local presbytery's censure and consequent imprisonment by the magistrates. The Act sought to grant limited privileges of worship to Scotland's oppressed episcopalians on the condition that they follow Greenshields's precedent and employ the recognised English usages. Its intended beneficiaries, however, were frequently ungrateful, resenting the implication that their ancient Scottish tradition was somehow merely an off-shoot of Anglicanism: only some, the so-called 'English' congregations, subsequently availed themselves of the Act's protection. Further, by also confirming their exclusion from the old parish churches, it effectively completed the consignment of episcopalians to the outer ecclesiastical darkness. Yet the presbyterians were even less happy. The Toleration Act curtailed the powers of the Church of Scotland's courts, preventing presbyteries and the General Assembly from punishing those non-presbyterians who took advantage of it. Moreover, and although this was unintended, by weakening the punitive authority of the established church it significantly increased the prospects both for successful future schism within the presbyterian community itself and for unfettered religious pluralism in Scottish society at large.

The Patronage Act of 1712 was, if this can be imagined, even more difficult for many presbyterians to swallow. A flagrant breach of the Union's guarantees, it also removed a central plank of Scotland's presbyterian church government as established, supposedly in perpetuity, as recently as 1690. The burden of the legislation was to entrench the rights of landowners, burgh corporations, the universities and the crown to exercise patronage in the presentation of ministers to parishes. If the elders (that is, elected senior parishioners) objected to the patron's candidate, as the Act still allowed, then the kirk session could appeal to the presbytery, though the understanding – usually, but not always, justified by events – was that the higher church courts would favour the patron's choice. The motives for thus circumscribing the rights of Scottish congregations to choose or 'call' their own clergy are easy enough to explain, given the crown's longstanding mistrust of this unpredictable and populist aspect of presbyterianism. But the legislation caused immense ill-feeling. Responses to it, whether conformism or ostentatious disobedience, became the touchstone of party affiliation within a divided church for most of the next two hundred years.

The implications of the Patronage Act were therefore enduring, and not only in the ways that Anne and the Tories wished. It promised, as the government had hoped and the evangelicals feared, to make the established Scottish clergy increasingly the creatures of the government, the political classes and the social elite: this had profound consequences to which we will later return. More immediately, it also called into question the value of the other assurances given to Scotland in 1707. Nevertheless, one thing above all others ensured that presbyterianism ultimately remained four-square behind the post-Revolution and post-Union state. This was the menace to Scotland's Protestantism and civil liberties, as to England's, seemingly posed by those who sought the restoration of the exiled Jacobite claimants to the British thrones. It is to this most perplexing product of the Revolution, and its formative impact on eighteenth-century Scotland, that we need now to turn.

Jacobitism: ideology and intrigue

Few themes in Scottish or British history have received so much attention, and yet been so thoroughly misunderstood, as Jacobitism. Partly this is because it remains difficult to gauge its true strength. Influenced by the scorn heaped upon them by sneering Whigs, historians long dismissed the Jacobites as a colourful rag-bag of optimistic no-hopers whose eventual defeat by the forces of progress was as inevitable as it was beneficial. The derision has recently abated. Yet there remains genuine uncertainty as to whether Jacobitism was really a viable ideological and military enterprise. In particular, there is controversy over whether the Jacobites would ever have been able to muster the resources necessary to resolve once-and-for-all not only the Scottish but also the English succession. This critical but imponderable factor, which probably deterred potential supporters at the time just as much as it has preoccupied historians, is central to the continuing fascination with Jacobitism among the wider public.

A second problem is the sheer complexity of the motives which might conceivably lead individuals to become entangled in its conspiracies. Those who believed in the validity of the Stuart claim to the British thrones can safely be classified as ideological Jacobites. Unyielding belief in James's absolute legitimacy was itself a natural part of a broader conservatism of social and political outlook, one which intuitively set God's inscrutable dispensations above the convenience of politicians or the short-term problems caused by the religious quirks or personal weaknesses of an individual sovereign. People comfortable with this view were, of course, densely concentrated within the ranks of the non-juring clergy who had always opposed the Revolution: thus Jacobitism was necessarily stronger north of the Tay, and especially in the Highlands and the north-east. Another obvious cluster of principled Jacobitism existed among the conservative intellectuals, especially but not exclusively among those with relatively backward-looking or nostalgic cultural preoccupations – men such as Thomas Ruddiman, the publisher and antiquarian, and Allan Ramsay, the collector and promoter of traditional Scots poetry, as well as, famously, numerous professors in the more traditionally minded universities of Aberdeen, where episcopalianism, for the same reasons, always remained strong.

Instinctive and sincere conservatism of this kind was also disproportionately likely to be encountered in the few surviving enclaves of the old Catholic religion; among the baronage and peerage across rural Scotland, many of them resolutely episcopalian in religion and acutely conscious of their own status within a feudal hierarchy (Lockhart of Carnwath very much answers to this description); and among the Highland chieftains,

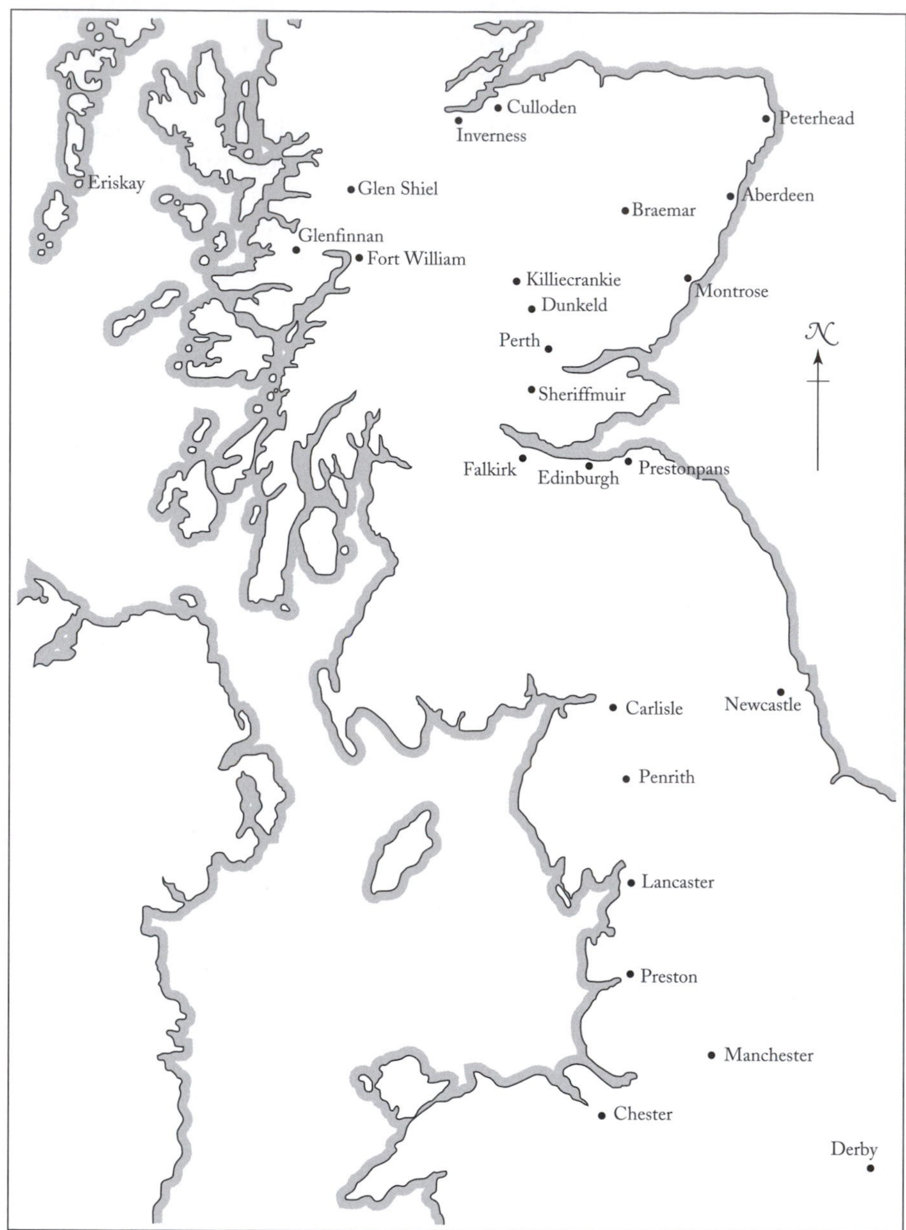

Map 2 Jacobitism and northern Britain, 1689–1746

mainly episcopalians like Maclean of Duart and Cluny Macpherson but sometimes Catholics like MacDonald of Clanranald, whose own exalted positions depended upon Gaelic society's greater attachment to notions of divinely ordained blood-right inheritance. Bound together in one way or another by a strong appreciation of timeless hierarchy, members of such communities were inevitably more receptive to the arguments for indefeasible hereditary succession in constitutional affairs proffered by silver-tongued Stuart apologists.

Yet many of those involved in Jacobitism demonstrably had less principled motives. Among them was John Erskine, 11th Earl of Mar, none other than the leader of the 1715 rebellion. Infamous as a turncoat and justly mocked by his contemporaries as 'Bobbing John', Mar's earlier support of Queen Anne and her Union treaty did not prevent his rapid defection to the Jacobites, in a brazen act of piqued opportunism, after his dismissal as Secretary of State by the recently installed George I. Another notorious trimmer, whose Jacobitism was in no sense rooted in faith or ideology, was Simon Fraser, 11th Lord Lovat. A ravenously acquisitive chieftain from Inverness-shire, his self-advancing progress from toadying Hanoverianism in 1715 to what he had calculated would be advantageous Jacobitism in 1745 ended with grisly inevitability at the gallows on Tower Hill in 1747. Thus for the historian to assert that an individual was a Jacobite – even that he or she manifestly played a leading part in a Jacobite rising – is not necessarily to say anything very useful about their theological or ideological commitments.

A third difficulty for the student of Jacobitism arises from the obvious fact that its supporters were obliged to disown or disguise their affiliations. By definition a treasonable commitment, open endorsement of the exiled dynasty's claims invited harassment and prosecution. Moreover, their sorry record of under-achievement scarcely encouraged potential allies of the Jacobites to believe that outright victory and thus immunity from retribution was likely. Most support therefore remained furtive, a matter for inward contemplation rather than ostentatious display. Vainglorious toasts to 'The King over the water' (or even just to 'The King', the monarch's identity being left pregnantly unspecific) failed time and again to translate into active support. Discussion of this shadowy movement's real dimensions, and so to a considerable degree of its contemporary viability, therefore ultimately founders on the rock of ignorance. Quite simply, we do not know, and are never going to know, how many Scots – or, for that matter, English people – contemplated a Stuart restoration with genuine enthusiasm.

The century opened, as we have seen, with Jacobitism already having assumed its classical form. It was throughout an underground and insurrectionary force with its focus overseas at the Continental court of the exiled

James VII and II – though in 1701 the Revolution's victim was succeeded by his son James Francis Edward, the Old Pretender, who lived, through a lifetime of more-than-usual disappointment, until 1766. Intrigue, plot and counter-plot were necessarily the essence of Jacobitism from beginning to end. Ceaseless manoeuvring and occasional extravagant planning within the fetid confines of the exiled Stuart court were the norm. High-political intrigue was also pursued regularly at the courts of assorted European princes, from whom diplomatic, financial and military aid was sought, always with more optimism than success. Rumour and deception were inevitably the currency of the numerous emissaries, secret agents and double agents at work for the cause. Internecine rivalry and faction-fighting was also rife. Activities were perhaps as often calculated to win favour or reward for the warring families, factions and individuals who were involved in the movement as materially to advance the cause of the Jacobite claimant himself.

If we discount the abortive plot of 1702, it was to be nearly twenty years before another Jacobite rising comparable with Dundee's failed counter-revolution of 1689–90 finally materialised. Its timing was actually determined by widespread hostility in Scotland towards the newly implemented Union, as well as by the strategic needs of Louis XIV of France, then at war with Britain. The resulting invasion of March 1708, however, like subsequent excursions, went off at half-cock. A naval force commanded by Admiral Forbin, and carrying the Old Pretender from Dunkirk to Scotland, found that the promised rising in northern England had failed to emerge. The Jacobites were then further discomfited by navigational errors and by the tenacious harrying of Admiral Sir George Byng of the Royal Navy, who pursued them up Britain's east coast. Eventually, exasperated by the lengthening odds against safe disembarkation, the flotilla was withdrawn by its French commander, failing to deposit James at Burntisland in Fife as had originally been planned.

Speculation has inevitably surrounded the potential for success in 1708. Genuine popular resentment of Union seems likely to have made Scotland propitious territory for an Old Pretender politically adept enough to make hostile noises about the treaty. It is also probable that elements within the nobility would have been prepared to lend their material support had James actually landed. But the longer-term prospects still look unpromising, even if we allow that the landed elite were in a position to force out significant numbers of their kinsmen, tenants and retainers in the Stuart cause. For an alarmed government had begun withdrawing regiments from Flanders, and it is frankly difficult to believe that the battle-hardened professionals who with Marlborough had recently defeated Louis's army in the field at Blenheim (1704) and Ramillies (1706) would not have proved murderously effective if brought to bear on James's far less practised forces.

This wider framework, with events in Britain inextricably linked to a wider European canvas, is in fact the key to understanding French interest in the Jacobite cause. For it greatly benefited France to foment domestic discontent within Britain. After all, both for a decade and a half at the start of the century and again through much of the 1740s and 1750s, France was pursuing an ambitious strategy of international expansionism in which the military, naval and financial rivalry of Britain was the principal obstacle: to this extent the familiar spectre of renewed Jacobite insurgency in Scotland – the mere threat of which could be almost as effective as a real rebellion in diverting London's attention and resources from the Continent, the Mediterranean, India or North America – was a precious gift to Louis XIV and his successors. Nevertheless, if France was willing periodically to promote successive conspiracies, then she assisted only to the extent that her own geo-political interests were served by a credible Stuart threat. It was a pity for Jacobitism that so many of its most intrepid supporters would be sacrificed before the strictly opportunistic nature of such foreign support finally sank home.

The limits to French commitment were seen clearly in Mar's bungled rising of 1715, which had to be undertaken entirely without Louis XIV's support. George I's arrival in London in the previous year had at first appeared to deal a body-blow to lingering Jacobite hopes that, somehow, the Hanoverian succession might be averted. But it had then proved instrumental in re-energising domestic support for Jacobitism. For the new monarch's narrow favouritism towards the Whigs and open disdain for the Tories marked a dangerous departure in royal policy. William's more equivocal approach, working pragmatically with politicians from both major groupings, and Anne's, which had openly embraced them, had divided and to some degree neutralised the Tories – a faction naturally more sympathetic towards monarchy and episcopacy – as a source of potential Jacobite recruits. But, excluded from office and influence for the foreseeable future, Scottish Tories in particular were now exposed to the blandishments and soothing words of the Old Pretender's agents. It was undoubtedly this factor above all which led the ousted Mar and other resentful colleagues like the Marquis of Huntly and the Earl Marischal to participate. The plan was for Mar, under the pretence of holding a hunting party on his estate at Braemar, to raise the rebel standard on 6 September. Thenceforward a victorious march on Edinburgh would be co-ordinated with a simultaneous rising by Jacobites in the Borders and northern England, the whole being timed to make possible James's landing in the English south-east and his triumphal progress towards London and the recovery of his patrimony.

The plan, however, went spectacularly awry from the start. Key interests in Scotland, like the established clergy and the Lowland burghs, were bristlingly hostile: the letter sent by the magistrates of Edinburgh to the loyal 1st Duke of Montrose, stressing that 'our utmost endeavours shall be used to preserve the peace of this place and prevent all insults from Jacobites and such as are enimies to his Matie and Government', encapsulates the formidable ideological obstacles facing the Jacobite cause in presbyterian Scotland. Furthermore, Mar was not even a competent leader of men: he dallied for two months at Perth before finally feeling emboldened to set his army of approximately 10,000 against the government's 4,000 men under Argyll. The outcome of the crucial engagement at Sherriffmuir in the hills near Dunblane on 13 November was tactically indecisive; but it was strategically disastrous for the Jacobites, among whom the MacRaes bore grievous losses. The battle left Argyll in possession of the key road to the south and the rebel cause effectively stalled. Crucially, it denied them the vital momentum that was imperative to boost confidence and attract further support from perennially reluctant allies.

Events in England, meanwhile, despite the active role played by Scottish forces under Viscount Kenmure and the dauntless William Mackintosh of Borlum, proved not much less of a damp squib. Instead of the intended march on Newcastle to secure the vital coal supplies on which London depended, the Jacobites marched west to meet an advancing government force. This quashed the rebels at Preston on 14 November. Government penetration of the Jacobite high command also easily detected plans for the invasion of Devon. It therefore had to be shelved. By the time the self-proclaimed 'James VIII' landed at Peterhead on 22 December, the rising was already in its death-throes. In February 1716 he was put back on board ship at Montrose, Mar accompanying him, a figure of ridicule to all sides and a symbol of a hopelessly inept cause.

If the failure of the 'Fifteen reflects badly on Jacobite competence, as well as on the utter necessity for the rebels to obtain serious foreign support, then what followed was even more disheartening. Kenmure was among those executed. The peerages of other key participants were forfeited (notably the earldoms of Mar, Seaforth, Nithsdale, Panmure and Southesk). Some Jacobite estates were sold to a speculative venture, the York Buildings Company, which emerged *ipso facto* as Scotland biggest landowner. Other properties were annexed to the crown and managed by government commissioners charged with applying their revenues to public use. The Disarming Act of 1716 also struck a blow against the martial traditions of the Highlands, imposing fines on those found in possession of weaponry. Meanwhile, the death of Louis XIV and the ascendancy of the regent Philippe, Duc d'Orléans, confirmed the recent revolution in French diplomacy. Determined to build bridges with Hanoverian Britain, the regent correctly deduced that providing aid and comfort for a pretender would be an insurmountable obstacle. James and his entourage, already ejected from Saint-Germain by the old king, were therefore forced to take refuge in Italy, where they threw themselves upon the mercy of another ambitious Continental power, the Spain of Philip V. This is why the next Jacobite rising made use of Spanish support, though unsuccessful overtures had even been made to Charles XII of Sweden, who had his own ambitions against the Hanoverians in northern Germany. The outcome, however, a characteristic mixture of wildly optimistic plans, grossly inadequate resources, a measure of genuine misfortune and more than a touch of absurdity, was no different.

In 1719, and co-ordinated with a planned invasion of southern England, two frigates deposited a small force of armed Spaniards, led by the returning exiles, the Earl Marischal, the Marquis of Tullibardine and the Earl of Seaforth, at the head of Loch Duich in the western Highlands. There they rendezvoused with a thousand men, raised by local Jacobite chieftains. But a storm off Cape Finisterre had already scattered the main fleet heading for the English coast: not for the first or the last time, the Jacobites, supposedly the Scottish diversion in a full-scale invasion of Britain, found themselves merely the stalking-horse for half-hearted foreign powers. A small government force from the Inverness garrison, under General Wightman, marched down Glen Shiel, and in the ensuing engagement on 10 June the invaders and their allies were put to flight – some of the Iberians fleeing up the mountainside to a peak ever afterwards known in Gaelic as *Spidean nan Spainnteach* (the Hill of the Spaniards). Tullibardine's subsequent letter to Mar, explaining how 'The Spaniards themselves declared they could neither live without bread nor make any hard marches thro' the Country', perfectly captured the sense of futility and frustration surrounding Jacobite adventures which were continually undermined by inadequate preparations and irresolute foreign backing.

The next twenty years were disappointing ones for Jacobites both in Scotland and elsewhere. A brief flurry of activity in the late 1720s culminated in yet more plots. But the absence of practical support from an interested Continental power rendered their threat largely nugatory. Indeed, it is unclear whether the British government now believed that Jacobitism, at least as a credible military threat, was dying a slow but inevitable death. Certainly there are signs that Hanoverian officialdom had begun to discount some of the dangers. Incorrigible rebels in exile, like Alexander Robertson of Struan, a legendary veteran of the 1689 campaign, and even the Earl of Seaforth himself, were allowed to return unmolested to their estates. Other Highland landowners of questionable reliability, with Lovat and MacDonell of Barrisdale suspiciously to the fore, were rewarded with key positions in the Independent Companies raised by the crown to police the Highlands. The military infrastructure designed by Wade to daunt any future risings, comprising an imposing network of garrisons, fortifications and roads, was also never completed to anything like the original specification.

Yet other aspects of policy do suggest continuing awareness of the Jacobite threat. While a further Disarming Act was imposed in 1725, pockets of government troops remained quartered, as a visible deterrent, in the vicinity of the more untrustworthy clans. The proximity of these garrisons to the fastnesses of the chieftains – Fort William, for example, was but a stone's throw from the home of Cameron of Lochiel at Achnacarry – nicely illustrated, but also continually exacerbated, the mutual mistrust between instinctive Jacobites in the Highlands and a still nervous Whig regime in Edinburgh and London. The activities of the Society in Scotland for the Propagation of Christian Knowledge (the SSPCK), the Lowland missionary agency founded in 1709 to sow the seeds of presbyterian orthodoxy among the obdurate Gaelic-speaking episcopalians and Catholics of the north and west, also suggested continuing official reservations about the underlying cultural alienation of the Highlands. Similar anxieties were arguably revealed in the excessive legal and political privileges granted to the Dukes of Argyll, who were identified – indeed, who actively encouraged others to recognise them – as the principal Scottish defenders of the Hanoverian order. Yet if the latter policy was a reflection of the government's nervousness, it was also to prove spectacularly counter-productive. For the Campbells' tightening grip across the southern and western Highlands, bolstering still further their family's traditional role as the acquisitive and assertive agents of central government, also served to push their many enemies and rivals, as well as a rapidly lengthening list of their resentful debtors and victims, into the welcoming arms of the Stuart pretenders.

The 'Forty-five

As things turned out, the government's anxieties were well-founded: the more dilatory aspects of recent policy were in fact to prove extremely costly. After 1739–40 the European scene once again brought renewed opportunities for the Jacobites to benefit from the Continental powers' strategic ambitions. France in particular was at daggers drawn with Britain amid the general conflagration known as the War of the Austrian Succession, provoked by the aggression of Frederick the Great of Prussia towards Austria and its vulnerable young monarch Maria Theresa. With France allied to Frederick and Britain's sympathies lying with the Austrians, by 1743, with the cautious Cardinal Fleury dead and Louis XV master of his own policy,

French interest in an invasion of southern England, to be facilitated once again by a Jacobite-led insurrection in Scotland, was revived. Well-placed to exploit this opening was quite the most intriguing product of the Jacobite court's enforced sojourn in Italy, the Old Pretender's son and heir Charles Edward, born at Rome in 1720. For the Young Pretender was an inspirational figure of boundless confidence and ambition – everything in the leader of a perilous undertaking that the insipid Mar was not. The French Channel fleet, however, was scattered off Brest in a storm: Whig historians were not slow to hail yet another 'Protestant wind' which had providentially nullified a Catholic power's assault on British liberties. Characteristically undaunted by what was in fact a desperate setback, Charles nevertheless took ship to Scotland, setting foot for the first time on the golden sands of Eriskay in the Outer Hebrides on 23 July 1745.

The story of the 'Forty-five, the last and grandest Jacobite rising, is well known. But the major problems encountered in gathering reluctant clansmen to Charles's standard at Glenfinnan on 19 August are worth emphasising. Key figures such as the Skye chieftains MacLeod of MacLeod and MacDonald of Sleat declined to bring out their clansmen, shrewdly assessing a rising without serious French participation as suicidal: coming from natural supporters, this should have been a warning that the cause once again lacked credibility. Donald Cameron, too, whose soubriquet 'Gentle Lochiel' was well-earned, studiously occupied himself in felling trees on his estate rather than rushing with open arms to greet the rightful heir to the throne. He endured an intense personal interview with Charles before being eventually cajoled into lending his and the Camerons' support. Forceful persuasion of this sort was critical in establishing momentum, and would clearly have been impossible without the overpowering presence and verbal dexterity of the Young Pretender himself.

It is difficult to say whether the Jacobites or the government were the more surprised by the outcome of the first encounter of the campaign. At Prestonpans, to the east of Edinburgh, on 21 September, Lord George Murray's army of 2,400 men, employed to effect in a classic Highland charge, comprehensively defeated Sir John Cope's roughly equal force, all that the government, with the British army heavily committed to campaigns in the Netherlands, had left for the defence of Scotland. Charles, who but for Cope's earlier anxiety might conceivably have been confronted in the Highlands before his momentum had become properly established, now had the luxury of spending October in Edinburgh, savouring the victory and preparing his forces for the long march into England. Some have regretted the decision to venture southwards on the grounds that it stretched the Jacobites' luck and resources too far, too soon. Yet long-term success in Scotland was inconceivable without an assault on England. In any case, it remains the golden rule of rebellion that momentum, once achieved, must at all costs be maintained. Charles was guilty not of unwarranted bravado but merely of pursuing what had been the explicit aspirations of his family for several decades past. Any Scot for whom the English expedition came as an unpleasant surprise had simply misunderstood the British nature of the Jacobite cause.

Accompanied by Murray, who would much have preferred a guerilla campaign in the Highlands, and a force of around 5,500 soldiers, including notable clan contingents from the Cluny Macphersons, the Camerons and the Robertsons, Charles passed through the Borders, capturing Carlisle on 15 November – another rude shock for a complacent government. By now the belated mobilisation of Hanoverian resources was underway. Front-line troops were hurriedly recalled from Europe and two large field forces assembled. One was placed under the command of Wade, whose army moved to block the rebels' progress through the north-east of England. The other was led by the king's third son, recently returned from Flanders, the young and brash Duke of Cumberland, who led his forces towards Chester, wrongly believing deliberately propagated Jacobite rumours that an assault on North Wales was in the offing. Not unexpectedly, Murray passed first through the English Catholic heartlands of Lancaster, Preston and Manchester, vainly hoping to recruit substantial additional forces. But thereafter he cut obliquely across the southern Pennines. In fact, Murray had completely outwitted both Wade and Cumberland: the road to London lay open and, with no major government army to block their path and Wade desperately scrambling to move his soldiers southwards to intercept the on-rushing Jacobites, it is, perhaps, not surprising that many Hanoverian politicians, City financiers and some of the metropolitan elite began preparing themselves for the arrival of the Young Pretender in the capital.

Even as a tell-tale run developed on the Bank of England, however, betraying the genuine fears of informed London opinion, a crucial decision was being taken in the Jacobite camp at Derby on 5 December – 'Black Friday'. At no stage had the considerable numbers of Lowland or English Jacobites promised by Charles materialised; nor had the French support, to which he had constantly alluded, been forthcoming. The mounting evidence that the army which had left Edinburgh was indeed alone – and, critically, that Charles's own repeated assurances to the contrary had been, at best, self-delusion – unnerved even some of his most loyal advisers. Furthermore, poor intelligence capability on the ground now exposed the Jacobites to government misinformation, leading them to believe that a large professional army still stood between themselves and London. Thus it was that the council of war finally outvoted a disgusted prince and determined upon an orderly retreat back to Scotland. There they would be closer to their own homes and their forces better able to sustain a guerilla campaign, ahead of a renewed offensive, perhaps with French help, in the spring.

The retreat was more successful than might have been hoped through largely unfriendly country and deepening midwinter. Following the road north through Lancashire and over the Westmorland fells, the Jacobites, though they evaded Wade's slow-moving countermarch from Yorkshire, were harried by Hanoverian dragoons – engagements occurring at places such as Hazelrigg near Lancaster and, on 18 December, at Clifton near Penrith, a skirmish in the mist, with the Macphersons prominent, the last battle ever fought on English soil. Back in Scotland, Charles's army met a sizeable government force of 8,000 men at Falkirk on 17 January under the command of Henry Hawley: again, a well-timed Highland charge on propitious ground scattered the rain-washed and wind-lashed Hanoverian soldiers. But Cumberland's relentless progress was unchecked. Taking advantage of the Royal Navy's command of the seas, he moved his soldiers by ship to Aberdeen, where they were rested, refreshed and, crucially, trained in battlefield techniques for bringing their superior experience and overwhelming fire-power to bear upon poorly armed clansmen.

The dénouement was short but brutal. In a last desperate step, on Charles's personal instruction and against Murray's professional advice, the Jacobites prepared for a set-piece confrontation on the boggy and exposed terrain of Culloden moor, on high ground to the east of Inverness. The engagement lasted little more than an hour: Hanoverian artillery ripped through the Jacobites; the government's 9,000 men, including large numbers of Lowland presbyterians in the 1st Foot (Royal Scots) and 21st Foot (Royal Scots Fusiliers), together with the Argyll militia, rebuffed the withering onslaught by the tired, hungry and poorly managed clansmen. After the ensuing massacre, perpetrated by accurate musketry and government cavalry, around 2,000 Jacobites lay dead in the heather. By nightfall on 16 April 1746, Jacobitism, at least as a serious military threat to the Anglo-Scottish state, was finished.

It is worth noting, however, that this was by no means apparent at the time. Some Jacobites expected the fight to continue. A force even gathered at the captured government fortress of Ruthven on Speyside some days later. But Charles had fled, along with his immediate entourage. He spent the next several months famously as 'the Prince in the heather', hiding among the Gaelic-speaking peasantry and Jacobite sympathisers in the west, with a price on his head, tracked by government ships and hunted by Hanoverian soldiers until he was finally spirited away by a French vessel on 27 September, never to see Scotland again. For his erstwhile supporters, the aftermath of Culloden was much less romantic. The government, yet to be convinced that Jacobitism was indeed a spent force, sought to make any repetition impossible. The considered opinion of presbyterian Scots, like John Home, the minister of Athelstaneford, whose later *History of the Rebellion* ably summarises this view, was crucial in shaping the policies imposed first by Cumberland's soldiers and then by parliamentary legislation: this was that the very nature of Highland society in its awful primitiveness – 'no cities nor populous towns', Home observed, 'no trade or commerce, no manufactures but for home consumption; and very little agriculture' – had made such dangerously reactionary politics virtually inevitable.

A permanent resolution to the problem of Scottish Jacobitism on this reasoning required not only exemplary punishment in the short term but also a raft of wide-ranging measures which over a longer period would bring the Gaelic-speaking communities into convergence with the law-abiding, polite and commercial values prevailing elsewhere in mainland Britain. This meant accelerating the gradual process of eradicating the traditional tenurial and judicial systems of the Highlands, in effect reducing chiefs like Lochiel or Clanranald from their problematical status as feudal warlords to being mere landowners and recipients of cash-rents like proprietors in the south. It also meant specifically prohibiting those customs and cultural forms among the clans which seemed to perpetuate or celebrate a violent and lawless lifestyle, where 'depredation and petty war', as Home alleged, were the accepted norm. It ultimately required civilising and improving the supposedly ignorant and backward Highland population through an earnest campaign of presbyterian missionary activity, the extension of basic schooling and a programme of enforced economic development.

Many of these imperatives are, of course, familiar in the aftermath of any civil war, brutal suppression gradually giving way to processes of restructuring and rehabilitation. Some of the government's victorious troops indulged in violent retribution in the Highlands. Instances of murder, rape, the burning of homes and the theft of animals were visited on the innocent as well as the guilty: their commander's endorsement of these activities has earned him opprobrium as 'Butcher Cumberland', his desire to intimidate potential future Jacobites meaning that even equivocal figures like John MacDonell of Glengarry, as well as uninvolved peasants in the glens, had their houses ransacked or the roofs burned from over their heads. Inevitably the judicial aftermath of the 'Fifteen was also mirrored, with several rebel peerages forfeited – notably the earldoms of Cromartie and Kilmarnock. Certain estates, such as those of Cameron and Fraser, were again placed under government control by the Annexing Act of 1752 and subjected to experiments in enforced improvement: it was to this scheme, for example, that the introduction of the tanning and bleaching industries to Crieff and the foundation of the new town of Callander, both on the Drummond estates in Perthshire, are owed.

The legislative package as a whole has achieved infamy in some quarters. But two totemic measures of 1747, the new Disarming Act and particularly the Act of Proscription (which prohibited the wearing of the tartan plaid, with similar exemptions for government soldiers), have in the popular imagination tended to obscure more fundamental changes like the final abolition of wardholding (i.e. land tenure in return for military service) and the imposition of the Heritable Jurisdictions Act. Certain parts of this programme have also been represented as brutish vandalism directed indiscriminately against an unfamiliar culture. Yet the government's response to large-scale Highland involvement in this almost-successful rebellion was far from being mindless. Instead, it rested, as Home's analysis emphasises, upon an elaborate political sociology which made various assumptions about cultural practices and social structure and their likely ideological consequences. Nor were the systematic dismantling of clan society after Culloden, and the attempt to use education and commerce as agents of civilisation, simply the crass impositions of an alien, English administration. To the extent that they were not in any case merely the result of long-term developments already evident in the Highlands (which, as we shall see, were bringing substantial change to Gaelic society by the 1740s), they were carried out with their accustomed zeal by the sort of presbyterian Scots who peopled well-meaning bodies such as the Committee for Forfeited Estates and the SSPCK. The aim throughout, as Tobias Smollett of Dunbartonshire patiently explained to his wider British public just fifteen years later, had been simply 'to prevent any future insurrection in the Highlands of Scotland, by diffusing a spirit of industry among the natives' and in particular to liberate them 'from that slavish attachment by which they had been so long connected with their landlords and chieftains'.

The ultimate fate of Jacobitism itself was not what either Charles or Cumberland would have anticipated. The movement continued, amid further intrigues and manoeuvrings in the courts of Europe, for perhaps another fifteen years, though never again managing a significant rising. Its last serious scheme was probably the abortive Elibank Plot of 1751–53, in which Alexander Murray, before his betrayal by a kinsman of Glengarry who was a British agent, was meant to have murdered or incarcerated George II and so precipitated another invasion by the Young Pretender. By 1760, however, any remaining French confidence in Jacobite plotting had disappeared. Even before that time, and not surprisingly given the disasters of the 'Forty-five heaped on those of earlier decades, virtually all remaining Jacobites had abandoned the delusion that either France or indeed any other Continental power would intervene decisively on their behalf. Charles Edward, who formally inherited the Stuarts' claim on his father's death in 1766, was reduced to an embittered and dissipated old man, devoted to sexual excess and hard drink, the sad man of Europe.

Contributing to the eventual eclipse of Scottish Jacobitism were undoubtedly several factors. But a principal one was the demise of the peculiar domestic environment in which both excluded episcopalians and incorrigible anti-Unionists had for different reasons thrown their weight behind a Stuart restoration. The reconciling of the Tories to the House of Hanover after 1745, not least through the Prince of Wales's increasing intimacy with opposition politicians, certainly helped heal wounds. So too did relative official leniency towards episcopalianism, as by mid-century Scotland began to enter an age of growing religious toleration and diminished interdenominational strife: indeed, by 1792, Dundas, pursuing patriotic unity following the French Revolution, was able to force through the lifting of the remaining penal sanctions against them. Meanwhile, the unmistakable economic benefits and tempting career opportunities which the Union had also begun to open up to most men of consequence in Scotland by the later 1740s provided ample incentive for belated accommodation with the Anglo-Scottish state: for example, the raising of Highland regiments for British service overseas permitted several leading members of disgraced families such as the Frasers and the Camerons to secure rapid rehabilitation by a reliable and remunerative route. All of these developments seriously reduced the competing attractions of what had always been a patently risky enterprise with uncertain prospects of success. Simultaneously the government's determined response to the 'Forty-five, coupled with the accelerating commercialisation of relations between Scottish landowners and their tenantry, made it less likely that a disaffected nobleman would be either able or willing to mobilise a sizeable private army for a rebellion.

Less easy to trace, of course, is the impact of creeping ideological change. Yet it is likely that sincere Jacobite principles, based on devout commitment to the legitimacy of the Stuart claim, were the last to fade away. The rights of heritable property remained axiomatic in Scotland's political, legal and social life even in the 1790s, as Lord Braxfield reminded Thomas Muir in his notorious trial speech. Moreover, with the pretenders convincingly cast in the emotive role of dispossessed feudal superiors, Jacobite protestations to be merely the innocent victims of wrongful disinheritance can only have retained real intellectual credibility. But without the encouragement of foreign powers and without the support provided by other, more opportunistic groups within Scotland who had previously lent critical mass to incipient plots and risings, Jacobitism as a serious political commitment was rapidly reduced to an eccentricity among a diminishing minority of the older generation. Indeed, in 1784 the Disannexing Act could safely be passed, allowing government-controlled estates to revert to their rightful owners. By

1788, when news of the Young Pretender's death reached Scotland, even the episcopalian clergy decided that they might now pray for the Hanoverians with good conscience. People by this time were learning to romanticise 'Bonnie Prince Charlie' and his intrepid band of Highland adventurers: the Jacobites had in effect completed their surprisingly swift journey from history into myth.

Moderatism: toleration and civility

Even by the time of the 'Forty-five, the Church of Scotland was fast becoming a rather different creature from the sometimes unpredictable animal, tetchy and introspective, which had emerged from the Revolution of 1689–90. Partly the changes were wrought simply by the passage of time: those who had known the 'Killing Times' were slowly but surely replaced by a new generation of more self-confident ministers and laymen who had known only a Scotland in which presbyterianism enjoyed an unchallenged legal monopoly. But other factors were also significant. The Union had progressively introduced a different outlook. A modus vivendi with Anglicanism, as with mainly non-presbyterian British politicians in London, was gradually achieved. Scotland's clergy also became less inward-looking. Increasing numbers, particularly younger ministers, were exposed to English literature and to a religious culture in the south in which toleration and moderation were beginning to be much more widely valued.

Nor was this all. As the principles enshrined in the Toleration Act of 1712 won over an increasing proportion of Scotland's parish ministers, so their predecessors' obsession with strict Calvinist doctrine and a unique presbyterian ecclesiology began to seem less germane to the life of a modern church. The Patronage Act, as its hard-line critics had originally feared, also gradually worked its effects. As the appointees of the Hanoverian monarchy, the political elite, the burgh corporations and the landed classes, it was almost inevitable that some of the best-placed and most influential ministers would cease by the 1740s to be moved primarily by their profession's traditional commitment to populist preaching and theological dogmatism. It was also probable that they would instead be supporters of the prevailing secular order, concerned to moderate the previously destabilising effects of religious controversy in Scottish life and to employ the pulpit both to counter the Jacobite threat and to promote social stability and political cohesion.

At the same time, a succession of senior clerical administrators emerged to help patrons deploy appointments in this way. Reverend gentlemen like

Patrick Cuming, Robert Wallace, William Robertson (Principal of the University of Edinburgh) and later Dundas's associate George Hill (Principal at St Andrews) ensured that the choicest posts went to deserving individuals of sober politics, restrained religious sentiments and good breeding. The changing nature of the clergy and the more relaxed character of clerical life in much of mid-century Scotland is typified by the unruffled demeanour of the very personable George Ridpath, minister of Stitchill in Berwickshire. An excerpt from his diary for two days in the late summer of 1752 conveys something of the agreeable tenor of his ways:

> Tuesday, August 19th – Read some of the *Philosophical Transactions*, and *The Art of Sinking*, and *Cadenus and Vanessa* in Swift's *Miscellanies*. In the former there are many fine strokes of humour and raillery, though on the whole it is but a hungry composition. Mrs. Pollock and her son Thomas here at tea p.m.
>
> Wednesday, August 20th – Revised some of *Philosophical Transactions*, etc. Diverted myself an hour or two with looking at places in the neighbourhood through Mr. Waite's reflecting telescope. Mr. Dawson called and sate a while before dinner. P.m. walked to Ednam with my sisters and drank tea.

With no appearance of theological concern or devotional passion, and seemingly based on literary and scientific pastimes punctuating a relaxed social round of tea-drinking and polite conversation, this existence was precisely what the Patronage Act had made more likely. The Welsh traveller Thomas Pennant, visiting the country in 1769, only exaggerated slightly when pronouncing Scottish clerics like these 'the most decent and consistent in their conduct of any set of men I ever met with of their order . . . at present much changed from the furious, illiterate, and enthusiastic teachers of old times'.

The emergence of such emollience at the very heart of the presbyterian church is conventionally dated to a meeting which took place in an Edinburgh hostelry (the venue speaks volumes) immediately prior to the General Assembly of 1751. It was provoked by the fear of some of the younger generation that the established church might be willing to acquiesce in an evangelical congregation's flagrant illegality. In rejecting the patron's presentation, the kirk session of Torphichen in Stirlingshire had not only shown themselves sympathetic to a more traditional interpretation of presbyterianism. They had also been openly scornful of the clear legal requirements of the Patronage Act. With the Presbytery of Linlithgow having effectively colluded with the parish by declining to censure them, several members of the upcoming Assembly – including Robertson, Home, Gilbert Elliot of

Minto (an Edinburgh lawyer and politician) and George Drummond (sometime Lord Provost of Edinburgh) – sought to engineer a more robust stance and thus to ensure that the Church of Scotland and its constituent congregations would remain submissive to the will of Parliament and the civil law.

That this was effectively the inaugural meeting of what soon became known as the 'Moderate' party in the Church of Scotland is now generally accepted; and both the strong links between like-minded clergy and laymen, and the underlying conviction that a highly organised caucus with connections in and around Edinburgh might impose itself decisively upon the more orthodox but disparate majority within the national church, were to be strongly characteristic of their largely successful career over the next forty years. For Moderatism, from its initial victory in another patronage dispute at Inverkeithing during the 1752 General Assembly, never achieved numerical preponderance in the church at large. It was quality rather than quantity that permitted the Moderates to exercise such a strong influence over the church from the 1750s onwards: influential academics, leaders and socialites, they were typically the incumbents of the more important parishes in south-east Scotland, and also closely associated, through men like Cuming and Robertson, with the traditional political and social elite.

A useful way of gauging the nature of Moderatism is to consult the stinging polemical rebuke directed at them by a contemporary critic of rather more orthodox outlook, John Witherspoon, then minister of Beith in Ayrshire but subsequently President of the College of New Jersey, the later Princeton University. Witherspoon's *Ecclesiastical Characteristics* (1753) stands in the grand tradition of eighteenth-century satire, its power arising from an uncanny knack of identifying significant facets of his subjects of which they themselves may have been but dimly aware. Above all, this view of the mental and cultural world of the Moderates reveals them as men characterised by growing embarrassment at the theological purity and moral rigour for which the Church of Scotland had until recently possessed such a fearsome reputation. As Witherspoon claimed in one especially vicious aspersion, this powerful new group within the church seemed 'never to speak of the Confession of Faith but with a sneer' and to 'avoid all unnecessary exercises of religious worship, whether public or private'.

Witherspoon's insinuation was, of course, that the Moderates actually wished to abandon, subtly but decisively, most of the defining features of traditional Scottish Protestantism. In place of proper Christian teaching, he suggested, they wished to install the pragmatic social psychology developed by the Glaswegian professor Francis Hutcheson and other 'heathen writers'; they saw God's Creation merely from the soulless perspective of modern science, as nothing more than 'a huge machine'; they preferred to keep the company of atheist philosophers like Hume and cynical politicians like

Ilay and Dundas, rather than mingling with their humble parishioners and evangelical brethren; they positively welcomed the authority of the British state over the Scottish church; they privileged the legal rights of lay patrons over the moral prerogatives of congregations, seemingly assuming that 'the inclinations of the common people are to be utterly despised'; and they sought to replace the strenuous preaching of salvation and the condemnation of immorality with a more agreeable amalgam comprising a smattering of blameless truisms and a mess of undemanding moral compromise.

Such criticisms, it must be said, have a certain validity: to read the once-popular sermons of Hugh Blair, minister of St Giles's, Edinburgh, is indeed to feel that no moral problem is insurmountable, no sentiment too bland to go unuttered. His sermons were perceptively mocked by his younger friend James Boswell for appearing to supply 'comfortable solutions'; and pulpit pieces such as 'On Gentleness', where Blair advised his congregation merely to 'Let determined integrity dwell in a mild and gentle breast', exude a coolness and vacuity fundamentally alien to the muscular and provocative demagoguery of what was still formally a Calvinist church. For many nineteenth- and twentieth-century commentators sympathetic to the evangelical standpoint, Moderatism thus seemed a disastrous cul-de-sac. It was a regrettable phase when the Church of Scotland had prostrated itself before the government and the elite, callously shirking its responsibilities for the nation's moral health and spiritual well-being in the deadening pursuit of conformity and quiescence.

There can be little doubt, moreover, that Moderatism did indeed hamper the church in tackling what was by the end of the century its most urgent problem. Rapid urbanisation was producing large concentrations of migrants living in conditions of increasing squalor. Often such people also lacked access to the religious, social and educational facilities traditionally provided by the national church. Yet the latter was fatally handicapped in its response, governed as it was by a caste of sociable but essentially lukewarm clerics closely allied to the propertied classes and largely devoid of missionary impulses. The other factors threatening the conventional pre-eminence of the Church of Scotland were also not ones against which the Moderates were inclined to act. The defence of patronage, the growth of pew renting (charges imposed to cover the costs of new facilities for worship) and the appearance of 'laird's lofts' (segregated accommodation for landowners in parish churches) all sat well with Moderate principles but contributed to the permanent loss of some adherents and the failure to recruit others. Each was also a gift to other Scottish churches which increasingly drew members away. Overall, from more than 90 per cent nominal adherence among the population as late as the 1760s, the established church could claim the allegiance of only around 30 per cent of Scots by the 1850s – a historic failure for which Moderatism must take its full share of the blame.

Yet it would also be grossly unfair to argue that the Moderate party did not contribute some striking achievements to Scottish life. Above all, their determination to end the church's lamentable record of persecution and political controversy over matters of religion, and so to draw a line in particular under the violent upheavals of the seventeenth century, was to be of immense long-term value. Their instincts, if never remotely democratic, were characterised by a kind of idealistic elitism: a willingness, in other words, to run ahead of public opinion, to adopt stances which were not yet widely credited by most of the contemporary population but which were already favoured by advanced thinkers in Britain and Europe and which would in due course be strongly endorsed by the great majority.

The whole question of intellectual and religious toleration is the outstanding instance of Moderate precocity. Under the influence of men like Robertson and Blair, the Church of Scotland ceased by default to exercise many of its more savage legal prerogatives. Just fifty years after Aikenhead's demise at the hands of recrudescent Calvinism, the philosopher and unbeliever Hume survived a concerted attempt by Edinburgh's evangelical faction in 1755 to have him tried for heresy. Hume's friend Lord Kames evaded a malicious prosecution the next year, while liberal clergymen fended off attempts by their more censorious brethren to punish their supposed impiety in attending the theatre. Several of the Moderates, including Blair, even became active freemasons: in other words, they were members of a social organisation with deep Scottish roots, which attracted respectable men from a wide variety of backgrounds with its emphasis on friendship, mutual toleration, moral propriety and a belief in a fundamentally benign Supreme Being. As we shall see, the rich intellectual culture which blossomed so dramatically in mid-century Scotland would certainly have been very different, and might well not have happened at all, without the protection afforded by this new generation of open-minded and gregarious clergymen who found themselves irresistibly attracted to such enlightened ideals.

The liberal aspirations at the heart of Moderatism, but also the practical problems of being in a numerical minority, were nowhere better seen than in 1778–79, when, under Robertson's leadership, attempts were made to bring the church behind the government's Relief Bill, supported by Dundas, which would remove most of the legal disabilities still imposed upon Scotland's Catholics. Amid the resulting row, the flames fanned by London's apparent obliviousness to the stronger reactions which were inevitable in presbyterian Scotland, evangelical clerics found it easy to whip up crowds of protesters in Glasgow and in the capital. At one point, faced by the mob, Robertson's family even took refuge in Edinburgh Castle. Ultimately the bill foundered, under pressure from a distinctly immoderate organisation, the Protestant Association. This was an important lesson to the Moderates – as to the historian, perhaps – that their contemporary successes were always likely to be limited, and would usually depend upon careful incremental change pursued within the church structure, where their personal authority and impressive contacts could be brought to bear.

Evangelicalism

The crucial division within the eighteenth-century Church of Scotland, the rift rendered almost irreparable by the Patronage Act, was over the system of clerical appointments imposed and upheld by successive governments. It was this, more than anything else, which set the Moderates apart from the evangelical or 'Popular' party with whom they contended. The former ritually protested their distaste at every General Assembly but ultimately obeyed the law. The latter sided enthusiastically with those kirk sessions and presbyteries, notably in celebrated cases such as Torphichen and Inverkeithing, and at St Ninian's near Stirling between 1766 and 1773, who rejected the claims of the civil power to jurisdiction over Christ's followers. The very fact that some patrons trafficked profitably in parish appointments was, of course, the reddest of rags to the evangelical bull: 'In obedience to your command . . . I find they have four presentations to sell – viz Tillienessle, Auchindoir, Newmachar and second minister of the old town. They say the lowest they incline to come in, is £150 for the two first and £200 for the two last . . .', reported one of the 2nd Earl of Fife's agents in 1769.

Yet while it long remained the defining controversy, eliminating the influence of venal landowners over appointments was never the only bone of contention. Political and doctrinal as well as merely ecclesiological differences distinguished the opposing clerical factions, even as in other respects they also had surprisingly much in common. In the first place, those who resented patronage were more likely, as traditionally minded presbyterians, to favour a stricter interpretation of Calvinist doctrine. Consequently they were more willing to oppose theological divergence wherever they perceived it. Many continued to think like John Mill, a conservative Shetland minister in the 1770s, who complained bitterly to his diary about his less orthodox colleagues: 'so double and deceitful, so great a scandal and disgrace to their function', he fulminated, 'that I would be loath to admit people of such dispositions to a Sacrament or to the office of a lay elder'. Above all, the Popular party was willing to conceive of the national church as a preaching, ministering and proselytising force for the advancement of Protestantism, and so were more obviously at ease with the customary rhythms of Scottish presbyterianism. Unlike most Moderates, its members were also evangelical by inclination, tending to be in tune with the sacramental and devotional cycles culminating in the conversion experiences and dramatic re-affirmations of faith which occupied the devout each annual communion season.

Ministers like Aeneas Sage of Lochcarron, and, of course, the SSPCK as an institution, also enjoyed some notable missionary success for the established church, winning over significant numbers of Gaelic-speaking episcopalians and Catholics to presbyterianism. Indeed, in so far as a Moderate-led institution remained capable of gathering new converts within Scotland, it unsurprisingly did so where its local activities, particularly in Highland districts and among urban and industrial workers, were in the capable hands of the more active evangelical clergy. The communion seasons, such as those at the heart of the great Cambuslang 'revival' in the early 1740s, were very much the living, breathing spirit of this energetic and enthusiastic brand of presbyterianism: certainly these phenomena owed little to complacent Moderatism. Yet it must be remembered that it was precisely this zeal for the preservation and extension of Protestant piety in Scotland that also saw the Popular party take the lead in mobilising public opposition to the Catholic Relief Bill in 1778–79. Their burning vision of a godly society not only entailed a punishing programme of ministering and conversion. It also made them implacably hostile to what they interpreted as a legislative assault upon the historic achievements of the Reformation, which had initially rid the Scottish people of the scourge of Popery.

Divergent impulses separated the established church's two parties in their responses to other touchstone issues. The fact that so many Americans were evangelical Protestants as well as having strong connections with Scottish presbyterianism in particular naturally encouraged many in the Popular party to support the rebel colonists after 1776. Such disloyalty to the British state inevitably caused offence among the church's establishmentarian leadership. Yet Popular ministers like James Muir, minister of Urr in Dumfriesshire in 1778, and William Porteous of Glasgow's St George's parish in 1782 (the latter also a leading opponent of Catholic Relief) confidently presented declarations at synods or General Assemblies which demanded a speedy restoration of peace, and, by implication, an end to the government's aggression. Certain pieces of American literature, notably fast-day sermons by Witherspoon, were also much re-printed. These predictably gained a strong reputation among the evangelically inclined, with whom their familiar mingling of Calvinist theology and demands for freedom from government persecution struck a powerful chord. Popular ministers within

Scotland even made their own contributions to the controversy. None better captured the sense of evangelical fellow-feeling with the colonists than John Erskine's famous *Shall I go to war with my American brethren?*, which first appeared in 1769 and was many times re-issued.

Simultaneously the Popular party were distinguished by their markedly stronger instincts towards social egalitarianism and pastoral vigour. The former, arguably a natural corollary of the broadly democratic ethos of strict presbyterian church government, also had obvious affinities with their inclusive approach to the saving of souls. Indeed, in a famous sermon to the Synod of Perth and Stirling in 1732, Ebenezer Erskine made this connection in the clearest terms: 'I can find no warrant from the word of God', he insisted, 'to confer the spiritual privileges of His house upon the rich beyond the poor.' The problems of poverty and the legitimate uses of wealth were also more likely to be discussed in the sermons of the Popular clergy – at least before public utterances smacking of ideological radicalism became less respectable after the late 1780s. Witherspoon, for example, had a great deal to say on the subject of the obligations of the rich to employ their personal resources for the benefit of the poor. So had evangelical ministers operating in increasingly deprived urban environments, like John MacFarlan of Edinburgh's Canongate parish.

Nevertheless, the traditional distinction between evangelicalism and Moderatism can be overdrawn. After all, much of the commentary from which this familiar picture of a strongly polarised eighteenth-century Scottish church is derived, from Witherspoon to his successor at Princeton, James McCosh, a hundred years later, is itself obviously partisan in nature. One result is that it exaggerates the Moderates' alleged faults with the clear intention of distinguishing them from the mainstream presbyterianism which these authors and their evangelical brethren themselves claim uniquely to represent. In reality, however, neither the political nor the cultural affiliations of the two clerical parties were necessarily antithetical. Often they amounted only to a difference of emphasis. Many evangelical clergymen, for example, were impeccably cultivated and learned. Some were almost as familiar with advanced philosophy and polite secular literature as their Moderate rivals. Certainly they were not in general a class of blinkered philistines. Indeed, it is impossible to imagine Witherspoon's satire having been quite so effective had it not rested on an insider's knowledge of the cultural milieu with which the Moderates in particular openly associated themselves.

The evangelical clergy, especially in Edinburgh, plainly included several men of great scholarly distinction. Alexander Webster, the mid-century minister of the Tolbooth Kirk, was one of the best known: an accomplished statistician who founded the Church of Scotland's pension fund for the widows and children of ministers, Webster's great fondness for claret earned him the affectionate nickname 'Dr Bonum Magnum'. Another was Robert Walker, one of Blair's colleagues at St Giles's in Edinburgh (though not to be confused with his rather younger namesake, minister of Cramond and then of Canongate Kirk, who was immortalised as the ice-skating clergyman in Raeburn's much-loved painting). A third evangelical minister of note was John Erskine, a respected classical scholar who served the city's Greyfriars' Kirk. Such men in practice conceded little to the likes of John Home in secular erudition and refined taste, even if anti-Moderate polemics have tended to downplay the similarities.

The two parties in the Scottish church also shared more than merely cultured personnel. Before the end of the century a sincerely shared humanitarianism would see them standing side by side against the iniquities of slavery. The General Assembly of 1788 itself welcomed overtures on the subject from three separate regional synods. Among the overwhelming majority of members of the established church who found themselves in agreement on this burning moral and political issue, differing only over methods for advancing the common cause, were not only Henry Erskine, opposition politician and prominent lay member of the Popular party, but also 'Jupiter' Carlyle, minister of Inveresk, and even Henry Dundas, the Lord Advocate himself, for the Moderates. Conversely, their typical responses to political radicalism reveal yet more of the unremarked common ground between ostensible clerical opponents. For the Popular party's growing reluctance by the 1790s to tease out any social implications to their spiritual egalitarianism tended to bring the parties even closer together. Moreover, neither had much truck with the French Revolution once its early liberalism had begun to mutate first into political extremism and then into godless atheism.

The similarity of approach was typified by men like Thomas Somerville, the minister of Jedburgh, who took the Popular side on patronage but who was also theologically close to the Moderates: his *History of Political Transactions* (1792) claimed fairly that it sought simply to nourish 'the ardour of patriotic reflections'. John Dun, minister of Auchinleck and sometime tutor to James Boswell, likewise pronounced Britain's existing constitution superior to the dangerous innovations of the Estates-General. Nor did either party entertain radical calls for domestic reform: the conservatism of the Popular party, as of the Moderates, was boundless. Perhaps we should not be entirely surprised. One party, enlightened and elitist, was tied by interest and inclination to the political and landed classes. The other, more spiritually energetic and populist in temper, was nostalgic for a sixteenth-century world of theological certainty and strict moral orthodoxy – even if this had never really existed. Both commitments were, however, essentially conservative in inspiration, and thus capable of pushing the Church of Scotland's warring clergymen unwittingly in the same ideological direction.

Dissent and Popery

Outside the established church remained other Protestants who, pushing the principles of the Popular party to their logical conclusion, declined to live under the yoke of the state. The figures are necessarily imprecise, but a total of no fewer than 100,000 presbyterian dissenters (based on an anguished claim made in the General Assembly in 1766) is often suggested. Not all of these belonged to the large-scale dissenting churches which emerged during the eighteenth century. The remnants of those radical Covenanters who had never embraced the 1690 settlement long survived as a separate tradition: one sect, the Cameronians, remained strong in Lanarkshire, and after 1743 they constituted the Reformed Presbyterian Church – a standing indictment, as they saw it, to those who conformed to the dictates of the politicians.

More significant, though, were the eighteenth-century departures from the Church of Scotland which occurred in the aftermath of the Patronage Act. One of the more interesting was the dissenting community founded by John Glas, deposed minister of Tealing near Dundee, in 1728. Known thereafter as the Glasite church, it actually managed to enjoy some success in America following the emigration of the Sandemanians, named after his Perth disciple Robert Sandeman. Like the Old Scotch Independents, established in the 1760s, the Glasites confirmed the attractions to some Scots of full-blown independency or congregationalism on the English model, in which the autonomy of each parish community was entrenched. Yet the most substantial departures from the eighteenth-century Church of Scotland were actually still fundamentally presbyterian in both organisation and ethos.

The first was led by Ebenezer Erskine, the Stirling minister, who, along with three colleagues, including his brother Ralph, minister of Dunfermline, organised the 'Original Secession' – a name used to distinguish it from subsequent further haemorrhaging from the establishment. The Erskines had impeccable Covenanting credentials. Ebenezer himself had been a 'Marrowman', and much of his motivation in challenging and eventually abandoning the national church came from a growing suspicion that it was moving away from the orthodox Calvinism in which he was steeped. In 1733 he and his colleagues were suspended by the General Assembly following a disagreement over patronage. This they took at first as justification for a degree of self-imposed segregation. Anxious about the taint of schism, they were careful to proclaim that their newly formed Associate Presbytery still remained formally within the establishment. But predictable tensions over this unusual arrangement eventually culminated in their final deposition by the General Assembly in 1740.

Within just two years, the Associate Presbytery had attracted twenty ministers and thirty-six congregations. By 1745 it had successfully reproduced itself, amoeba-like, to form three distinct presbyteries. Although characterised by a visceral dislike of patronage, it was also marked by an intensely evangelical spirituality. This entailed an emphatic re-affirmation of the Solemn League and Covenant of 1643 as the true standard of Protestant piety, and a strenuous pastoral commitment to the welfare of parishioners, these trends helping make the new church particularly attractive to those caught up in Scotland's contemporary social and economic upheavals. Doctrinally obsessed and, like Erskine himself, temperamentally unyielding, it is not surprising, however, that the Secession Church which eventually emerged from the Associate Presbytery should itself be riven by continued controversy. By 1800 it had split into no fewer than four factions: the Burgher and Anti-Burgher sects differed over whether adherents could decently profess a burgess oath which appeared to contain veiled references to the established church; the New and Old Light variant of both then separated because the former persuaded themselves that the Covenant's near-fusion of church and state had become a dangerous anachronism.

Thomas Gillespie's schism, the second major presbyterian departure from the eighteenth-century Church of Scotland, was similar to Erskine's in some of its origins. Entering the ministry at Carnock near Dunfermline in 1741, he had been involved the following year in the famous revivals, centred on Cambuslang to the south of Glasgow and at Kilsyth in Stirlingshire, in which the traditional communion seasons had given rise to perhaps the century's greatest outpouring of popular piety, devotion and ritual. In due course Gillespie also became an outspoken critic of patronage and of the church's political conformity and growing laxity. In a noteworthy passage in his *A Treatise on Temptation* (1774), he defended the right of congregations to choose their own clergy, specifically condemning those 'patrons, heritors, town-councillors, tutors, factors, presbyteries . . . whose station or office afford them weight or influence in the matter of settlement of ministers'. The similarity with Erskine, however, ends there. For the well-liked Gillespie was rather more the innocent victim of the Church of Scotland's fear of destabilising spiritual fervour within its own ranks.

Initially called to account at the General Assembly in 1752 for his resolute opposition to the settlement at Inverkeithing, he was deposed the following year. In 1761, after continuing to minister in the Dunfermline area (at times without recompense, having insisted that his stipend be distributed among the poor), and having been joined by Thomas Boston, son and namesake of the original 'Marrowman', Gillespie finally founded the Presbytery of Relief – the 'relief' in question being from the tyranny of an overbearing establishment. Strongly influenced by the strand of English liberal nonconformity associated with Philip Doddridge, with whom Gillespie had studied at Northampton, the Relief Church was less doctrinally precise than Erskine's church. It was also less preoccupied with the Covenant. This so-called 'Second Secession' notably displayed greater latitude than the first, freely communicating with other reformed churches and even favouring the granting of civil rights to Catholics. Yet in its evangelical piety and strongly anti-establishmentarian orientation it remained quintessentially presbyterian in character. It proved especially successful in southern and central Scotland, forming nineteen congregations by Gillespie's death in 1774.

The two secessions effectively transformed the landscape of eighteenth-century Scottish presbyterianism. Rarely by 1800 did dissenters of various kinds comprise less than 2 per cent of any Lowland parish: usually it was considerably more. Even in the furthest-flung reaches of the kingdom – such as Orkney, Shetland and Tiree, where the leaders of the Society for Propagating the Gospel at Home, James Alexander Haldane and his brother Robert, converted communities to a form of non-denominational evangelicalism – a variety of preachers acting independently of the established church were winning the hearts and minds of growing numbers. But presbyterianism, for obvious reasons given Scotland's history, remained the most common basis of dissent, the churches founded by Erskine and Gillespie often achieving such extraordinary local success that they totally swamped the remaining adherents of the Church of Scotland. At Orwell in Kinross-shire by the 1790s, for example, a largely weaving population contained 712 Burghers, 590 Anti-Burghers and 40 members of the Relief Church: just 401 of the parishioners still professed the established church.

Another point worth strongly underlining is that those attracted to dissent were by no means always simply the poor or the oppressed. Many had successful occupations and professions: industrial workers and tenant farmers mingled with merchants, shopkeepers and the self-made. Noteworthy individual adherents included not only the radical Dundee weaver George Mealmaker but also plutocrats like David Dale, the Glasgow textile entrepreneur, who was actually an Old Scotch Independent, and John Jamieson, the lexicographer and antiquarian, who was himself a Secession Church minister in Forfar. The Glasites too included James Morison, the Perth publisher, as well as many of the more important Perth and Dundee linen manufacturers. Indeed, only the Anti-Burghers really failed to recruit significantly from among the prosperous sections of society. More commonly the dissenting churches received an enthusiastic response from all those groups outside the traditional landed and professional elites who wished to assert a degree of control over their own religious lives and who suspected that the participatory ideals so dear to Scottish presbyterianism were being traduced by a lukewarm Moderate establishment.

Of course, all Scottish presbyterians, whether dissenters or the members of the rival factions within the established church, believed that they alone were the true inheritors of their nation's spiritual heritage. Yet other Scots always remained unambiguously beyond the outer margins of this deeply divided Protestant community. Catholicism – 'Popery' as it was still pejoratively known – had survived all earlier attempts by a hostile civil and ecclesiastical establishment to stamp it out. In most of central and southern Scotland by the eighteenth century it was rare, excepting where it had been sustained by incurably recusant aristocrats like the Drummonds in southern Perthshire and the Maxwells in Peebles-shire. Overall, there is no good reason to cavill with Alexander Webster's estimate in 1755 which put Scotland's Catholic population at just 16,490 people (or 1.3 per cent of the total). He also believed that these were densely concentrated in a few localities: roughly 2,300 of them lived in Aberdeenshire, a similar number in Argyllshire and as many as 5,700 in Inverness-shire. By contrast, the counties of Ayrshire, Berwickshire, Kinross-shire, Nairnshire, Roxburghshire, Sutherland and West Lothian, together with the islands of Orkney, at least on Webster's calculations, contained precisely no Catholics at all.

Structures were, however, in place which served to buttress what little Roman observance remained in a country once proud to be known as the 'special daughter' of the Papacy. In 1694 a Vicar-Apostolic had been appointed with specific responsibility for Scotland. By the end of the 1720s separate Lowland and Highland vicariates were also in operation. Overseen ultimately by the office of Propaganda Fidei at the Vatican and employing a constant trickle of graduates from the exiled Scots Colleges at Paris and elsewhere – and also, after 1717, from an underground seminary at Scalan in Banffshire – a succession of post-holders like James Gordon and later George Hay and John Geddes supervised small-scale but determined endeavours to minister to the faithful. In remote and potentially fruitful areas like Morar, where seaborne access was favoured and contact with Ireland well-established, there were even some attempts at missionary work, involving perhaps forty active priests by mid-century. Underfunding, however, together with rivalries between the Highland and Lowland missionary operations and continuing tensions arising from the French Jansenist heresy within the Scottish Catholic community in the 1730s and 1740s, created serious obstacles.

Even more so than non-juring episcopalianism, moreover, Catholicism was fatally handicapped by the Jacobitism which its adherents almost universally endorsed. Indeed, following successive rebellions in which priests had been clearly implicated, Catholic chapels were destroyed, Jesuit missionaries imprisoned and prominent supporters pressured into conversion. Only with the final elimination of the Stuart cause did the political imperatives for suppression begin to disappear. Accordingly, the fortunes of Catholicism improved steadily after mid-century. While the Relief controversy of 1778–79 revealed how hostile popular opinion remained, the heady atmosphere of patriotic unity amid the Revolutionary wars, in which Catholic soldiers served courageously despite their technical disqualification from public service, allowed similar legislation to be imposed on Scotland by Pitt's government in 1793, finally removing the worst disabilities. From 1796, Dundas, who favoured comprehensive toleration of the various churches to which loyal British subjects subscribed, even engineered a secret £1,000 Treasury subsidy which enabled Scottish Catholicism to survive during the European wars which cut it off from Rome's direct support.

Popular superstition

If commitment to each form of institutionalised Christianity tended to be determined by a range of local and communal factors which resulted in very substantial geographical variations, other kinds of belief occurred more uniformly across Scotland, with adherence determined principally by a combination of social status and educational background. Even to use the word 'superstition' is, of course, to risk treating popular convictions with the scorn to which they were increasingly subjected by better-educated contemporaries. Yet among the Highland peasantry and rural tenantry of the Lowlands during the eighteenth century, the existence of fairies and demons, the ability to predict future events and the efficacy of spells and charms was still generally taken for granted. Nor had these beliefs entirely disappeared even among the elite – at least at the start of the eighteenth century. After all, Sir Isaac Newton's lifelong obsessions with astrology and numerology are now well-known. But we might also do well to recall that his colleagues included George Sinclair, professor of mathematics and philosophy at Glasgow, who specialised in hydrostatics (particularly the provision of water supplies for Edinburgh and the drainage of coal mines) and who even managed to invent a primitive diving-bell. This eminent and practically minded intellectual was, however, the author of *Satan's Invisible World Discovered* (1685), in which a range of natural phenomena were presented as certain proof of diabolical forces at work in the world.

Two other educated men provide further compelling evidence of the sheer pervasiveness of strictly non-Christian beliefs around the turn of the eighteenth century: Robert Kirk, minister of Aberfoyle in Perthshire, who in 1691 wrote *The Secret Common-wealth*; and Martin Martin, the Dutch-educated steward to the Macleods at Dunvegan on Skye, who published a *Description of the Western Islands of Scotland* in 1703. Neither was remotely ignorant by contemporary standards: indeed, each was very likely the best-educated man in his own parish. Yet Kirk and Martin sympathised with the living superstitions of the common people around them. Kirk even testified emphatically to the existence of whole species of fairies, including brownies and elves: for many decades after his own funeral in 1692, local people continued to maintain that his coffin was filled with stones and that the overly inquisitive clergyman had in fact been spirited away to Fairyland. Martin too had much to say about the prevalence in Gaelic society of powerful beliefs only distantly related to the theological teachings of the Christian churches, whether Catholic or Protestant.

Belief in second-sight – a psychic power defined by Dr Johnson during his 1773 visit as 'An impression . . . by which things distant or future are perceived, and seen as if they were present' – remained particularly deeply rooted. Indeed, it was frequently said that the gift was hereditary in certain families. The folk motif of precognition, though not uncommon in other societies, was, however, sufficiently characteristic of the Scots in this period that it is found time and again in literature and anecdote. Scott's *Waverley*, for example, reaches its momentous climax with the fictional hero of the 'Forty-five, Fergus MacIvor, having been visited by the *Bodach Glas*: the appearance of this ancestral presence is proof-positive of the chieftain's own impending doom, which he therefore embraces with dignified resignation. Similarly, in North America in 1758, Duncan Campbell of Inverawe, a kinsman of the Duke of Argyll, recalled that years earlier he had been upbraided by the spectral image of a murdered cousin whose assailant Campbell had unwittingly sheltered: the ghost promised they would meet again 'at Ticonderoga' where he too would meet an early death. When the apparition duly re-appeared on the eve of a military engagement at a place known to the natives as Ticonderoga, Campbell told his commanding officer that his fate was already sealed – as things proved. Boswell and Johnson, while sceptical of what they heard, simply reported what remained a widespread belief in the ability of certain individuals in certain circumstances to foresee the future, and usually its grimmer aspects.

Many superstitions, of course, had more benevolent implications. Most had origins in the immemorial human relationship with nature: they explained the weather, the seasons and the agricultural cycle on which people depended; they concerned the woods and forests, the mountains, the rocks and the sea in proximity to which an overwhelmingly rural population in Scotland still lived; they legitimated the use of herbs, potions and spells to heal the sick and nurture the crops and livestock on which a mainly agrarian society depended. This was the world in which a church court in Strathblane in Stirlingshire in 1723 heard how Catherine Cameron and William McIldoe had passed a cat three times around the belly of a sick horse, evidently persuaded of its curative powers. It was also a world in which modern medical practice was largely unavailable to the wider populace; where prayer and the invocation of supernatural assistance was the normal – not least because usually the only – recourse for ordinary folk in the face of disease or misfortune.

A further factor in the survival of such beliefs into the eighteenth century might also be that they had rarely been effectively suppressed. Indeed, for many within the Christian churches, particularly local clergymen like Robert Kirk, whose immediate responsibility it would have been to confront the problem, it may not have seemed worth conducting a serious campaign against such deeply rooted and almost universally credited popular superstitions. Moreover, since in general terms they encouraged a conviction that events in the visible world were affected by an unseen conflict between the forces of good and evil, folk beliefs almost certainly had the important practical advantage of rendering the population more susceptible to the supernatural teachings of Christianity itself. This was doubtless what Kirk meant when he argued that his own attempts to prove the existence of fairies, rather than threatening theological orthodoxy in Scotland, would actually help to 'suppress the impudent and growing Atheisme of this age'. Only with increasing scientific understanding and the wider diffusion of veterinary, medical, agricultural and meteorological knowledge did natural explanations begin to replace supernatural interpretations – though inevitably more quickly among those social groups with access to advanced education and publications.

Belief in witchcraft, above all other popular convictions encountered into the eighteenth century, has attracted a substantial recent literature. Partly this is because it implies something about social tensions in early-modern European society (since elderly women were the preponderant though not the exclusive victims of the accompanying 'witch-craze' persecutions). At the same time, the legal depositions generated by prosecutions also provide a rare documentary insight into the mental world of ordinarily illiterate people. Moreover, the decline of the witch-craze – and in fact nowhere more clearly than in Scotland – starkly delineates the growing cultural division between an increasingly sceptical elite minority and the still-credulous majority. For even in the later seventeenth century, sophisticated Scottish thinkers like Sir George Mackenzie of Rosehaugh, Charles II's Lord Advocate, had registered doubts about the excessive use of torture by their over-enthusiastic judicial colleagues, as well as about the uncorroborated confessions – Mackenzie dubbed their typical content 'a thousand other ridiculous things, which have no Truth nor Existence, but in their Fancy' – upon which witchcraft cases so often seemed to rest.

Yet despite growing doubts of this kind among the educated, the persecution of supposed witches continued in Scotland, to evident public acclaim, for several decades. It took place in many parts of the country and, like most other popular beliefs, without any obvious reference to the formal religious complexion of a particular locality. One noteworthy execution occurred at Pittenweem in Fife in 1705, where the victim, Janet Cornfoot, was crushed to death. The last took place at Dornoch in 1727, the sheriff-depute of Sutherland himself overseeing the strangling and incineration of a woman, Janet Horn, convicted of turning her daughter into a donkey. No less preposterous allegations were still being levelled as late as the 1750s at Kenmore in Perthshire, though the relevant Scottish legislation (the Act Anent Witchcraft of 1604) had actually been annulled at Westminster in 1736 – to the great dismay of the more zealous, who instinctively rationalised the British state's leniency towards witches simply as further proof of its moral and theological laxity. Late in the century, many people, particularly in the more remote rural reaches of Scotland, remained convinced that witches and witchcraft were a reality. Reports suggest, for example, that even beyond 1800 nervous people in eastern Sutherland still held Janet Horn's descendants in suspicion.

Eighteenth-century lives, then, were dominated by convictions which both transcended and gave special meaning to ordinary experiences. Some form of presbyterian Protestantism for most, and either episcopalianism or Catholicism for the remainder, supplied the institutionally sanctioned cornerstone of people's spiritual lives. But beyond these safe generalisations, a widening division between elite and popular belief must be recognised. The never-ending disputes between Scotland's presbyterians exhibited a significant measure of social definition: evangelicals and especially dissenters achieved discernibly greater success among those groups experiencing, for better as well as worse, the most disorientating demographic and economic change. Other beliefs even more clearly reflected social stratification: in particular, the supernatural commitments of the rural poor increasingly came to seem just one more indelible mark of their lowly rank and deficient education. The dynamic intellectual culture to which better-educated Scots themselves subscribed in growing numbers in the decades after 1707, and which progressively encouraged them to re-think their attitudes towards traditional beliefs, is something to which we shall later need to return. It is to the transformative economic forces underlying these widening fissures in Scottish society that we must immediately look.

CHAPTER THREE

Lives

In the course of the eighteenth century, Scottish society was greatly altered. As was claimed in 1814, 'the present people of Scotland [are] a class of beings as different from their grandfathers, as the existing English are from those of Queen Elizabeth's time'. Sir Walter Scott's observation is important not so much for its confirmation of change as for its judicious sense of compressed chronology. For Scotland's economic transformation was more rapid even than England's, often thought of as the classic instance of precocious modernisation. It catapulted Scotland in just three or four generations from one of western Europe's more rural societies to one of its most urbanised. It altered the Scottish people's farming, their trade and their manufactures, their patterns of business and their employment. It dramatically increased the national wealth, as well as redistributing it between different groups. It also raised the incomes and living standards of most Scots, while introducing new and enduring social evils. In sum, the eighteenth century changed forever the daily lives, horizons and expectations of an increasingly numerous, diverse and mobile population. These processes justify our closest attention.

Population and settlement

The basic proportions of Scotland's contemporary population are obscured not just by the inevitable issues of interpretation but by the sheer inadequacy of the raw data. For the civil registration of births, deaths and marriages in Scotland dates only from 1855 while the decennial censuses of the United Kingdom as a whole did not begin until 1801. Scottish historians are therefore slave to a variety of surrogate methods for estimating the size, composition and location of the eighteenth-century population. Nevertheless, recent efforts have made it possible to speak with some confidence about many parts of the larger picture. Above all, what emerges is a story of consistent aggregate growth, from a modern estimate of somewhere around one million people in the years immediately prior to the Treaty of Union to a recorded total of 1,608,420 returned a century later by the inaugural census. This general picture of substantial population growth through the period is reinforced by a third source, the first serious effort at scientific demography in Scotland, Alexander Webster's survey of 1755, which, resting on reports from parish ministers, arrived at the spuriously precise total of 1,234,575.

These three figures, together with the further evidence in Sir John Sinclair's *Statistical Account of Scotland*, compiled from similar sources to Webster in the 1790s, provide the base-line for an understanding of the physical dimensions of eighteenth-century Scottish society. To start with, they establish beyond doubt that the greater part of the century's overall population increase occurred in the decades after 1750: in other words, the rate of growth accelerated strongly in the second half of the century. Crucially, the same data also show that Scotland's demographic regime was gradually diverging through this period from the general patterns found elsewhere in the British Isles. In particular, they confirm that the Scottish population grew at an average rate of 0.3 per cent per annum before Webster and around 0.5 per cent afterwards. Yet England, which had previously been comparable, was increasing by around 0.8 per cent per annum during the later eighteenth century, while by 1800 the population of Ireland was expanding every twelve months by as much as 1.6 per cent. An obvious conclusion is therefore that, notwithstanding their accelerating demographic growth after the 1750s, the Scots actually represented a steadily diminishing proportion of Britain's total population, a trend which would actually continue well into the twentieth century.

The detailed contemporary calculations for different parts of the country in both 1755 and 1801, placed alongside our current best guesses for the local picture in 1700, also make possible a credible reconstruction of Scotland's shifting demographic geography. This insight is in fact crucial, given that substantial regional variations emerged during the eighteenth century. Overall, it is clear that what had always been an overwhelmingly rurally based Scottish population was now moving in increasing numbers towards the towns (though it is vital to recognise that even in 1801 still only 20 per cent of people lived in settlements of more than 5,000 people). This trend particularly affected the Central Lowlands, traditionally the seat of most of Scotland's significant urban communities. The region as a whole received substantial in-migration from both the Highlands and the Borders (the latter region grew by just 9 per cent through the entire second half of the century). It also generated significant natural population increases of its own. Furthermore, a closer inspection of local trends reveals that the epicentre of demographic increase actually lay in the western parts of the Central Lowlands. Here the population grew by 82 per cent between 1755 and 1801, far outstripping the growth rates for Scotland as a whole.

These trends also provide a context within which to understand some of the more extraordinary individual instances of demographic change. The royal burgh of Glasgow, for example, had a population of only 32,000 people in 1755, not much more than half of Edinburgh's 57,000. But by 1801 – that is, within less than many inhabitants' lifetimes – it had become, as it still is today, the largest town in Scotland, nearly tripling in size to 84,000 people against the capital's 82,000. Growth rates were no less remarkable elsewhere in the west. Greenock more than quadrupled from fewer than 4,000 people to more than 17,000 between Webster and the first census. The older townspeople of Paisley in 1801, who might still have remembered living in a tight-knit community of fewer than 7,000 souls in the mid-1750s, now contemplated life in a town of 31,000 – a 350 per cent increase in less than fifty years. Even in some of the traditional county towns, growth could be phenomenal: Perth, for example, doubled from 7,500 in the mid-1760s to 15,000 by 1801. At the other extreme, largely rural counties outside the Highlands, like Banffshire and Moray in the north-east and Peebles-shire in the Borders, were actually contracting. Such conflicting fortunes provide striking illustrations of how a combination of large-scale internal migration and differential rates of intrinsic growth were enhancing regional disparities across Scotland even within a picture of overall national expansion.

Explaining these demographic patterns, and in particular the unprecedented increase in Scotland's total population through the eighteenth century, is not simple. But it is clear that immigration can largely be discounted as a factor. The great wave of Irish migration to Scotland, which would eventually transform the ethnic and religious mix among the Scottish people, especially in the west and in the towns and cities, was substantially a nineteenth-century phenomenon. Moreover, at least until the 1780s, arrivals from Ireland were probably more than offset, as we shall see, by the departure of native-born Scots in great numbers to England and to North America. In other words, population movement into and out of the country between 1700 and 1800 tended, if anything, to reduce rather than to increase the total Scottish population. It is therefore to the changing eighteenth-century relationship between birth rates and death rates within Scotland itself that historians must look for the mechanism delivering long-term population growth.

Scotland's natural rate of increase (that is, the surplus of live births over deaths in a given population) was certainly sizeable in this period – especially so from the 1760s. Webster's data, for example, suggest a birth rate in 1755 in the region of 34 per 1,000 people but a death rate of only around 30 per 1,000. Using the *Statistical Account* to calculate similar indices for the 1790s, this vital excess of births over deaths, which necessarily produces natural population growth, had clearly widened, to somewhere around 35 and 24 respectively. As these figures underline, however, Scottish birth rates (unlike those in contemporary England) were not in themselves rising significantly. Female age at marriage and a woman's willingness to marry, along with intrinsic fertility, remained the dominant factors (as in all societies lacking widely used and effective contraception) in determining the actual number of births. And with remarkably few fluctuations, Scottish women in the eighteenth century wed on average somewhere around the age of 26, with perhaps 15–20 per cent not marrying at all. It must therefore be the greater longevity of the average Scot, who at birth might have expected to live for little more than thirty years in 1755 but who would seemingly survive for nearly forty by the 1790s, that mainly accounts for the population's overall expansion.

Yet even this deduction is, of course, only a partial answer. For knowing why death rates actually declined, especially among small children in the second half of the century, is the real key. A crucial factor in this process, as we shall see, was almost certainly the improvements in Scottish agricultural productivity, diet and incomes (and, accompanying this, in the standard of much rural accommodation, clothing and sanitation) throughout this period. Another cause may well have been those medical innovations which reduced the people's vulnerability to disease. In particular, the use of inoculation to combat the greatest of child-killers, smallpox, can only have improved average life expectancy in the population at large: first introduced in Dumfries-shire in the 1730s, it was especially favoured by the people in the Highlands and some parts of the Borders. Yet it was also slow to spread and long remained less popular in the Lowlands and in the larger towns: 'they say it is an encroachment upon the prerogatives of providence', reported one clerical writer of his evidently unimpressed parishioners at Coldingham in Berwickshire in the 1790s; 'To inoculate is here regarded as criminal', claimed another, the minister of Portmoak in Kinross-shire. In other words, the real demographic impact of inoculation in the eighteenth century may actually have been both late and rather patchy.

Other deliberate medical contributions to the declining death rate of eighteenth-century Scotland are no easier to identify. The major burghs were certainly acquiring public hospitals: the outstanding example, Edinburgh's Royal Infirmary, received its charter in 1729; Glasgow's opened its doors in 1793. Scotland's universities, as we shall also see, were fast becoming renowned for their medical education. Yet the immediate benefits for the wider population must be seriously doubted. Provision remained grossly inadequate, and what existed was frequently beyond the financial means of ordinary people: 'There is not a single surgeon in this parish', noted the same minister of Coldingham. In any case, the dubious ministrations of the physicians, surgeons and apothecaries were still as likely to kill as to cure the unfortunate eighteenth-century patient.

Other explanations are therefore needed for the increasing longevity of the Scottish people, and these may lie not so much in the familiar history of institutionalised medicine as in the less certain field of historical epidemiology. We know, for example, that bubonic plague had died away in Britain after the 1650s. Typhus also clearly went into abeyance before re-appearing for a time in the overcrowded nineteenth-century Scottish towns. But the critical relationship between bacterial and viral agents and the human populations on which they have preyed so savagely until very recently in our history – governed by key variables such as people's changing resistance to infection and alterations in the behaviour of the micro-organisms themselves – remains frustratingly opaque at the present level of scientific as well as of historical knowledge.

Whatever the fundamental causes, however, one key demographic trend, with its roots deep in the eighteenth century, is beyond dispute. Infant crude mortality had been rather more than 200 per 1,000 before 1755, still much higher than in England. It had fallen to 175, significantly lower than England's, in the space of just fifty years. Even the adverse impact of rapid urbanisation and worsening conditions of domestic sanitation for many of Scotland's poorer town-dwellers by 1800 had not yet reversed this most benevolent of long-term trends. As we shall later discover, the fact that Scotland was becoming not only a larger but a younger society was to be of profound importance for people's everyday lives. It underlay all manner of new material and cultural energies in an age of innovation, Enlightenment and empire. At the same time, it also posed new and difficult questions for the prevailing social order and its traditional institutional fabric. Most immediately, however, we need to investigate the key agency of social change in this period: the causes and nature of Scotland's contemporary economic transformation.

National crisis and economic change

The condition of Scotland's economy around 1700 is central to an understanding of the country's history over the next hundred years. As we know, the perception among politically literate contemporaries was usually that it was chronically underdeveloped. This assessment, of course, guaranteed the effectiveness of England's Alien Act when it threatened to snuff out what little commerce had already emerged. Moreover, the twenty-five clauses of the Treaty of Union included no fewer than fifteen in which the English made specific fiscal and commercial concessions to Scotland in return for acceptance of a full incorporating union: these too can be seen as tacit acknowledgement on both sides that economic concerns dominated Scottish calculations. But not least because it obviously bears upon the continuing controversy as to how much of Scotland's subsequent transformation might still have occurred even without the Union, the state of the economy in and around 1700 has been subjected to a great deal of recent scrutiny.

Above all, it is increasingly possible for historians to set the material difficulties which undoubtedly faced the Scots before the Union against credible evidence of worthwhile independent economic activity that made crucial contributions to Scotland's advancement. It is also clear that, despite the many advantages to Scotland's incorporation into the world's largest free-trade area, with access not only to England's vast domestic market but also to its overseas territories, these were largely concentrated in the final two-thirds of the century. Indeed, modern research has emphasised that there was a prolonged phase in the wake of Union marked chiefly by Scottish disappointment and frustration at the failure of the anticipated benefits to materialise – even, it seems, by significant short-term dislocation and economic hardship. Thus if they had exchanged their national sovereignty for the untold riches dangled before them, then the Scots were to make the unwelcome discovery that the English had in fact purchased their independent parliament with a post-dated cheque.

Scotland's economy in 1700 was overwhelmingly based on the productive capacities of the land. The soil provided most regular workers with their incomes and even more of the Scottish population with occasional labour. Most trade and many industries, such as leather-working, brewing, woollen production or flax spinning, were also dependent upon its raw materials. Fields or pasture were the resources close to or on which the vast majority of Scots lived and worked and died. The economic exploitation of the land was therefore the sine qua non of personal as well as of national wealth, whether one was a peasant labourer in Lanarkshire, a burgess maltman in Edinburgh, a hard-pressed village wife in Perthshire engaged in weaving linen, a Gaelic-speaking cowherd on Raasay, or, for that matter, a belted nobleman contentedly counting his rentals in Berwickshire. Without the crops, the animals and the various income streams yielded up by their country's often unforgiving soil, lingering death awaited most Scots, since agricultural produce fed, housed, clothed and provided gainful work for the large majority.

That rural life was inextricably linked to the soil will not be surprising. But by comparison with the modern city, limited surpluses and poor transport systems ensured that the prosperity of the Scottish town in 1700 was also still largely contingent upon the agricultural success or failure of the surrounding hinterland. People in the larger burghs, to be sure, had their own distinctive culture. A wealthy minority had the corporation, the magistracy and the merchant guilds, with all their proud privileges and rituals. Among the plebeian multitude, urban life uniquely generated large-scale crowd events, including regular markets and fairs, periodic alcohol-fuelled revelries on the king's birthday and occasional carefully targeted rioting against high-handed officials or against unpopular or unreasonable merchants. Such things to some extent set the culture of townspeople apart, as contemporaries increasingly remarked. Yet the main economic function of most of Scotland's towns remained as a market for local agricultural produce and a supplier of goods and services to the surrounding population. All of this made it even more likely that the state of Scotland's rural economy would be of overriding importance to the last Edinburgh Parliament, packed as it was with the representatives of the landowners and burgesses, as its members debated the nation's future in the difficult years before 1707.

The famines of 1695–99, in which more than 100,000 Scots probably died and the national population fell by perhaps 13 per cent, cast a baleful shadow over these deliberations: Andrew Fletcher's severe schemes for economic restructuring ultimately rested on the bleak premise that, for many, servitude might be better than starvation. Poor weather had also precipitated a subsistence crisis right across western Europe (though significantly not in agriculturally advanced Holland or England). Yet an important underlying cause in Scotland was without doubt the state of the rural economy. Through good times and bad, most Scots struggled in a damp and cool climate to extract a living from an earth which was too often boggy, rocky, hilly, sandy or acidic. Nature, then, was a crucial limiting factor, the more so at a time when Europe was still experiencing the 'Little Ice Age' of the post-medieval period. Winters in the decades either side of 1700 – memorialised in numerous Dutch paintings of ice fairs and in Samuel Pepys's descriptions of the frozen Thames in London – were discernibly harder than today. The growing season, particularly as far north as Scotland, was shorter and less friendly. Perhaps 40 per cent of seventeenth-century harvests had been significantly deficient. Full-scale famines had periodically hit the whole country, as again in the 1690s. Regional dearths occurred more frequently, particularly in the Highlands.

To the indifferent climate and inauspicious landscape were added Scotland's poor internal communications. It was still difficult in 1700 to transport agricultural produce any distance by land, hampering urbanisation and stunting the development of a market-orientated agrarian economy. Even the first and third largest towns, Edinburgh and Aberdeen, rather less than one hundred miles apart, were in practice separated by two unbridged sea-firths and several days of uncomfortable road travel. Scotland's contemporary settlement patterns and relative under-population also inhibited development. It had a strikingly low population density: just 11 people per square kilometre against France's 34, Italy's 44, and England and Wales's 40. Moreover, perhaps 25 per cent of the people were still spread thinly across the Highland zone. There was therefore little sign, in many parts of the country, of the concentrated consumer demand that might attract commercially minded proprietors. Indeed, even where saleable surpluses arose, whether by dint of tolerable harvests, improved techniques or plain good fortune, the problem might well be how to dispose lucratively of perishable produce for which insufficient markets existed.

The broad outlines of this depressing picture remain incontestable. Yet modern scholarship has painted in many details, adding to our understanding of Scottish agriculture in 1707 and suggesting that in crucial respects there already existed clear signs of progress. Most importantly, the age-old regional contrasts – between the mainly pastoral Highlands and Border hills, a mixed agriculture prevalent in the upland boundary zones and a largely arable regime around the coasts and plains in the south and east – seem already to have been matched by pronounced variations in both output and advancement. Crop production was necessarily restricted in the mountainous regions: even when arable land use in Scotland peaked around 1800, still only 10 per cent of the total surface area of the Highlands was actually under cultivation. In the other two zones, however, but particularly in the Lowlands, significantly different trends were already emerging by 1700. In Ayrshire, East Lothian and Fife, and in the Merse (the Berwickshire plains), the Mearns (the coastal strip to the east of the Grampians) and around the Moray Firth coastline, the existence of towns and better transport systems, superior soil conditions and a relatively more congenial climate had all helped make progress in the arable sector more likely.

It should not therefore be wholly surprising that at the time of Union there is mounting evidence of agricultural innovation in some Lowland districts, resulting in normal years in a surplus. Indeed, research reveals that the number of authorised markets had doubled between 1600 and 1700, with small settlements like Dunning in Perthshire and Kennoway in Fife among the many beneficiaries. Oats remained the Scots' characteristic crop well into the new century: in the 1750s Dr Johnson could still define it, not untruthfully, as a food that 'in England is given to horses but in Scotland supports the population'. Yet even in 1700 it was increasingly being supplemented, even supplanted, by new staple crops. Bere or bear (a rough barley) was found in many places; the better two-row barley in the Merse and the Lothians; wheat in parts of eastern Scotland; nutritionally rich legumes, including peas and beans, in some Lowland areas. Allied to these crop innovations were a range of other devices increasingly recognised as improving both soil fertility (especially nitrogen levels) and the efficiency of cultivation. These included seaweed manuring near the coast, the ploughing-in of stable litter and human effluent ('night soil') near towns, and vigorous liming on some estates. The traditional eight-oxen wooden plough was also being abandoned in some parts of the Lowlands in favour of the lighter and more effective four-horse plough.

More substantial exercises in landscape engineering also seem to have been occurring around 1700. Peat cover was already being burned-off in Fife, land reclamation was taking place on the Forth coastline and in other districts deforestation was opening up valuable new farmland. At the same time, increasing local experimentation in land management was evident. In the Lothians, Berwickshire and Roxburghshire, a growing acreage was being treated as 'infield' (intensively cultivated farmland supporting a variety of crops, usually situated close to the settlement); in much of the Highlands, meanwhile, 'outfield' cultivation practices remained preponderant, the farmland being commonly sown only with oats and often reduced to pasture. New crop rotations were also being introduced. These too raised yields and improved the chances of a surplus. A typical example might see the infield subjected to one year of bere and two of oats, with no intervening fallow course. But peas, beans and other crops, as well as fallow periods, were increasingly being employed, especially in the eastern Lowlands, by the time of Union.

There is also strong evidence that Lowland proprietors in particular were already looking to lever up cash incomes. Chiefly this involved diversifying the economic uses to which land was put. Tree plantations had begun on a significant scale from the 1650s (useful thrice over, for commercial forestry, for amenity and for the protection of crops and animals from the piercing Scottish winds): Yester in East Lothian, home of the Marquises of Tweeddale, had probably the largest plantation in Scotland by 1707 and over a million mature trees just twenty years later. Extractive industries, still essentially rooted in the economy of landed estates, and including the mining of coal (such as by the Earl of Dundonald in Lanarkshire and the Earls of Rothes and Elgin in Fife), salt (especially in Ayrshire and along the Firth of Forth) and lime (notably on the Earl of Leven's estates at Raith in Fife), were increasingly being developed at the turn of the eighteenth century. So too were expensive embellishments, such as ornamental landscape gardens and 'policies' (enclosed parkland), for which the more utilitarian innovations helped to pay: Lennoxlove in East Lothian, home of the Duke of

Richmond and Lennox, was among the leading examples at the end of the seventeenth century.

Some Scottish proprietors had by the time of the Union also begun to modify the conditions on which those who cultivated the soil and reared livestock actually occupied the land. Increasing numbers of single-tenant leases, with rent payable in cash rather than in labour or in kind, were being issued: these created larger holdings for individual tenant-farmers, invariably selected for their proficiency in new agricultural techniques and granted a secure fixed-term lease of reasonable duration, typically nineteen years. Older forms of customary tenure, based on tacit collective understandings, were slowly being confined to the Highlands: data from Aberdeenshire in the 1690s, by no means a wholly Lowland county, confirm a pattern evident from Fife and Angus in the east to Lanarkshire in the west. The vociferous approval of observers like Fletcher and Belhaven for the monetisation of rents and formalisation of single-tenant leases, which they introduced enthusiastically on their own estates, usefully underlines that even those who opposed the treaty accepted that root-and-branch reform of the nation's traditional economic structures was necessary.

Secure, exclusive and essentially commercial tenure was therefore widely seen by 1707 as an antidote to Scotland's ills. With the stroke of a lawyer's pen they seemed to increase the chances of profitable innovation, simultaneously helping transform landowners into entrepreneurs, tenants into self-sufficient farmers and the surplus customary occupiers of their estates into either paid agricultural labourers or prospective migrants. Related to these changing attitudes among landowners, the old 'runrig' system, a form of pre-modern open-field management whereby arable land was divided into individual strips with both cultivation and herding being organised collectively within the 'fermtoun' (the communal agricultural settlement), was already beginning to fall into disfavour. The generally lower yields under 'runrig' were, of course, a glaring fault. But the greater long-term difficulty was increasingly believed to be the veto which collective farming of this kind imposed on innovation or improvement, effectively obliging all participants to proceed only at the pace of the most reluctant. The future, it seemed clear to most proprietors in the age of the Union, lay with turning over Scotland's soil to consolidated single-tenant farms: there enterprise and innovation would at last be given their head.

Agricultural improvement

More conducive wider circumstances, rather than direct English transformation of hitherto moribund Scottish practice, were therefore the principal advantages bestowed upon native agriculture by the Union. In fact, experimentation largely continued along the lines already determined prior to 1707 by legislative changes and the emerging new proprietorial wisdom. Yet now it also seemed to accelerate, particularly from the 1740s and even more so from the 1770s. Post-Union agriculture throws up many names rightly hallowed in the history of Scottish enterprise: innovating patricians like John Cockburn of Ormiston and Thomas Hamilton, 6th Earl of Haddington; erudite authors of agricultural tracts, such as Dempster the MP, Kames the judge and William Barron, otherwise an obscure professor of rhetoric and logic at St Andrews; and many dozens of landowners who combined sincere patriotism with profitable self-interest by joining the Honourable Society for the Improvement of Agriculture in Scotland after its inception in 1723. But Archibald Grant of Monymusk will perhaps always be the most memorable: an aggressive speculator and investor in the York Buildings Company, the complete physical overhaul of his Aberdeenshire estate involved colossal investment over many years – in just 1718–19 alone, no less than £1,198 was spent on measures like the digging-out of boulders, the construction of dykes and the shooting of troublesome rooks which had been preying on the crops. On such unglamorous practicalities did the legendary achievements of improved Scottish agriculture invariably rest.

By 1740, and assisted by the example and exhortation provided by luminaries such as these, the transformation of the Lowlands in particular was perceptibly quickening. Continued crop innovation was central, encouraged not least by rising consumer demand in England: yields accordingly improved even more dramatically from mid-century. Soil-improving species such as clover, sown grasses and turnips were now being added to increasingly complex rotational systems. The potato, remarkably tolerant of Scottish conditions and also highly nutritious, was certainly the most important innovation. From the 1760s it supplemented – and sometimes replaced – oats as the poorer classes' staple food, especially in the Highlands, where its ability to thrive even in low-quality soils was a gift from heaven to landlords and tenants alike. Not all of the fashionable new crops, however, were for human sustenance. Afforestation expanded rapidly, stimulated by the insatiable appetite of Britain's shipyards, which constructed the world's leading merchant and naval fleets: by the end of the century the 4th Duke of Atholl in Perthshire had planted around 27,000,000 new trees, mainly larches; at Monymusk perhaps 5,000,000 were planted by the Grants. Some ambitious and enlightened landowners even erected model villages for their newly prosperous commercial tenantry and estate workers, and in certain cases to create elbow-room for their own grandiose landscaped policies: Newcastleton in Roxburghshire was constructed in 1793 by the 3rd Duke of Buccleuch; Tyninghame, the best-known of all, was Haddington's elegant brain-child.

Enclosure of 'commonties' (customary common land), resting on Scottish enabling legislation dating back to 1695, also accelerated greatly after mid-century. This provided new field divisions more suited to the occupancy patterns and cropping practices of a commercial agricultural regime. It also allowed segregated policies to multiply. Delineated and protected by walls, ditches and dykes, these plantations physically imprinted the new imperatives of proprietorship on the improved Scottish landscape, indicating tangibly the translation from the fermtouns and open-fields to individual tenancy and competitive enterprise. Changing economic priorities were accompanied by increased dependence upon expert assistance. The profession of surveyor emerged as landowners sought to identify and exploit the full potential of their estates. Proprietors also benefited from the recent growth and sophistication of Scottish banking. Along with the more traditional borrowing from merchants, this allowed agricultural innovation to be appropriately financed. Towards 1800 even prosperous tenants were taking a hand in speeding the pace of change, assisting landowners with both investment and implementation.

Meanwhile lawyers were being employed to challenge 'tailzie' or entail, the strict Scottish system for predetermining future ownership which served to hinder the rationalisation or mortgaging of heritable property. The Montgomery Act of 1770, named after the Lord Advocate of the day, significantly relaxed the legal constraints on disposal originally imposed during the turmoil of the seventeenth century. Enabling bank borrowing against as much as six years' rental, in principle the Act allowed Scotland's landowners to invest more ambitiously in the modernisation of their estates. In practice, however, entail survived well into the next century. After all, despite its drawbacks, it still fulfilled its original purpose, providing a guarantee against the breakup or loss of a family's precious patrimony. Indeed, the period from 1760 to 1800 saw the further consolidation of the major Scottish holdings through an aggressive acquisitions policy: in Aberdeenshire, for example, the 621 owners of heritable property assessed at the introduction of the land tax in 1667 had been reduced to just 236 by 1802. A reduction in the total number of proprietors in Scotland as a whole, from perhaps 9,500 at the start of the eighteenth century to around 8,500 at the end, was a further indication of the tightening grip, in bountiful times, of those who dominated landownership.

As we have seen, the Union was not the fundamental cause of any of these further developments. Most if not all had discernible roots in the years before 1707. Yet the treaty was nevertheless crucial in that it made much more congenial the general climate in which Scottish agricultural improvement was now being pursued. After all, insufficient demand had formerly been as much of an impediment to reform as any failings in land management, cultivation, stock-rearing and infrastructure. Unfettered access to England's own swelling urban markets therefore necessarily facilitated further advances in Scotland. Enhanced internal communications following the Union also allowed these opportunities to be properly exploited. To Wade's military roads, probably Westminster's most tangible early achievement in many parts of the country, were added after mid-century a succession of private Scottish turnpikes: roads from Edinburgh to Berwick, Queensferry, Stirling, Moffat and Glasgow all appeared during the 1750s. A spate of bridge-building also arose, further reducing delays and speeding travel at crucial points: John Smeaton's across the Tweed at Coldstream and the Tay at Perth, completed by public subscription in 1767 and 1771 respectively, were among the most useful as well as the most elegant constructions of the age.

In the Highlands in particular, some of the most remarked-upon agricultural developments were certainly facilitated by the much wider post-Union market for Scottish produce as well as by the introduction of commercial practices already established in the south. Above all, through the 'trysts' (i.e. markets) at Crieff and, by the 1770s, at Falkirk, vast numbers of black cattle were herded for English consumption: it was this which enriched proprietorial entrepreneurs like the Earls of Breadalbane in Perthshire, as well as the industry's shady parasites, such as the infamous rustler Rob Roy MacGregor. The exploitation of Highland property also received an early boost at the hands of the York Buildings Company, with its large holdings of forfeited Jacobite estates: the company's activities ranged from forestry to mining, as well as establishing the Invergarry smelting operation in the 1730s. And just as in the Lowlands, Highland commercialisation accelerated perceptibly in the second half of the century, symbolised by the foundation in 1753 by a Lancashire entrepreneur of the Lorn Furnace Company's famous facility at Taynuilt in Argyllshire. Yet the adaptation of Highland proprietors themselves to profit-motivated enterprise also entailed greater social trauma than in the Lowlands. The chieftain, conventionally accepted as the unchallenged overlord of his Gaelic-speaking people, protector of his kin and dispenser of hospitality and welfare to his tenants, could only with difficulty be transformed into a mere proprietor and collector of rent after the southern fashion.

It needs to be emphasised that the commercialisation of Highland landownership which gathered pace after Culloden was in no sense the exclusive preserve of those most closely affiliated to the Hanoverian state: Cameron of Lochiel had long had investments in commercial forestry, in iron-smelting and even in the Jamaican plantations, while his fellow-Jacobite, Mackintosh of Borlum, had published an enthusiastic tract on enclosure in 1729. Yet it remains true that, in applying the latest economic thinking to their properties, the Dukes of Argyll, with their myriad personal and political connections in Edinburgh and London, were naturally pre-eminent. The 3rd Duke's difficulty in raising armed forces from his estates to counter Charles Edward Stuart's threat in 1745 ('I used many arguments to convince them', explained a mystified ducal agent on Tiree, 'but all to no purpose') was merely the predictable result of the family's precocious success in translating their relationship with their clansmen from a feudal to a largely commercial one, based on monetised, written, single-tenancies. Above all, he and his brother had been effective, again assisted by the ferocious legal talents of Forbes of Culloden, in eliminating the 'tacksmen', the traditional middle-men who had held a 'tack' or lease directly from the chief and who had formerly provided both intermediate community leadership and military organisation in Highland society.

Proprietors closest to the Lowlands, both physically and culturally, were almost inevitably responsible for the swiftest changes. In 1769, Breadalbane had his Loch Tay estates surveyed in expectation of being able to invoke the impending legislation on entail. His two operatives recorded almost no tacksmen at all in this part of the Perthshire mountains: most people already held written and monetised leases directly from the landowner. The 5th Duke of Argyll emerges similarly as a progressive and ambitious entrepreneur during the century's closing decades, extending the tenurial revolution out into the Hebridean islands, with tacksmen nowhere in view. As he wrote to his chamberlain on Tiree in 1791, he craved reports on 'the true value of each farm . . . considering and pointing out the best mode of disposing of it so as to improve the farm, encourage industry, and at the same time give me a reasonable rent'.

The quickening progress of entrepreneurship among the Highland elite was measured not only in the reduction of the tacksmen. As Argyll hinted, it was also evidenced in rising estate incomes: an increase of 300 per cent or more between the 1750s and 1800 was not uncommon; at Torridon in Wester Ross rental returns grew tenfold betwen 1777 and 1805. It was this all-embracing upheaval in the basis of tenancy rather than the much more emotive phenomenon of forced deportation overseas, or merely the arrival of sheep, that underlay most of the large-scale Highland emigrations of this period. When a body of Macdonald tenants on Skye departed for North Carolina in 1771 led by their tacksmen, or when the MacDonells left Glengarry and Knoydart for Canada through the 1770s and 1780s, emigration was not simply the consequence of eviction by the landlords. Rather it was motivated in substantial part by optimism about the opportunities available in the New World and justifiable pessimism about their prospects within the swiftly commercialising agriculture of the Highlands.

Colin Maciver, minister of Glenelg in Inverness-shire in 1793, may well have been right in his first-hand assessment that emigration in his locality was 'owing in a great measure to the introduction of sheep'. Yet it was no less true, as Maciver added, that 'the high rents demanded by landlords, the increase of population, and the flattering accounts received from their friends in America do also contribute to the evil'. Josiah Tucker likewise observed of emigrant Highlanders in 1773 that a mixture of motives lay behind the exodus: 'it was not Poverty or Necessity which compelled but Ambition which enticed them to forsake their native Soil'. Some worried proprietors, including both Breadalbane and Argyll, who feared the excessive haemorrhaging of labour from off their estates, even organised campaigns against emigration, authorising rent reductions to tempt reluctant people to stay. But the spread of competitive tenancies and rising cash rents, together with the transfer of traditional communal grazing land to other uses, led many positively to seek to leave. Such changes were also divisive enough to create intra-communal tensions among those who remained. This was particularly so between those larger leaseholders who might well share in the profits of improvement and the smallest tenants and landless cottars who were increasingly being squeezed out.

Most late eighteenth-century Highland proprietors fully understood the benefits of altering the whole productive structure of their estates – ironically the very strategy which resulted in the emigration that some of them then sought desperately to counteract. This contradiction was clearly seen in the effects of increased stock-rearing and, more specifically, the introduction of large-scale sheep farming in many districts. Using the Cheviot or later the Blackface breeds from the Borders, it proved possible greatly to increase the quality and efficiency of Highland wool production in the decades before 1800: the motives are not difficult to discern, for between the 1770s and the early decades of the new century the market price of wool increased by as much as 400 per cent. In many places the former inhabitants were displaced as sheep runs filled the inland straths and glens: as another parish minister sombrely observed in one part of Wester Ross, 'where formerly hundreds of people could be seen, no human faces are now to be met with, except a shepherd attended by his dog'.

Rather than being thrown off the estate or allowed to emigrate, the tenants were where possible relocated, often to the coastal fringes, where it was hoped that their labours would be more profitable both to themselves and to their landlords. Thus it was that an entirely new social and economic organisation – 'crofting' – emerged to provide sustainable employment for the still-growing Highland population. Potatoes rapidly came into their own in the north and west of the country, often cultivated in the famous 'lazy-beds', small plots of poor-quality land crudely manured with seaweed or shell-sand. At Eddrachillis in Sutherland, the minister, blissfully unaware of the impact that the potato blight would have on the crofters just two generations later, reported in 1791 that 'though less than 30 years ago scarcely known here, they constitute a considerable part of the food of the inhabitants'.

Fishing was another activity sustaining a growing population. It provided gainful employment in crofting townships where the people, with insufficient land to subsist solely by agriculture, were meant to be morally and socially uplifted by the unfamiliar rigours and rewards of paid employment. Even more important in this vision of beneficent commercialisation was 'kelping'. The labour-intensive harvesting and burning of seaweed found in abundance on the shores of the mainland and the islands, this not only provided agricultural manure. It also supplied the soap, glass and textile industries of the Lowlands and England with an important ingredient. On North Uist in the 1790s it was claimed that 'All the inhabitants . . . are employed in manufacturing kelp from the 10th of June till the 10th of August.' By 1800, its price inflated by the European wars which shut out foreign competition from Britain's vast internal market, kelp was a critical source of income in the Highlands and islands. Yet it was not only a major contributor to unprecedented landlordly wealth. Through an expanding population's over-reliance upon its extraordinary short-term success, as upon the sustenance provided by the seemingly miraculous potato, it was also storing up unforeseen disasters for the region in the next century.

Commerce, trade and manufactures

Developments elsewhere in the Scottish economy cannot be understood independently of agricultural change. Partly this is because land underlay most contemporary trade and industry. Partly it is because the patterns of agricultural development tell us much about the wider context in which commerce and manufacturing also progressed. Certainly, the broad trends are similar. Modest but discernible growth and diversification occurred from the mid-seventeenth century onwards. Signs of crisis emerged in the last decades before the Treaty of Union, worsening rather than abating in its immediate aftermath. Further movement forward began about a generation later. The greatest advances, however, although resting on earlier achievements, were significantly delayed and not unambiguously seen until after the 1740s. By 1800, dynamism, output and profitability in Scotland were reaching previously unimaginable levels.

Trade was, of course, in the doldrums in 1707. Indeed, for many Scottish politicians Union was to be recommended or denounced primarily for what they judged would be its likely impact on a depressed position. The low trading volumes, not only for export but also internally to Scotland, are largely explained by the arrested development of the agricultural economy. Limited surpluses, and in some years none at all, meant that the Scots struggled to be substantial and consistent exporters of primary produce. But their trade also suffered from an immature pre-industrial manufacturing sector: generally unattractive goods, usually produced in small quantities and often of poor quality, made it difficult to win major export earnings. At the same time, at least in terms of an unflattering comparison that Scottish contemporaries tended instinctively to make, the country patently lacked the colonial and international footholds exploited so lucratively by the English, the Dutch and the French.

The main contact that the Scots had around 1700 with the sort of high-value goods which were now becoming of critical commercial importance in western Europe – spices, silks, exotic timber, wines, tea, coffee, tobacco and the like – was as dazzled consumers rather than as prospering carriers, wholesalers or re-exporters. This had two consequences, both of them loudly lamented. Superficially, a wave of hedonistic self-indulgence and credit-driven ostentation seemed to have arisen. To some in a poor society long inured to austerity (and with its recently triumphant Calvinist clergy urgently reinforcing such puritanical leanings), this appeared the very road to hell. The gloom of George Crawfurd, a Glaswegian scholar, was typical: 'All trades which import commodities of mere luxury and pleasure into a country', he complained, 'and tend to heighten the expense of living, to debauch the manners of the people . . . , are imminently destructive to the nation; and the hands employed in them are acting to the ruin of their country.' More damaging in reality, the taste for expensive imports ensured that Scotland was bled dry of hard currency. Much of what little could be earned by export was sunk into conspicuous consumption, to the detriment not only of further structural investment at home but even of the Scots' capacity to buy basic food supplies to supplement unreliable domestic production.

The 1690s heightened awareness of these interrelated problems. Disastrous harvests had savagely underlined Scotland's need to import essential foodstuffs: the shortage of good coin contributed significantly to the resulting dearth. Wars between England and France had also damaged traditional, hard-earned Continental trading connections. Linen exports to Flanders, one of the Scots' few successful commercial staples, were particularly badly hit by England's blockade. Meanwhile, their efforts on the colonial front were disastrous, the Darien scheme spectacularly imploding with the loss of £133,000 – as much as one-quarter of the nation's total liquid capital. Yet despite simmering resentment at England's role, the debacle actually proved an important catalyst for the Union. In effect, it confirmed the sheer impossibility of the Scots securing independent access to overseas produce and oceanic trade. If just one rash investment decision could inflict such a crippling blow upon Scotland's close-knit business and landed communities, it is not difficult to appreciate why contemporaries feared for the material survival of their nation.

Even so, and as with agriculture, the later seventeenth century had actually seen important developments in commerce and trade – ones that would suffer further setbacks between the 1690s and the 1720s before eventually prospering again and evolving in unexpected ways in the long-term wake of Union. Linen production had already expanded before 1700 in the well-populated counties of the Central Lowlands, particularly Lanarkshire, Renfrew, Angus, Perthshire and Fife. Literally a cottage industry, the workers – mainly women – would spin locally grown flax and weave linen essentially as a natural extension of their traditional household activities. Indeed this pre-industrial pattern of production was so well-established that it long survived in certain localities, the minister of Kennoway in Fife reporting in 1793 that 'Every person almost that is not engaged in the labours of the field is employed at the loom.' Woollen manufacturing too had emerged in a rural and domestic setting, notably in Aberdeenshire. Under the 'putting-out' system, merchants co-ordinated the production of finished goods by individuals working in their own homes. By 1700 both woollens and linens supported small but useful export trades. This fact, of course, makes even more understandable the anxieties of the last Scots Parliament when Westminster threatened them with the Alien Act.

Fishing and the coastal trade also had a significant pre-Union history. Communities had for centuries harvested the rich stocks off Scotland's shores: the herring and haddock fisheries were particularly important, while shellfish (the Firth of Forth contained some of Europe's most prolific oyster beds) were widely gathered and consumed by all social classes. Scottish vessels also regularly plied the routes to and from the major English ports, France, the Low Countries and the Baltic. Many harbours, like Aberdeen, Dundee and Leith in the east, and Greenock and Port Glasgow in the west, experienced growth and some prosperity in the seventeenth century, at least before the shocks of the 1690s when Scotland's patterns of trade fell victim to the crown's strategic ambitions in Europe. It is therefore less surprising that some of the most trenchant opposition to the proposed treaty came from the royal burghs. Indeed, it came particularly from ports which, if they had not exactly grown fat on Continental exports, had at least warded off immediate starvation. Above all, they feared the commercial consequences of what they interpreted as Scotland's even greater subordination to England's political and commercial interests.

Another commercial development with tangible roots in the pre-Union period was the emergence of a banking system. The Bank of Scotland had been founded by Act of Parliament in 1695, the familiar modern duopoly being completed in 1727 with the appearance of the Royal Bank of Scotland, sponsored by Ilay and Argyll and utilising the Equivalent funds payable under the treaty. Both institutions, together with a growing number of provincial and industrial banks (notably Douglas, Heron & Co., the Ayr Bank, whose sudden collapse in 1772 was the greatest Scottish commercial crash of the century), were to prove important to wider economic development, a legacy of the Williamite and Union era with the most far-reaching consequences. The limitations of traditional inter-personal lending, or indeed of individual capital accumulation, had long been a firm brake on Scotland's commercialisation. But organised banking now made funds available in substantial quantities, in effect recycling the growing profits of landholding and trade more widely. Several technical innovations by the Scottish banks, such as new accounting techniques, overdrafts, interest-bearing deposit accounts and the issue of credible paper money (by the early 1770s, as much as £864,000 was in circulation across the country), further assisted in the establishment of a monetised economy by making possible both long-term investment and more complex credit arrangements.

Union, then, was neither the sole nor the immediate cause of rising prosperity among Scotland's merchants and manufacturers. Indeed, as the burgh petitioners had feared, it created problems for many of these existing areas of economic strength. East coast towns faced a particularly difficult time: Dundee, one of Scotland's leading ports, experienced static trading levels after 1707; others which had prospered on the European coastal trade in fish and malt, such as Crail and Pittenweem in Fife, also declined. The minister of nearby Anstruther-Wester summarised the local effects from the clearer perspective of the 1790s: 'It is evident that that event did undoubtedly give a great shock to the trade of these towns.' Even the linen trade suffered. Vibrant enough to attract the malicious attentions of the Alien Act, it was initially nowhere near strong enough to compete with superior English goods within Britain's dynamic single market. Of the pre-existing areas of Scottish commercial development, only the incipient banking system, which would long remain immune to English competition, comfortably rode out the turbulence after 1707.

In general terms, therefore, the opportunities for the Scots to enrich themselves in England's market-place had a crucial reverse-side: the exposure of their manufactures to high-volume, low-cost and better-quality English competition. This was a bitter lesson for linen. It was so also for some ardent supporters of Union whose calculations of immediate advantage were proven woefully misplaced. Whisky, a dietary staple for Scots of all classes, was itself an unexpected victim of the treaty – or at least of its abrogation by Westminster. The malt tax, finally applied by Walpole in the

1720s, provoked the Shawfield Riots, violent witness to the impact of government levies on a Scottish industry less profitable and less well-developed than its southern counterparts. More widely the commercial taxes imposed by Parliament, disproportionately irksome to the Scots for the same reasons, led during the early post-Union decades to attacks on excise officers and widespread tax evasion. It was truly 'an era of misfortune and distress to the trade of Scotland', when, as another minister recalled in the 1790s, exaggerating only to a degree, 'commerce everywhere declined; in spite of the attempts which were made to support it by the wretched resource of smuggling'.

But as years turned to decades and the other provisions of the treaty worked their hoped-for effect, clear signs of Scotland's aggregate economic benefit from the Union began to emerge. Agrarian improvement, as we have seen, not only continued but accelerated after the 1740s, assisted by the widening market horizons for Scottish producers. By 1760, in a quite remarkable turnaround from the parlous position in the 1690s, grain and meal accounted for no less than 8 per cent of Scotland's own primary produce exports, going chiefly across the North Sea to Scandinavia. This transformation was no less evident in the booming black cattle trade to England, enriching Highland as well as Lowland proprietors to an unprecedented degree. Yet improvement and expansion was also taking place in non-agricultural sectors, again as a by-product of Union and the access which it gave to a much larger market. John Gibson, a west-coast merchant writing in the mid-1770s, was clear that the treaty lay at the root of this successful diversification in the regional economy of Clydeside: 'from this aera', he insisted, 'date the prosperity of the city of Glasgow; whatever efforts the inhabitants had made, for the introduction and extension of commerce and manufactures, prior to this time, they were but trifling and unimportant'.

By the 1730s, as Gibson explained at length, Glasgow's merchants had substantially penetrated the Chesapeake tobacco trade, importing this most profitable of American commodities and re-exporting it into Europe, especially France and the Netherlands. This development was indeed seminal. It established the Scots within a key imperial trade. It also brought prosperity and economic vigour to the Atlantic ports of the Clyde. Greenock reaped great profits. Glasgow itself, the 'Merchant City', was home to the entrepreneurs, usually operating in syndicates, who became known as the 'tobacco lords' – men like James Buchanan and John Glassford, the latter alone the owner of twenty-five ships. This lucrative oceanic commerce helped confirm a trend resulting in a situation that today seems characteristic of Scottish life: already by the mid-eighteenth century, the nation's demographic and economic centre of gravity had shifted away from the Lothians and towards west-central Scotland, where the clear majority of the country's modern population would live and work.

The spectacular growth of Scotland's tobacco trade is the classic instance of a type of large-scale global import–export business which would not have developed without the Union. Yet it also benefited from specifically Scottish circumstances. Clearly the ease with which Atlantic shipping could enter the Clyde, as well as the greater security from French interference it afforded during the periodic warfare of the eighteenth century, assisted enormously. An illicit pre-Union trade carved out with the West Indies and North America, despite Westminster's protectionist Navigation Laws, had also blazed the trail. But post-Union colonisation of the tobacco trade by the Scots was also furthered by the ability of their traditional trades and manufactures to expand to meet the specific reciprocal needs of the Virginia and Maryland colonists. Linen and ironware were staple Scottish goods. They provided ideal cargoes for outward voyages. Similarly the need for working capital not only involved the two main Edinburgh banks but also stimulated the growth of private and provincial banking in Glasgow itself. The tobacco trade thus delivered a potent multiplier effect, boosting other emerging sectors of the domestic economy.

For a time at least, it was crucial. Tobacco accounted for 52 per cent of Scotland's total exports by 1762. In 1775, the last year before the Declaration of Independence, Glasgow imported fully 21,000 tons from America – a weight which, in a telling comparison, slightly exceeds the total tonnage of all Scottish shipping afloat at the time of Union. Political and military events in Britain's colonies not surprisingly proved vexing for the Scottish syndicates in the 1770s. Initially, their factors feared the worst. But in the event a combination of prudent diversification (especially into coal and cotton), the charging of premium prices to offset declining volumes and the retention of control within a traffic increasingly bypassing the Clyde and importing directly into Continental Europe allowed Glasgow's merchants largely to insulate themselves from the constitutional drama unfolding between George III and his American subjects.

Linen production, a more deeply rooted Scottish specialism, showed not dissimilar flexibility. It gradually re-invented itself after the 1720s as a growth industry that not only brought important trading benefits to the wider economy – for example, supplying exchange goods for tobacco buyers – but also pointed the way towards new and more efficient forms of manufacturing. Lord Milton's brain-child, the British Linen Company, a banking, sales and marketing operation chartered in 1746, was an important contributory factor. But curiously, Scotland's soil also helped. For while in Ireland flax grew plentifully, allowing manufacturing to remain tied to the domestic economy of its rural workers (whose flax was indeed often grown locally), the difficulties of growing sufficient raw material in Scotland forced the expanding linen industry to import it in increasing quantities: flax accounted for 10–15 per cent of total national imports by the 1760s; by the 1790s, the Kirkcaldy district was drawing six-sevenths of its flax from overseas, the large bulk from the Baltic, particularly Bremen and Hamburg. This process severed over time the traditional connections between linen manufacturing and rural agriculture. It ensured that Scottish linen production would achieve denser concentrations of manufacturing, increasingly undertaken in workshops and sheds, giving way more smoothly in due course to technological change and factory organisation – in short, to full industrialisation – throughout the textile sector.

With textiles comprising 75 per cent of Scotland's home-produced exports by 1750, linen, which accounted for perhaps 50 per cent alone, was central to post-Union economic growth. Output levels were also much higher, and quality considerably improved: Scottish linen was now proving capable of ubiquitous use – including for tablecloths, shirts, underwear, sailcloth, socks, bags or ropes. Technical achievements included 'Osnaburgs', imitations of prestigious German linens, which just in the decade between 1747 and 1758 helped push annual output from 500,000 yards to more than 2,200,000. Calculations of the human scale are more complex. But a minimum of at least 100,000 linen workers across Scotland (perhaps 15,000 loom weavers, the balance spinners) seems reasonable by the 1760s: total national output may have hit a staggering 13,000,000 yards in the next decade. Significant social changes resulted. Rural women increasingly found it possible to spin or weave rather than labouring in the fields. The steady concentration of production also stimulated some of this period's remarkable demographic growth: Paisley, with its four-fold population increase between 1755 and 1801, was a notable centre of specialist manufacturing for high-value fine linens and silks.

Other textile products also figured prominently in Scotland's rapidly expanding manufacturing output. Woollen goods, another traditional staple, accounted for up to 10 per cent of home-produced exports at mid-century, again providing a significant domestic occupation for female workers. Moreover, as sheep progressively replaced cattle in much of the Highlands, some landlords actively encouraged manufacturing and Inverness emerged as an important centre of the British wool market. The non-textile sector, responsible for the other 25 per cent of home-produced exports by 1750, also depended largely upon the expansion and diversification of existing activities. The fisheries delivered notable success, strongly encouraged by enlightened officialdom. The Board of Trustees for Manufactures and Fisheries, established under Ilay's all-embracing patronage in 1727, disbursed development funds promised in the treaty. The British Fisheries Society was founded in London in 1786 under the chairmanship of the 5th Duke of Argyll: it projected the model fishing port of Ullapool in Wester Ross in 1788 and contributed to the development of Tobermory on Mull, Lochbay on Skye and Pulteneytown at Wick in Caithness. Fish exports fluctuated, however, from an extremely impressive 21 per cent of Scotland's total in 1755 to a perfectly respectable 9 per cent in 1760. Herring and salmon were dominant, followed by cod. Scottish catches were even sent as far as the Caribbean, where fishmeal nourished the slaves. Scotland's inshore and estuarine fisheries were also important to local economies, the Tay famously providing cured and, eventually, iced salmon for the London market.

Some trades and industries that were expanding rapidly by the 1750s had their roots directly in the proprietorial experimentation and estate management of the early agricultural improvers. Lead, mined in the Lanarkshire hills for centuries, emerged as a significant export: in 1755 it accounted for 18 per cent of Scottish exports, before falling to 5 per cent in 1770. The same process of more concerted exploitation to satisfy growing eighteenth-century demand also accounts for the small-scale but eye-catching export of arable products, especially grain, into mainland Europe. But Scottish trade and commerce, again profiting from expanding post-Union vistas, also grew by re-exporting on the tobacco model. Thus by the 1760s around 10 per cent of imports were actually of finished linen goods – remarkable given Scotland's own strengths, until it is realised that these were mainly specialist productions destined for lucrative shipping-on overseas. More interesting still were the increasing quantities of rum, sugar and rice passing through Scotland. These other products of the plantations made up perhaps 10–15 per cent of imports by mid-century – notably through Greenock and Port Glasgow – and again were profitably carried on to the rest of Britain and to Europe.

Industrialisation

As late as the 1770s, Scotland's economy was still primarily agricultural in nature. But farming was being supplemented – and in some of the most rapidly urbanising localities in the Lowlands, largely supplanted – by other activities. These included an ever more diverse and profitable trading culture; the provision of ancillary professional services; and, crucially for the next stage in economic development, the growth of still mainly domestically based, but increasingly high-volume and densely focused, manufacturing. This is in fact a fair description of an economy on the brink of industrialisation – of what some scholars refer to as an 'Industrial Revolution'. Parts of Scotland were reaching this stage by around 1780. This was a little later than England. But the Scots were still only the second people in history to experience industrialisation; and, because proximity to England encouraged convergence, they industrialised even faster than their southern neighbours. It remains to ask where, when, why and with what consequences this most important formative process in the creation of modern Western society finally imposed itself on Scotland.

In one sense it is easy to describe the process of Scottish industrialisation. For a broad characterisation, derived from abstract models of economic development, is something about which, after decades of furious academic debate, it is possible to offer some cautious generalisations. First, it occurred where productive activities, such as the extraction or processing of raw materials, or the manufacture of finished goods, were being undertaken on a scale sufficient both to dwarf comparable earlier endeavours and to make a swiftly increasing contribution to total economic output. Second, and closely related to the first, it was to be found not in the scattered domestic workplaces of the pre-industrial phase but in consolidated, specialised working environments – such as factories (or 'manufactories' as they were still described), mills and large workshops. Not least for this reason, industrialisation sooner or later came to be linked with urbanisation. Third, industrialisation occurred where labour-saving mechanisation was being introduced. This factor reinforced the need for increased business capitalisation and the tendency to seek economies of scale through the concentration of production. (Of course, it also explains the prominence in traditional accounts of an 'Industrial Revolution' given to ingenious technologies like Samuel Crompton's 'Mule' and James Hargreaves's famous 'Spinning Jenny'.) Finally, industrialisation carried with it profound implications for economic change itself. So far-reaching was the progress made that, once the acceleration or 'take-off' had begun, production levels, output, profits and further innovations and refinements were carried remorselessly onwards and upwards. As a result, industrialisation was sustainable and apparently irreversible: it was a self-replicating process whose unparalleled dynamism eventually swept away the old order, replacing it with something immediately recognisable as very different.

To determine when and where Scottish industrialisation actually happened is a rather more thorny question. Indeed the periodisation already proposed, putting 'take-off' around 1780, is only a very crude generalisation. In practice, the pronounced regional variations within the eighteenth-century Scottish economy ensured that it occurred in different parts of the country at different times. For industrialisation itself rested on a successful 'proto-industrial' phase, marked by those rurally based developments in manufacturing most clearly seen in the growth, concentration and increasingly complex organisation of linen production. Proto-industrialisation, in turn, could not have happened without progress in the agricultural and commercial sectors, which freed labour for seasonal or part-time manufacturing and provided integration with a more sophisticated trading network through which supply and demand could be mediated. Given the contrasts between the global economic horizons of Clydeside and those of improved rural agriculture in the Lothians, not to mention the subsistence-based crofting economies of Wester Ross, it will be obvious that the combination of capital, labour, technology, markets and entrepreneurship necessary to achieve industrialisation would be brought together much more readily in some places than in others.

A more fruitful approach to Scotland's industrial chronology is therefore to acknowledge the danger of sweeping generalisations and to proceed instead by reference to specific local and regional examples. This naturally directs attention to some of the outstanding instances of early Scottish industrialisation, not only in textile manufacturing but also in the metal industries, which we have so far overlooked. For if one single workplace, quintessentially industrial in character, symbolised for contemporaries the sudden emergence of a different scale and kind of productive activity, it was the Carron Ironworks, founded in 1759 on an advantageous site near Falkirk in eastern Stirlingshire. This was an enormous complex. An Anglo-Scottish enterprise created by a Birmingham businessman, an Edinburgh-educated English doctor and a merchant from Prestonpans, it brought together a cheap power source (the Carron Water) and abundant raw materials (drawn from iron ore deposits at Bo'ness and coal at Kinnaird) to supply furnaces, forges and mills on a single integrated site. Carron's products were as varied as its scale was daunting: cannonballs, cylinders, pipes, nails and fire grates (the last designed by fashionable architect John Adam), but, most famously, the 'carronade', a shorter and lighter piece of ordnance which, gradually refined and then purchased by the government from the 1770s, became the weapon of choice for Nelson and Wellington. By that time Carron was the largest iron works in Europe with an immense workforce in excess of 2,000 people. It was also a tribute to what was possible when native resources and business acumen, allied to a substantial input of English expertise, were able fully to exploit the huge markets increasingly available to Scottish manufacturing in a British and imperial context.

Carron will always remain the best-known instance of precocious Scottish industrialisation, unambiguously displaying all of its classic features. Yet it was for precisely those reasons exceptional. A more important sector, as might be expected, was textile production. In 1800, as in 1740, this still employed vastly more people and contributed far more to Scotland's national output. The crucial development here was that linen, the classic proto-industrial product and Scotland's principal manufactured export in the 1750s, was after the 1780s overtaken by cotton, whose meteoric rise again exemplifies much that is characteristic of an economy's 'take-off' into full industrialisation. Unlike linen, cotton's story has no real proto-industrial phase. Most of its raw material was imported from North America and the West Indies. With its focus in west-central Scotland, it rested instead on the reserves of capital, expertise and connections already accumulated by merchants engaged in the Atlantic and European tobacco trade.

Close business links with England, created initially in linen production, were as important as at Carron, locking Scotland's entrepreneurs into a wider network of British industrialisation. This gave the west-coast textile manufacturers privileged access to the latest Lancashire technology. It also gave them an opportunity to carve out an early mass-production niche in Britain's vast domestic and colonial market. Combined with the Scottish experience of concentrating production into mills which had latterly increased linen output even more dramatically, this lent the infant cotton industry a dynamism that it is almost impossible to exaggerate. The first mill opened at Penicuik to the south of Edinburgh in 1778. By 1795 there were thirty-nine, the most famous being at New Lanark. This was a combined mill complex and model workers' settlement founded in 1786 by David Dale, a Glasgow textile merchant and sometime local agent of the Royal Bank, whose connections in northern England also facilitated the rapid importation of Richard Arkwright's water-frame.

Other important early mills were located at Catrine in Ayrshire, Deanston near Doune, and Stanley outside Perth (in whose foundation Dempster the local MP was involved). Outlying examples were established as far afield as Rothesay on the Isle of Bute and Spinningdale on the Dornoch Firth (another of Dale's creations). Annual imports of raw cotton into Scotland, averaging just 430,000 lb in the early 1780s, were exceeding 7,000,000 lb annually by the end of the century. The estimate shortly after 1800 that perhaps 257,900 jobs were provided by Scotland's textile industries owed a great deal to the cotton boom. In a society of only 1,608,420 people at the 1801 census, and if we exclude young children and the elderly from the workforce, the material importance of textiles in general and cotton manufacturing in particular to a growing proportion of Scotland's families, especially through female employment, can readily be imagined.

Continuous large-scale change, as production was transformed by new technologies and by the progressive concentration of activity within specialist factories and mills, was also being experienced in the woollen industry. Here too, as at Carron, Scotland's natural resources were invaluable. After mid-century, the spread of the more efficient Cheviot and Blackface breeds, together with new forms of productive organisation in the textile sector, particularly in spinning, permitted manufacturers to expand to satisfy a growing market at home and overseas. Newcastleton emerged as a planned village for wool weavers, as did Carlops to the south of Edinburgh. Towns like Galashiels and Hawick also expanded and modernised their production to meet increasing demand for woollens and hosiery. At Innerleithen in Peebles-shire in 1788, Alexander Broadie, a local blacksmith whose wealth derived originally from the Shropshire iron trade, established the first properly mechanised wool-spinning mill in Scotland, the first of many and the forerunner of the Borders' later tweed industry.

A range of other industries closely associated with textiles were also prominent in early Scottish industrialisation. Some had long histories in a country where abundant natural resources and centuries of textile production provided a diversity of ancillary occupations. Commercial bleaching began in 1727. In 1749 a factory at Prestonpans run by the later founders of the Carron Ironworks became the first to employ sulphuric acid instead of natural agents; the use of chlorine followed in 1787. By the turn of the next century, Scotland had upwards of 200 bleachfields in operation, the largest at Luncarty on the River Tay above Perth. Turkey red dyeing was also introduced: a facility on the Water of Leven, west of Glasgow, led the way. It is important, however, not to exaggerate the advances made in the eighteenth-century textile industry. Spinning technology was significantly ahead of weaving. As late as the 1820s the large majority of Scotland's weavers still operated handlooms rather than powerlooms. Most worked in villages rather than in large towns. Crucially, moreover, the steam engine, that Promethean symbol of man's ingenuity, forever associated in the popular imagination with the 'Industrial Revolution', powered its first integrated Scottish textile mill only in 1798. Water was still the commonest source of motive power in the early nineteenth century. Its availability in Scotland – cheap, clean and plentiful – would long remain an important factor in shaping the topography of the country's distinctive industrial development.

An enterprise which further demonstrates the limitations of eighteenth-century industrialisation – again decisively placing Scotland's development behind England's – was coal-mining. Originating in the small-scale exploitation of landed estates, its progress towards genuine industrialisation was slow. Demand rose steadily through the century. Iron works required increasing quantities of coke. Coal was also needed in lime preparation, salt-extraction, glass-making, domestic consumption, and, in time, the steam engines in the mills and factories. Output duly rose from less than 400,000 tons in 1700 to perhaps 2,000,000 tons a hundred years later. Yet the size of workable seams and so of individual collieries remained limited. Innovation was inhibited, capital-intensive change in the mines usually uneconomic. In any case, Scotland's miners, like the salt-panners, were bound in a form of indentured servitude established during the labour shortages of the seventeenth century, obliging miners to work for their employer in perpetuity. Compounded by the induction of their children at birth, this had created a virtually hereditary workforce – though it also led to higher wages than in England (for the solidarity and collective bargaining power of Scotland's indentured colliers was legendary). This was only ended by Westminster legislation in 1775 and 1799, creating a free labour market over bitter opposition from the miners themselves. Mining technology was also stubbornly traditional. The tools for hewing and carrying coal were little changed, despite the availability of the Newcomen engine in Scotland from 1719 onwards and horse waggon-ways after the 1720s. Proper steam-engines for pumping and winding were rare even in 1800, and confined to the few larger pits.

Industrialisation, because of the bewildering array of goods made available to consumers and because of the increasing pull it exerted on the whole economy, affected all people, whether they were personally involved in the cotton mills or the iron works, or whether they were shopkeepers, proprietors, farmers or Highland peasants in the remotest glen. The industrial 'take-off' propelled national output – and material consumption among all social groups – to new heights. As manufacturing expanded in certain districts, it sucked in workers, further accentuating regional demographic divergence. Late eighteenth-century industrialisation was, of course, mainly a rural phenomenon. Yet it underpinned some dramatic instances of urbanisation: manufacturing boom-towns like Paisley, just like new settlements such as Stanley and New Lanark, swelled with migrant workers; traditional centres like Edinburgh and Perth grew as a result of the more complex trading networks and unprecedented agricultural surpluses of the period. By the 1780s these same forces were also transforming many other aspects of people's lives, undermining traditional social institutions both in rural communities and in the towns. They introduced a more individualistic, innovative and competitive ethic to much of the population. Many people embraced new roles or had new ones thrust upon them. The experiences of the Scottish people, individually and collectively, were altered forever. It is with these far-reaching consequences of economic change that the remainder of this chapter is concerned.

Social structure and social experience

In 1700 Scotland was recovering from disastrous harvests in which at least one in ten of its inhabitants had starved to death. In 1740–41 poor weather again produced shortfalls and consequent hardship, especially in the Highlands; but this time there was no nationwide population crisis – nor would there ever be again. By 1780, as we have seen, crude death rates were declining relentlessly and infant mortality in particular was falling. Despite further harvest failures, notably in 1782–83, the population grew by more than 50 per cent between the 1750s and 1800 and the average person's life expectancy increased markedly. Vital data such as these provide the basic parameters of human experience in a period of unparalleled economic change. They confirm that conditions in Scotland were improving in one overwhelmingly important respect: the ability of the country to support a growing population, and, for the first time, to do so without triggering a corrective Malthusian crisis. But what else can we say about the social consequences of economic development and about the lives on which it impacted? Clearly they must differ depending upon the social group about whom we are talking.

Unsurprisingly, this was a golden age for Scotland's landed elite. Most of the leading proprietors exploited rising incomes in the customary manner, extending their patrimony by purchase as well as increasing their personal expenditure. The Earls of Aberdeen, members of the illustrious Gordon family, expanded with breathtaking rapidity. Sixteenth-largest landowners in their eponymous county in the 1660s, they were comfortably in top place by the 1770s. Across the country by the same decade, two-thirds of the 123 estates with rentals in excess of £4,000 (Scots), as conventionally expressed in the mid-seventeenth-century values, were owned by titled noblemen. These largest proprietors included all nine Scottish dukes and 33 of the 40 earls. Overall, the total number of owners with valuations in excess of £2,000 was just 336. This small group of men and their dependants also gained considerably in other respects. Income streams from land diversified: sheep, timber, mineral extraction, grain exports, industrial production, overseas investments and so forth.

The palatial residences of the Duke of Roxburghe at Floors and of the Duke of Buccleuch at Dalkeith testify eloquently to the sheer liquidity increasingly available to the leading proprietors. Nor is it accidental that the great Scottish estates so often expressed their eighteenth-century achievements in a timeless vocabulary – neo-classical pediment, capitals in the ancient orders and generous acres of lush sward. For such idoms affirmed the continuing pre-eminence of land and blood in spite of quickening commercialisation. Indeed, coupled with further political or military achievements under the Hanoverians and further assisted by advantageous marriage alliances in the south, an Argyll or, later, a Sutherland could begin to move without embarrassment amongst the Devonshires, the Newcastles and the Portlands. Italian art, English porcelain, French furniture, oriental exotica, fine clothes, excellent food, extensive libraries and grand London town-houses: these were the elegant confirmation of modern Scottish aristocratic success.

Other hereditary landowners also enjoyed great prosperity. In the 1770s the lairds of real substance, those owning property conventionally valued in the range £500–£2,000, numbered a thousand or so; those with less than £500 of land, the minor lairds and so-called 'bonnet lairds' (essentially owner-occupiers), probably nearer seven thousand. Here too political or professional success in London, India or the armed forces might add to both standing and income. But a Scottish laird's principal asset remained his land. By 1800 most had begun to exploit their property's full economic potential, seeing this as a patriotic as well as a dynastic duty: Henry Home, Lord Kames, took as much pride in his wife's estate at Blair Drummond in Perthshire, where he reclaimed swathes of fertile farmland from the Forth, as he derived from his legal and scholarly accomplishments. Dynasties like the Hopes of Rankeillour from Fife (one of whom led the Honourable Agricultural Society) and the Clerks of Penicuik (Midlothian mine owners with a penchant for fine art) similarly experienced consistently rising incomes and could affect a lifestyle comparable with Europe's lesser nobility: the Clerks, living to the south of Edinburgh, also emerged as key patrons of the brilliant cultural awakening that adorned Scotland's capital by mid-century.

Closely related to the landed classes, usually as younger sons, brothers and cousins, were the traditional professions whose working lives focused on Edinburgh and the major provincial towns. The law was pre-eminent, with its axial position in post-Union government and its continuance as an all-pervading social institution. Scots law and its well-heeled professional communities – the Faculty of Advocates, whose denizens pleaded in the courts, and the Writers to the Signet, who transacted most legal business – rode the crest of the wave of the country's economic progress. Individual practitioners sprung from minor landed stock were able to reach new heights of status and prosperity. Whole kinship-groupings, like the Dalrymples and Dundases, became Lords Advocate and judges in the Courts of Session and Justiciary. They acquired considerable wealth that could be ploughed back into estates such as Arniston, Melville Castle, Dunira, Newhailes and Oxenfoord. In towns like Perth, Kilmarnock and Dumfries, too, the legal classes expanded and profited as economic developments increased demand for conveyancing, advice and representation. By 1800 there were approximately 200 advocates and perhaps 1,600 writers and other lawyers in Scotland – perhaps one for every eight hundred people.

Other professions found their opportunities similarly increased, not least as a result of the Union. Younger sons often found military service a useful route to independent status. Nor were openings scarce. There were many like General James Grant of Ballindalloch, a laird's brother who served in Flanders and America before acquiring his own estate and becoming MP for Sutherland. It has been calculated that by 1794 more than one-quarter of all officers in Britain's line infantry battalions were Scots. Numerous supposedly English regiments (like the 9th Foot, East Norfolk Regiment, and the 19th Foot, The Green Howards) had a predominantly Scottish officer corps. Even more tellingly, they comprised no less than 40 per cent of full regimental colonels by the time of the Revolutionary Wars. In the greatly expanded British armies which fought successive wars against the French right through the century, the Scots clearly found it relatively easy to turn the patronage system to their own advantage.

A different form of patronage, from the proprietors and politicians to whom after 1712 they frequently owed their appointments, gave those who entered the presbyterian ministry a leadership role in local communities across Scotland. This too might well bring a substantial income. For the eighteenth-century clergy benefited from the customary linkage of their stipends to agricultural productivity: the 'teinds', a statutory levy of one-tenth of parish output, were actually what maintained rural clerics like George Ridpath in Berwickshire in their undemanding lifestyle of preaching, reading, visiting and conversation. But, of course, the ministers of the established church accounted for a diminishing part of Scotland's clerical population by the end of the century. All told, by 1800 there were probably approaching 2,000 clergymen across the different denominations, or roughly one for every seven hundred people. Most were men of learning; virtually all earned a decent living.

Hundreds of eighteenth-century academics and authors also prospered. This was an age of growing cultural vitality in Scotland. Intellectual or literary aptitude created important economic opportunities through publishing, criticism and journalism. These occupations in turn opened up new avenues to wealth and even made a career as a man of letters for the first time both possible and desirable: learning, as Dr Johnson noted approvingly, had at last become a trade. It remained true, of course, that no minister, scholar or scientist purchased a country estate on his professional earnings. None, needless to say, received a peerage for his pains. But most had an instinctive affinity with the landed class from whose junior ranks they often sprang: Hume, the greatest of them, was, after all, the son of a minor Berwickshire laird; Scott, comfortably Scotland's most bankable author by the early years of the next century, was proud to be descended from a long line of Border landowners. Frequently intermixing with the cultivated proprietors and learned lawyers of the age, and sharing their ideas and opinions, some of Scotland's intellectuals by the 1760s could realistically hope to add a measure of social status and genuine influence to their financial rewards.

Because Scotland was experiencing both an increase and a diversification in economic output, there were also unparalleled opportunities for upwards social mobility. It was probably inevitable that the phenomenon of 'new money' should arise, challenging – indeed, sometimes affronting – the effortless superiority of the traditional landed elite and their progeny who trod the well-worn track into the old professions. Men like the commodity merchants and other international traders, themselves often younger sons of minor propertied families who had prospered through American or West Indian commerce, exploited their purchasing-power to re-colonise the countryside: Alexander Speirs, a Glasgow tobacco entrepreneur, sank more than £100,000 into numerous estates in Renfrewshire, Lanarkshire and Stirlingshire. By the 1750s, tycoons were emerging in expanding commercial sectors such as banking, shipping and provisioning. Such self-made men not only established business dynasties. They also sought to buy their way into local landed society. Sir Lawrence Dundas, draper's son made good, made his fortune as a supplier to the British army through the 'Forty-five and then the Seven Years War. In due course he managed to purchase Orkney and Shetland and part of Stirlingshire; he even entailed his estates in a display of dynasticism the equal of any ancient proprietor.

These magnates were joined from the 1760s by a new breed. The 'nabobs', much commented upon at the time though probably fewer in number and less substantial in influence than paranoid contemporaries liked to imagine, acquired their frequently ill-gotten gains in India before repatriating themselves back to Britain ('No man ever went to the East Indies with good intentions', observed Horace Walpole sagely in 1783). In Scotland they were represented by brash and worldly interlopers like John Johnstone and George Paterson. Making ostentatious inroads into the heartlands of old money, they respectively purchased Alva House, an old Erskine of Mar property, in 1775, and Castle Huntly near Dundee from the Earl of Strathmore in 1777. By the end of the century, manufacturers had also begun to buy land. David Dale, who came originally from a weaving family, marked his social arrival with a substantial Lanarkshire property. A decent acreage clearly remained the ultimate affirmation of status. This was despite the fact that many of the *arrivistes*, and virtually all of the Scottish industrialists, actually came from non-landed backgrounds, the ambitious sons of tenant-farmers, merchants, tradesmen and engineers.

An expanding and more diverse middle class – entrepreneurs, employers, minor professionals, and others whose income did not depend on their own manual labour – was a further consequence of economic development.

This remains a safe generalisation, even though we need to remember that the language of 'class' was itself unfamiliar to contemporaries, who, like the clerical authors who compiled the *Statistical Account* in the 1790s, still invariably thought of social gradations in looser concepts such as 'order' and 'rank'. Commercial and productive activity inevitably delivered substantial prosperity for many owners. Grain shipping, woollen exports and ale brewing were just some of the traditional businesses to benefit from this general growth. Small undertakings involved in supplying and servicing key growth sectors, like specialist equipment manufacturers to the textile industry, also shared in rising profitability.

Comparable growth and rising incomes touched other skilled and respectable occupations long pre-dating the Union. Schoolteaching expanded, with increased demand for the broader education of an increasingly youthful population – and even though it was still usually abysmally paid. Printing and its ancillary trades (particularly in Edinburgh, Britain's second largest publishing centre) was a notable Scottish growth sector, eventually producing major operators like Andrew Bell and Archibald Constable. Instrument-making, whether for factories or for ships, was another expanding and innovating specialism. Nor should we forget the parallel growth and diversification across a range of conventional skilled artisanal activities, manual in character and certainly not middle-class but also not yet dominated by wage-labour: each in fact still included many small employers and the self-employed. In shoe-making, tailoring, carpentry, ironmongery, victualling, furniture-making and most forms of retail or wholesale shopkeeping, there were thousands of such practitioners throughout Scotland's towns, villages and hamlets.

For members of all of these occupations, the ever-more-diverse people who filled the great social chasm between the minor lairds and the mass of wage-labouring employees and unemployed, the experience of economic change could still, of course, be destabilising. Some, unable or unwilling to adapt, or just plain unlucky, fell by the wayside. But in broad terms those with a business, a profession or a trade were best able to exploit the new conditions. Not surprisingly, this broad intermediate segment of the population – with handloom weavers like George Mealmaker at one end and junior members of the literate professions like Thomas Muir at the other – also dominated those aspirational political movements which emerged with the French Revolution. In most cases they were motivated by the desire to extend the parliamentary and burgh franchises to people like themselves. Their relatively limited and sectional campaigns therefore need to be distinguished from the overt social egalitarianism and much greater radicalism of organised and industrial wage-labourers – and the precondition of such phenomena, the growth of a wide-ranging working-class consciousness among an urbanised proletariat – which only really began to rear its head in Scotland in the next century.

Improvement extended even to those still involved in the agricultural economy but who, in strict legal terms, owned no landed property at all. Single-tenant farmers almost anywhere by 1800 were still humble compared with a Buccleuch or a Clerk. Yet like the 'bonnet lairds', they would be far better-off than their predecessors on the same estate. James Robertson, minister of Callander, surveying Perthshire in 1794, left us a vivid impression of the lifestyle now possible even among the rural tenantry:

> What an astonishing change has taken place even in the memory of man! About half a century ago the country was uninclosed, the fields uncultivated and the farmers spiritless and poor. . . . Then the farmer went on foot to market; now he rides well dressed and mounted: formerly he ate his food off his knee, and it consisted of meal, vegetables and milk: now his table is covered, his knife and fork are laid down before him to dine on meat . . . he sleeps comfortably on feathers with his curtains drawn snugly around him.

A further striking indication of growing affluence in eighteenth-century Scotland was a socially stratified divergence in female roles. Poor women benefited from increased employment opportunities. But the disproportionate wealth accruing to property-owning and professional members of the middle class allowed their female relations to withdraw entirely from the world of work. Rising family incomes led these women increasingly to inhabit a separate sphere from their menfolk, becoming purely domestic in their function, overseeing a growing number of paid household servants and standing as the guardians of family morality, religion and culture.

Statistical measures of the impact of economic change across Scottish society as a whole are also available to some extent, and they shed invaluable further light upon the consequences for the less well-off. Above all it is likely that, as commercial and industrial development accelerated, some of the key variables affecting even the humblest lives improved markedly. Between the 1750s and the 1790s, the price of oatmeal in Scotland probably increased by around 50 per cent and of other basic foodstuffs by around 100 per cent. But the average pay earned by typical groups such as agricultural workers and Edinburgh printers increased by at least 150 per cent in the same period, helped by a relative shortage of skilled labour in Scotland, on the land as much as in industry, which imposed upward pressure on the cost of labour. Real wages – defined as the purchasing power of actual wages – therefore also rose, falling back only with the onset of the Revolutionary Wars and renewed price inflation after 1790. Moreover, it should not be forgotten that women's paid employment was increasingly providing opportunities for supplementation: then as now, total family income, rather than the wages of individual male 'breadwinners', was the key determinant of living standards among the working poor.

Non-monetary improvements in the basic conditions of Scottish life can also be tracked to some extent. For example, new and cheaper crops like the potato and a greater diversity of grains and vegetables were becoming much more widely available through the eighteenth century. Together with increased quantities of dairy produce in particular (this was the period when Ayrshire developed its famous Dunlop cheeses) and more mutton and beef, these innovations enhanced the diets of large numbers, especially in the Lowlands. Farm servants may have been particularly advantaged by these changes, being largely paid in kind. Rural housing conditions also generally improved. Employment in farm service again carried entitlement to accommodation, especially for married workers and their families (known as 'hinds' in southern Scotland): starting in places like Midlothian and Fife, the old construction methods for rural residences were being abandoned, as cottage walls made of stone and mud-mortar and roofs covered with sods gave way to masonry and straw thatch, as well as to ceilings and timber floors in some instances. Even unmarried servants, typically boarded within the farm steading itself, benefited from the re-designed and enhanced facilities which were appearing as an integral part of eighteenth-century estate reform. All of these trends help us make sense of the generally upbeat assessments of post-improvement rural life routinely found in the *Statistical Account*: his parishioners, said one Fife minister, were 'remarkably sober, industrious, and economical, so that even the dearth of 1783 had no visible effect upon the poorest and lowest of the people; nothing was done for them by the heritors, yet all supported themselves in their usual manner'. In search of the elusive mechanisms explaining Scotland's declining death rates in this period, we could clearly do worse than concentrate our inquiries on real incomes, diet and housing as the areas likely to yield the richest pickings.

Yet all of this can only be part of the story of the human impact of economic change. In particular, it tells us little about those people, buried within the overall favourable aggregates, to whom little or no material benefit accrued, or for whom this was offset by other disadvantages. After all, many who had attained modest self-sufficiency within the old tenurial and cultivation systems – groups like the Highland tacksmen and many customary tenants – simply had no place within a very different agrarian regime. Certain skilled artisans, like the handloom weavers who found their craft guilds eroded and their status and bargaining power diluted by an influx of new workers, could also identify disadvantages to recent changes. Agricultural labourers and industrial workers alike, bound by contracts and dependent for their living on the wages they could earn, risked redundancy or summary dismissal. Those employed in commerce and manufacturing were particularly exposed to the increasingly unpredictable trade cycles characterising an industrial economy. All groups also faced growing expectations of productivity and managerial discipline in the eighteenth-century workplace. Some not surprisingly resented things enough to articulate their feelings in ways which can still be traced.

The best-known example of active resistance to economic change in this period remains the 'Levellers'. These were small tenant-farmers and labourers in Dumfries-shire and Galloway, a region with popular traditions of Covenanting anti-establishmentarianism, who in 1724 reacted against proprietorial engrossing of land designed to expand lucrative stock-rearing. Defying eviction, they threw down some enclosures. A few cattle were killed. Military suppression ensued, together with a couple of exemplary deportations, before officialdom wisely pursued a more lenient course. This was not a unique event, however. In 1718, the Lanarkshire JPs had confronted twenty-two miscreants who 'in a violent manner . . . [had] entered upon the said new dike and rifled and pulled down some parts thereof at several places . . .'. While the demolished enclosures had on this occasion belonged to another JP, the bench was sufficiently mindful of popular sensitivities, and nervous enough about the scope for future outbreaks, that the peculiarly Scottish criminal verdict of 'not proven' was returned. Indeed, most of their forensic scrutiny was in fact devoted to ascertaining the original legality of the dyke.

The Highlands also saw sporadic resistance to the new landlordism, particularly in the later eighteenth century as the pace of change accelerated: in Lochaber in 1782, a sheep farmer was attacked by local women; ten years later, animals were driven off Sir Hector Munro's new sheep farm in Easter Ross and an incoming farmer again roughed-up. Yet another kind of direct action against unwelcome commercialisation was the excise riot. Involving attacks on excisemen and customs warehouses, these popular protests, like those culminating in Edinburgh's Porteous Riot in 1736, tended to be short in duration and specific in their application, though until the 1750s they may have been relatively frequent throughout the Lowlands and certainly always worried the edgy authorities. Even coastal smuggling, illicit distilling and widespread tax evasion are with somewhat less plausibility often interpreted as yet another form of resistance to commercialisation. But they may well have been encouraged by the fact that, until Dundas finally re-captured the posts for native talent in the 1780s, the Barons of the Court of Exchequer, Scotland's fiscal overlords in Edinburgh, were predominantly English, appointed on the provocative premise that the Scots were incapable of operating an efficient taxation system for themselves.

The considerable expansion of paid employment also brought with it inevitable disputes over wages and conditions, both between employers and their workers and between the traditional craft interest-groups of masters and journeymen. Increasingly this agitation and negotiation was organised collectively through trade societies, like the early union of Paisley weavers in 1768, whose legal rights Dundas actually defended as Solicitor-General, or the Journeyman Shipwrights of Leith, who secured a pay-rise for themselves in the late 1790s. The most celebrated instance of industrial action, however, was the strike of the cotton handloom weavers at Calton near Glasgow in September 1787. Beginning in a dispute over wage-rates which escalated into a rash of loom-breaking and the cutting of threads by a crowd of thousands, it culminated in the Lord Provost and magistrates being stoned. Eventually the Riot Act was read and six people were shot dead by soldiers.

Scotland was still, of course, less prone than England to economically inspired protest of these miscellaneous kinds. Rising incomes and unaccustomed plenty almost certainly served to defuse tensions. The more paternalistic approach of Scottish JPs and sheriff courts (seen, for example, in their continued regulation of prices and in their preparedness to recognise legitimate grievances) may also have helped. It is remarkable, for example, given the long parallel history of anti-landlord violence in Ireland, that such a profoundly disturbing phenomenon as the transformation of the Highland rural economy, in which physical force was certainly employed on occasion by proprietors and their agents, seems not have provoked a single murder. Yet traditional communal expressions of displeasure did survive. The classic example was the bread or 'meal' riot in which merchants who hoarded, profiteered or transported grain out of a needy district in effect found their supplies being requisitioned and re-distributed by well-organised groups of inhabitants. Women often played a leading role in these crowd-scenes, not least because this made it much more difficult for even the most bullish authorities to respond aggressively. Such traditional phenomena long remained an intermittent feature of Scottish life, with particular peaks of activity during the 1720s (with more than a whiff of anti-Unionism also in evidence), following the very poor harvests of 1740–41, and again through the 1770s. They are a potent reminder that, particularly with some groups increasingly cut off from an agricultural system upon which all Scots still ultimately depended, the intra-communal tensions caused by economic difficulties could sometimes be acute.

Although defining the experience of only a minority, it is again with urban Scotland that we should end this survey of the negative effects of economic change. For the rapid and chaotic growth of centres like Glasgow, Paisley, Edinburgh and Dundee, together with unregulated conditions in the newly established industrial and commercial workplaces, produced an environment that was increasingly dangerous for those who had to endure it. Water supplies were inadequate. Sanitation systems as a whole were primitive and becoming overloaded. Housing conditions in the towns were poor and increasingly cramped. Burgh councils, as we have seen, were ill-equipped to respond. The return of tuberculosis (the 'white death') and the emergence of other contagious diseases such as cholera, typhus and measles as major causes of death in Scottish towns after 1810 was only a delayed consequence of these eighteenth-century developments. It would be left to the Victorians, and to the reformed welfare and administrative systems that finally emerged after the 1830s, to begin to provide effective solutions.

At the heart of the economic and social transformation of Scotland in this period therefore lies a paradox. Unparalleled wealth enriched the few very greatly. Information on prices, incomes and demographic trends, together with evidence of material culture, shows that it also raised the basic living standards, and probably had some role in increasing the life expectancy, of most. For significant numbers, however, these gains were accompanied by the loss of property, of ownership, of self-determination, of health and of opportunities. Like other societies experiencing comparable processes over the next two centuries, eighteenth-century Scotland therefore teaches us a difficult lesson: inequalities readily widen as increased wealth is generated; and the ills accumulate for some as a direct consequence of precisely the factors which deliver rising incomes and better lives for the majority. Arguments over social benefit and social cost in such circumstances are, of course, likely to be resolved more by ideological preferences than by bald historical data.

Social institutions

Education brooked large in contemporary assessments of what was most praiseworthy about Scotland's distinctive social fabric. Since the Reformation, during which the schools and universities had been appropriated for the service of a presbyterian church and the creation of a pious Protestant society, teaching had been accorded paramount importance. Such views were famously expressed in the *First Book of Discipline* (1560). This articulated a vision of the Scots as a literate people, familiar with scripture and thus capable of fulfilling their destiny as a godly and, later, a Covenanted nation. The Williamite Revolution of 1689–90 empowered a new generation of presbyterian enthusiasts, leading to redoubled emphasis upon these aspirations, as well as to some further practical progress. An Act of 1696 duly confirmed the principle that there should be a school in every parish: the 'dominie' (the teacher) would be supported by a tax on the heritors, enforced, if necessary, by the commission of supply.

Apart from in the Highlands and islands, where widespread non-presbyterianism and the unmanageable size of parishes created intractable problems (Harris, for example, included seven inhabited islands and measured forty-eight miles by twenty-four), Scotland's rural schools actually functioned by 1700 in a manner similar to that formally envisaged. Children paid a small fee to attend: education was far too precious to be treated as a free good. It was expected, however, that the kirk session would support the very poor. This mechanism, reinforced by a combination of parental aspiration and clerical pressure, ensured that most rural Scots received some elementary education. Many burghs also had their own schools. Overseen by the council and the parish clergy, the 'grammar schools', many with medieval origins, delivered not only an elementary but a more advanced Latin-based education to boys moving towards university and the traditional professions. Large burghs like Edinburgh, with its endowed welfare institutions such as Watson's, Heriot's and the Merchants' Maiden and Trades Maiden Hospitals, also made supplementary provision for the children of needy burgesses.

All types of school, whether rural or urban, were, by our standards, somewhat limited in their aims. Yet constant emphasis upon a narrow range of attainments meant that basic literacy, numeracy and some knowledge of the catechism were already within the reach of many, and, in the Lowlands, most. Scottish literacy was by no means as exceptional as is sometimes thought: Highland literacy was among the worst in Europe; the Lowlands were comparable with northern England. But it was nevertheless impressive for a relatively poor and thinly populated country. In practice, literacy was much higher among males: in 1750 roughly 65 per cent of Lowland men giving evidence in criminal trials could sign their name, against 15–30 per cent of women. Predictably, it was also better among the respectable and the prosperous: in the period 1700–70, perhaps 97 per cent of lairds and 82 per cent of craftsmen and traders, but only 45 per cent of servants, could sign. Nor can literacy be interpreted simplistically. It is open to question whether signing one's name is really a useful or an accurate measure of meaningful literate competence, and whether, indeed, the emphasis on the measurement of writing capacity merely serves to underestimate the prevalence of the simpler skill of reading. It is also likely that formal education was not the only factor determining literacy. For Scotland's Protestant religious culture and the dynamic economic forces of the period almost certainly compelled many individuals to find out how to read and even to write. The schools were simply one means to acquiring a widely valued social good.

In the decades after 1700, the presbyterian clergy, especially through the SSPCK, exercised considerable influence in improving this inherited system. Their main strategy was predictably to plug the institutional gaps – above all in the Highlands, where education was also integral to the modernising and civilising mission conceived by Lowlanders. In practice this also entailed the suppression of Gaelic: its classroom use was expressly forbidden until the 1760s; no complete Gaelic bible yet existed. The success of this approach was mixed, though sometimes dramatic. In terms of scale, the SSPCK was running more than 150 schools by 1800. Many thousands of Highland children – perhaps 13,000 at any one time by this stage – were being brought for the first time within the educational fold. Lachlan Shaw, a Moray minister, claimed in the 1770s, with audible echoes of his Hanoverian presbyterian predecessors in the aftermath of the 'Forty-five, that the educational activities of the SSPCK had finally ensured that 'Christianity is increased, Heathenish Customs are abandoned, the number of Papists is diminished, disaffection to the Government is lessened, and the English language is so diffused, that in the remotest glens it is spoken by the young people'.

But the Highlands were not the only institutional pressure-point. Demographic change, together with legislative loopholes, was also rendering the Lowland parish school system gradually less effective. The numbers of children frequently overwhelmed the dominie. Some coped by providing only a bare minimum of three or four years' education. The strains particularly affected the ability to provide opportunities to girls. Absenteeism, too, was a growing problem: children's manual labour was precious to families and employers at certain seasons, the more so in a time of economic expansion. In many cases, non-statutory additional provision was the only solution, however much it was initially regretted by proud kirk sessions and burgh councils. The SSPCK helped a little even in the Lowlands, founding some schools in Fife and Edinburgh. Sunday or 'sabbath' schools, imported from England in the 1780s and usually run by interdenominational societies, were another option, since they neatly circumvented the obstacle of weekday child employment. But by far the larger part of supplementary provision – in some urban areas, the bulk of educational provision of any kind – came from other quarters.

The principal expedient was the 'adventure' school, a fee-paying private institution, soon embraced by both parents and officialdom as an important aspect of local educational provision. A similar welcome was extended to the smattering of new endowed charity schools, such as the one attached to the Tolbooth Kirk in Edinburgh, which emerged in response to the growth of personal and corporate wealth. It was still, however, becoming less and less likely by the 1780s that the poorest children would be schooled even at an elementary level. Partly this was a matter of sheer population expansion. But it was also a consequence of mass migration and Scotland's changing regional demography. In rapidly increasing urban centres like Paisley and Greenock, as well as in the new crofting townships of the Highlands and islands, conventional provision through burgh councils and parishes was simply swamped. Thus literacy in some urban areas was for the first time falling behind levels in the adjacent countryside. Localised factors such as the erosion of religious culture and impoverished social experiences probably contributed, but this unprecedented reversal also implies a degree of institutional failure in eighteenth-century education.

Yet all was not gloom. The middle and respectable working classes were growing in size and prosperity. There was rising economic demand for technical and business knowledge. Increased cultural importance also attached, as we shall see, to civilised behaviour and to literary and intellectual awareness. These powerful currents inevitably encouraged not only the expansion of existing provision but also diversification. Private tutoring increased greatly, particularly in the towns but also among the lairds and nouveaux riches. Leading scholars educated the aristocracy, even accompanying them on the Grand Tour: Adam Smith conducted the young 3rd Duke of Buccleuch across Europe; Hume laboured manfully with the insane 3rd Marquis of Annandale. Well-to-do women, for whom formal provision was limited and who were increasingly headed for a life of domesticity, benefited from an expansion of teaching in the home. Finishing schools for female boarders also emerged after mid-century, notably in Edinburgh, where there were several dozen: sewing and French were the principal curricular attractions, a useful mixture of the practical and the polite. Some workplaces, and in a few cases the SSPCK, provided 'spinning schools' for poorer girls: while honing remunerative skills, they also taught reading, further encouraging literacy beyond the male elite. Tellingly, many of the most sophisticated works published in Scotland after mid-century, including Hume's polite essays in the 1750s and the sentimental novels of the 1770s, explicitly addressed themselves to a female readership.

New forms of provision were accompanied by new modes of teaching. Most noteworthy were the Academies. Perth's was the first, founded in 1760 by a town council concerned to provide a more useful education for those at the cutting-edge of a commercialising society. Others followed by 1800 in towns as far apart as Dundee, Inverness, Ayr and Elgin, introducing a range of vocational and practical subjects, including navigation, geometry, chemistry, bookkeeping and surveying. Some of these disciplines also began to creep by parental demand into the Latin-based grammar school curriculum. The Academies, however, emphasised professional education for the middle classes. Just as in the senior years at grammar school, where university entrance was the principal objective, pupils needed a decent elementary education behind them. Eighteenth-century schooling, even as the Highland problem was at last being tackled, was thus becoming more clearly characterised by a diversity of provision and practice, with opportunities determined less by ability than by social and geographical position. Many in an expanding population clearly did benefit. But most, given the constraints of the system, did not.

At St Andrews, Glasgow, Edinburgh, and King's and Marischal Colleges at Aberdeen, two post-Revolution developments significantly affected those adolescent males from the middle and upper ranks of society who attended university – typically around 2 per cent of the age group in 1700. The first was curricular, involving the importation of advanced foreign thought. Traditional connections with Holland, whose vigorous Calvinist universities had long attracted a steady stream of presbyterians, as well as more recent links with England, led to Scottish university syllabuses quickly absorbing ideas from the cutting edge: thus the jurists Hugo Grotius and Samuel Pufendorf, the medical teacher Herman Boerhaave and the scientist Sir Isaac Newton were among the most important new influences on what was taught in Scotland by 1720. The reform of teaching practices was no less seminal, spreading outwards from Edinburgh in 1709 to include everywhere but King's by 1753. 'Regenting' (generalist supervision of a student cohort by a single professor) was abandoned. In its place, subject-specialist teaching was provided by an expert professor. Latin lecturing also began to fall out of use from the 1720s, consistent with a Europe-wide trend towards the vernacularisation of university teaching.

These reforms were not unconnected with the urge for national improvement also informing the political and economic debates of the Union era. But their practical consequence was that eighteenth-century Scotland possessed a particularly effective university system. At the same time, and no less happily, the country also began to produce academics of signal distinction. The first was probably Gershom Carmichael of Glasgow (regent from 1694 and professor of moral philosophy from 1727), who made Pufendorf's celebrated study of the laws of nature the standard text for his classes and introduced Newton's theory of light and colour into his teaching. Further developments followed: new academic disciplines like history and literary criticism emerged; the teaching of law was improved through a range of new specialist professorships; and a considerable increase occurred in overall student numbers (from perhaps 1,000 in 1700 to around 3,000 by 1800). Medical education was a particular focus for improvement: when Edinburgh opened its Faculty of Medicine in 1726, five of its first six professors were former pupils of Boerhaave at Leiden; competent physicians like Robert Hamilton also underpinned the emergence of Glasgow's medical school. But, as we shall see in the next chapter, this was merely a particular instance of the general intellectual advancement underway in the universities.

Other social institutions found it no easier to adapt to the challenges brought by Scotland's economic and demographic expansion. In particular, the traditional welfare regime based on the parish unit was tested to breaking-point and beyond. This had been designed to provide for a small number of needy cases in a comparatively immobile, intimate and overwhelmingly rural society where agriculture supplied a living for the able-bodied. But the poor law system, devised in the sixteenth century and bolstered by an Act of 1672, was unable to cope with the unforeseen social consequences of agricultural improvement, mass migration, rapid urbanisation and the cyclical bouts of unemployment characteristic of an increasingly dynamic economy. In parishes receiving substantial in-migration, such as many in west-central Scotland after 1750, the governing principle that each parish (or each general session in groups of contiguous urban parishes) should look after its own was manifestly unrealistic. Meanwhile, the invidious distinction between the able-bodied poor, whose condition was regarded as in large part self-inflicted, and the elderly, sick and disabled, whose plight was genuinely deserving of assistance, remained axiomatic.

As with education, supplementary localised welfare provision was a common response. Some parishes, especially in southern Scotland, invoked their legal right to impose a compulsory poor rate on taxpayers; others badgered the better-off to donate to a crisis fund. A few towns looked to find effective methods of separating the willing from the merely idle through the institutionalised linking of labour and relief: this was the logic pursued by Edinburgh through its workhouses. For certain classes of people, such as textile workers, tradesmen and fishermen, an alternative source of welfare was the friendly society, which afforded its humble subscribers and their families relief and mutual support in times of distress. There were eventually several hundred: even Dumfries, a small county town, had eighteen friendly societies with more than 2,000 members by 1800. The proliferation of such voluntarism merely underlined the shortfall in statutory provision as well as illustrating the increasing fear of cyclical unemployment. Yet major structural reform awaited the simultaneous economic depression and final implosion of the Church of Scotland in the 1840s, which effectively destroyed what remained of the existing system's credibility.

The other key social institution was Scots law. Administered by 3,000 different courts in an interlocking network of ecclesiastical, private and public jurisdictions, this served as the bulwark between the respectable and the deviant, as well as helping structure relationships, assign status and distribute power within the community. In 1700 the established church still retained a central role in social regulation, particularly in handling less serious offences. Kirk sessions, comprising the minister and the lay elders, functioned as, in effect, both investigating magistrates and summary petty courts. Small monetary fines were the normal punishment, but a public rebuke from the minister during Sunday service was also customary. Churches even employed a 'stool of repentance' on which certain categories of offender might humiliatingly be perched to exhibit their penitence. Sabbath-breaking, drunkenness and other puritanical obsessions were of interest, and minor secular infractions such as theft, assault and slander could also be dealt with under ecclesiastical jurisdiction.

But, perhaps predictably, sexual misdemeanours were the church's favourite province. Fornication and particularly adultery were the form of wrong-doing most commonly railed against by the ministers: breaches of the kingdom's law and sins against the holy institution of marriage, they were also likely to result in an additional unwanted burden on parish funds. The evidence, incidentally, suggests wild clerical exaggeration. Even allowing for under-reporting and the not infrequent occurrence of bridal pregnancy in times when betrothal was often regarded as a formal contract, illegitimacy rates suggest very low levels of extramarital activity, particularly when one also bears in mind the inadequacies of contemporary contraception. Fewer than one recorded Scottish birth in twenty actually took place outside wedlock in the mid-eighteenth century: in Fife and the Lothians it may have been as low as 2 per cent, rising to only around 6–8 per cent in the comparatively incontinent north-east and south-west.

Even had the church courts genuinely needed to confront a great torrent of immorality, however, their powers were being curtailed, as a conceptual distinction steadily emerged between criminality as a legitimate public concern and sin as a strictly private matter. The Toleration Act of 1712, giving qualified recognition to episcopalians, stripped the established church of its right to regulate the behaviour of all Scots. The more indulgent approach of Moderate clergymen also softened the church's former severity, even as the reinvigoration of the secular courts by the 1750s began to provide an alternative route for the pursuit of transgressors. In addition, the old 'testificat' system, by which new arrivals in a parish had to have their moral character certified by their previous minister, broke down in the face of unprecedented, large-scale migration. Kirk sessions dominated by evangelicals, and particularly those among the presbyterian dissenters, remained more willing to tackle their members' lapses. But the burgeoning size of many urban parishes, together with the growing problem of the 'unchurched' poor, who were effectively beyond the ministers' clutches, militated against the continuing behavioural regulation of Scottish society through ecclesiastical structures.

Ritual humiliation before the assembled community therefore steadily gave way to private upbraiding before the kirk session. Even a dressing-down behind closed doors was frequently not possible by 1800. Ministers as a result increasingly failed to detect, or perhaps simply chose not to see, indiscretions over which their own jurisdiction was diminishing, preferring instead to paint an unrealistic picture of innocence and sobriety: Andrew Grant, minister of Portmoak in Kinross-shire since 1784, claimed eight years later that 'During the residence of the present incumbent, there is no instance of any one being punished, either by fine, banishment, or death.' By this time, of course, no adult was obliged to attend church. More significantly, no one needed to submit to its discipline. Wrong-doers were more likely simply to be expelled from their congregation. This was, of course, tacit acknowledgement that church-going was becoming more like any other form of voluntary association. In effect, the godly society of the Reformation, an ideal still taken seriously in the decades immediately after 1690, had been overtaken as comprehensively as the poor relief system by the inescapable realities of social change.

Other courts, meanwhile, continued to impose the custom and statutes of Scots law. At first through a mess of private franchise jurisdictions, but increasingly after 1748 in the persons of the JPs, the bailies, the sheriffs-depute or, ultimately, even the Edinburgh judiciary, those charged with criminal offences, and particularly the more serious ones, found themselves answerable to secular authority rather than to the church. Scottish patterns of crime have not been subjected to anything like the detailed analysis undertaken for England. But it is clear that two types of offence dominated criminal business in this period: thefts and assaults. Precognitions, the investigations laid before courts by procurators-fiscal or sheriffs-substitute, show that the incidence of property crimes in particular fluctuated depending upon wider economic circumstances, the peaks coinciding with agricultural depressions, industrial crises or military demobilisation. It is also evident that in garrison towns such as Edinburgh, Perth and Inverness, soldiers were among the most frequent offenders. The migrant, the indigent and the unemployed similarly presented higher risks. Little of this is surprising given what is known about other contemporary societies. But further research can safely be expected to reveal much more of interest about the backgrounds, motivation and judicial treatment of those who fell foul of the criminal law.

Far greater numbers actually had contact with the courts in their civil capacity. The post-Reformation commissary system, with a superior court in Edinburgh and lesser courts in the regional 'commissariots', dealt with petitions for divorce: in Scots law the latter was permissible on grounds of adultery or desertion. Divorces increased in this period, probably another consequence of growing female economic opportunity and diminishing church censure. But from fewer than twenty per decade around 1700 rising to a hundred by 1800, the numbers remained negligible. The same courts also dealt with regular disputes over legitimacy and with the proving of people's final testaments. Two of the most famous and protracted civil actions of the century specifically concerned inheritance and both were only finally settled not in Edinburgh but on appeal to the House of Lords: the vindication of Elizabeth, daughter of the 18th Earl of Sutherland, as Countess and eventually 1st Duchess in her own right; and the celebrated 'Douglas Cause' in which Archibald, son of the 1st Duke of Douglas's sister, eventually defeated three rival claimants to his uncle's estates. These causes célèbres also attracted rapt contemporary attention through growing newspaper coverage of proceedings.

Local sheriff courts and the Court of Session dealt with innumerable other questions. One of their more difficult duties was to adjudicate when individuals were alleged to be suffering from the mental weaknesses that contemporaries usually described as either 'idiocy' (imbecility) or 'furiosity' (mania). Cases of 'tutors' and 'curators' (guardians) being assigned on these grounds trebled in Scotland between 1720 and 1790, perhaps as changing notions of acceptable behaviour, and views about how to deal with aberrations from it, took hold. Other legal matters were very much less intimate, and resulted in robust series of court judgments of wide-ranging application. A notably flexible view of joint-stock companies – which south of the Border were restricted to six partners – evolved in post-Union Scotland. The courts consistently defended the legality of the paper money issued by Scottish banks, despite frequent English objections. At the end of the century they refused to impose the Combination Acts on Scottish workers (Westminster legislation which outlawed employees' collective organisations). They also continued to intervene in some of the more sensitive aspects of economic activity, including the annual fixing of grain prices, known as 'fiars' prices', by juries in each sheriffdom. Scotland's civil courts to some extent adapted themselves to changing circumstances; but at the same time they often sought to preserve the nation's distinctive values and practices. It does not therefore seem unreasonable to conclude that the Scots law, at least in its civil department, may have been the social institution that responded most successfully to the extraordinary challenges posed by eighteenth-century developments.

CHAPTER FOUR

Ideas

Throughout Britain, Europe and North America by the 1780s, a truism had won wide acceptance. This was that Scotland, home to many of the acknowledged leaders in science, philosophy, scholarship and the arts, possessed an intellectual life of extraordinary brilliance. Praise showered down from admiring contemporaries. 'I can stand at the Market Cross of Edinburgh and take fifty men of genius and learning by the hand', gushed one English physician who came to the city in 1771. Carlo Denina, an Italian scholar, even suggested that the Scots had begun to rival the ancients, bringing 'to maturity, in the cold regions of the north, what had heretofore been foolishly supposed incapable of taking root but in the warmer climes of ASIA MINOR, GREECE, and ITALY'. Voltaire, the most famous author in France and perhaps in all Europe, hailed an important recent shift in the world's cultural geography: 'It is from Scotland', he pronounced, 'that we receive rules of taste in all the arts.' For Thomas Jefferson, founding father of the American republic, it seemed obvious that 'no place in the world can pretend to a competition with Edinburgh'.

The Scots were not slow to take up the refrain. 'Jupiter' Carlyle boasted in 1760 that 'Never has the genius of the Scotch shone with greater lustre than now.' Ten years later the novelist Tobias Smollett, long resident in London, could describe his native capital, without a trace of irony, as a 'hotbed of genius'. Even the normally unflappable Hume was taken aback:

> Really it is admirable how many Men of Genius this Country produces at present. Is it not strange that, at a time when we have lost our Princes, our Parliaments, our independent Government, even the Presence of our chief Nobility, are unhappy, in our Accent & Pronunciation, speak a very corrupt Dialect of the Tongue which we make use of; is it not strange,

> I say, that in these Circumstances we shou'd really be the People most distinguish'd for Literature in Europe?

Astonishment at the Scottish Enlightenment – particularly since it had emerged, to Hume's evident puzzlement, only *after* the Treaty of Union – has been only partially moderated by the passage of more than two hundred and fifty years.

Most remarkable must be the fact that so many of those involved were friends, relations, colleagues and acquaintances, moving in the same narrowly defined social circles. The Select Society of Edinburgh, active in the decade after its foundation in 1754 by the younger Allan Ramsay, one of Britain's finest portrait artists, boasted a membership with whose distinction few organisations, in any other country or period, could compete. It included men who were even then helping found political economy and sociology (Adam Smith and Adam Ferguson). It also embraced two of Europe's best-selling historians (Hume and Robertson), its greatest living philosopher (Hume once more) and some of its most eminent practising scientists (including Alexander Monro and William Cullen). To have any hope of explaining such a dense concentration of ability and energy, and also of understanding why several individual Scots were catapulted to international celebrity, we must begin by reviewing the peculiar social and cultural conditions in which this situation emerged.

Scottish society and polite culture

The unique institutional circumstances of the eighteenth century were critical both to the emergence of the Scottish Enlightenment and to the form that it took. For while their parliament was abolished in 1707, the Scots, as we have already seen, long retained the other cornerstones of their independent nationhood. In the first place, the presbyterian church had been re-energised in 1690: its subsequent exemption from the assimilationist provisions of the treaty preserved a key source of the country's distinctiveness, even as Westminster legislation helped foster within it a tolerant and cultivated clergy. Crucial too was the fact that the Union specifically preserved Scotland's separate legal system and legal profession. Indeed the status and influence of the lawyers within Scottish society waxed rather than waned in the decades after 1707. Given this, it should not be surprising that a battery of sharp legal minds based in Edinburgh – such as the judges Henry Home (invariably known by his courtesy title Lord Kames), James Burnett (Lord Monboddo) and Sir David Dalrymple (Lord Hailes), and learned professors like John Erskine and David Hume (the philosopher's nephew) at Edinburgh

– should have made the history, philosophy and sociology of law one of the country's peculiar intellectual specialisms.

Scotland's eighteenth-century universities also remained very different from their two somnolent English rivals. Specialist professorial teaching, gradually introduced after 1707, brought a steady stream of gifted scholars and pedagogues into the academic cloisters. At the same time new ideas triumphed, with revised curricula incorporating the latest English and Continental teachings in cosmology, mathematics, moral philosophy, law and medicine. The Scottish universities therefore not only survived the Union. They actually continued confidently into a golden age of unprecedented energy and achievement. Indeed, from the perspective of educated contemporaries, the relative importance of the universities, like that of the church and the law, as effective guarantors of Scotland's continuing national distinctiveness may have been significantly greater in 1750 than when the Scots Parliament itself had still been in existence.

Nor did the abolition of the parliament kill off the Scots' taste for public debate. This was perhaps one of the reasons why clubs and societies proliferated so rapidly in the decades after 1707. The Select Society, the Philosophical Society and the Cape Club in Edinburgh, the Political Economy Society and the Literary Society in Glasgow, and later the Literary and Antiquarian Society in Perth, were typical of the species. The Select debated many abiding issues of principle, including the problems of gender relations ('whether can a marriage be happy when the wife is of an understanding superior to that of the husband') and the desirability of field sports ('whether is hunting an exercise proper for persons of liberal Education'). Edinburgh's Poker Club – so-called by Ferguson because it would 'stir things up' – spent many years as a vehicle through which clergymen like Carlyle and politicians like Dempster pursued their desultory campaign for a Scottish militia. The Aberdeen Philosophical Society, haunt of the town's academic philosophers (hence 'The Wise Club'), also frequently aired topical concerns: in 1761 their debates included 'What are the Natural Consequences of high national Debt & whether upon the whole it be a benefite to a Nation or not' and 'Whether the determination by unanimity or a majority in Juries is most equitable'.

As Cockburn later recalled, Scots were inducted early into this vigorous culture of discussion and argument. Students at Edinburgh in the 1790s enjoyed the Academical Society, where 'more essays [were] read, and more speeches delivered, by ambitious lads, in that little shabby place, than in all Scotland'; but there was also the Speculative Society, where Cockburn himself acquired his 'first notions of composition and debate, and that delightful feeling of free doubting and independent discussion, so necessary for the expansion and manliness of young minds'. An earlier student generation, avid members of the Newtonian Society, had equally boasted in the 1760s of 'the Advantages as well as Pleasures which may arise from a more close Application to the Study of Natural Philosophy'. Nevertheless, despite the manifest para-parliamentary pretensions of some and the intriguing quasi-academic role of others, these societies had an even more vital function for their enthusiastic participants: above all, they were believed to promote 'politeness', a word that resonated profoundly in the vocabulary of British contemporaries.

To understand the eighteenth century's intense preoccupation with politeness is not merely to explain the vast range of social institutions that emerged in Scotland – or, for that matter, in London, the provincial English towns, most European cities, and as far afield as colonial North America and Bengal. Even more importantly, it brings us closer to understanding why debating political philosophy, or discussing poetry or the laws of gravitation, possessed a significance that today they have largely lost. For there had emerged a conviction that organised social interaction of this kind, which encouraged the free exchange of information and opinion, represented an unparalleled opportunity to spread moral insight and mutual understanding. This touching faith in the miraculous mechanism of intelligent conversation, shared by most educated eighteenth-century people, was closely linked to the influence and authority achieved among contemporaries by *The Spectator* (1711–12), Joseph Addison's collaborative venture with Sir Richard Steele. And the stunning success of this famous publication reveals much about why the Scots in particular pursued politeness with such optimism and devotion.

Issued as a daily magazine, *The Spectator* purported to be the journal of a fictitious gentlemen's club meeting in a London coffee-house. It offered thoughtful observations upon everyday topics, Addison promising, not entirely tongue-in-cheek, to enrich his readers' own discourse: 'I will daily instil into them', he boasted in an early volume, 'such sound and wholesom Sentiments, as shall have a good Effect on their Conversation for the ensuing twelve Hours.' Yet the aim was not to stimulate idle gossip or mere tittle-tattle. Better-informed and more judicious conversation entailed a deeper understanding of the human condition in all its complexity. Addison even claimed that his magazine, and the discussions it provoked, would help bring 'Philosophy out of Closets and Libraries, Schools and Colleges, to dwell in Clubs and Assemblies, at Tea-Tables and in Coffee-Houses': in other words, intelligent dialogue nurtured through structured social interaction would help spread throughout society a rational approach to human nature and morality.

Though also familiar across contemporary Europe, this hugely seductive manifesto was aimed with particular success at early eighteenth-century

British people increasingly conscious of their own changing economic, social and political circumstances. Addison's message certainly struck a chord in Scotland in those early disorientating years immediately after the Union. As John Ramsay of Ochtertyre, a keen-eyed Perthshire landowner, later explained, it had been more than anything else 'the appearance of *Tatlers*, *Spectators*, and *Guardians* in the reign of Queen Anne' that had helped transform the hitherto rough-edged Scot into a 'polite scholar'. As early as 1711 an imitative Scottish *Tatler* had emerged, ostensibly the creation of 'Donald MacStaff of the North'. For the rest of the century regular reprints of *The Spectator* were also issued, including ultimately several score editions in Edinburgh itself and at least a dozen in Glasgow.

Further evidence of early Scottish fascination with Addison's vision exists in the Easy Club, founded in Edinburgh in May 1712 by the poet Allan Ramsay and his friends. These young men resolved 'to Retire from all other Business and Company and Meet in a Society By Themselves in order that by a Mutual improvement in Conversation they may become more adapted for fellowship with the politer part of mankind'. Some subsequent fawning towards Addison in a letter that they despatched to London ('the 1st thing that induced us to join a Society was ye Readings of your Spectators') merely underlined how far Scotland's own dawning age of polite culture, based on the pursuit of individual and collective improvement through well-informed social interaction, was wrapped up in the determined mimicry of modish English culture.

But politeness, as retailed most beguilingly by *The Spectator*, was very far from being just a fashionable pretension. For, not only in England but increasingly also in Scotland, contemporaries were tiring of the narrow-minded bigotry and factional animosity which had so scarred Britain's affairs during the previous century of civil war and revolution. To increasing numbers of the respectable, the educated and the ambitious in the upper and middle ranks of society after the turn of the eighteenth century, polite culture promised what Addison explicitly called the 'wearing out of Ignorance, Passion, and Prejudice'. It would suppress those irrational and immoderate impulses which would otherwise, as *The Spectator* warned, 'naturally conduce to inflame Hatreds, and make Enmities irreconcileable'. Fostering toleration and mutual understanding between people, politeness would actually help establish a new kind of society – peaceful, prosperous and pleasant.

The extraordinary variety of Scottish clubs and societies in the eighteenth century, or for that matter of assembly-rooms, masonic lodges (there were more than 320 by 1799), subscription libraries and other meeting places and voluntary associations of all kinds, had no single cause. Rising wealth and an expanding middle class provided greater scope for recreation: the consumption of leisure, whether in spa towns like Moffat, the many new theatres – such as Edinburgh's Taylor's Hall, Concert Hall and Theatre Royal – or even in the innumerable taverns, oyster cellars and coffee-shops (like the one in which, fittingly, *The Spectator*'s fictional club supposedly convened) made sociability an important reality as well as an earnest aspiration. Urbanisation, concentrating people in close proximity, similarly created unprecedented opportunities for interaction: Edinburgh's mid-eighteenth-century environment, cramming tens of thousands of citizens of all classes into a warren of tenements, wynds and closes, was merely the extreme example of unavoidable social intimacy.

Nor should the historian underestimate the eternal temptations of pleasure. Surviving accounts of institutions such as the Cape Club and the Aberdeen Philosophical Society leave little room for doubt that good company, especially when lubricated by claret and further enlivened by a hearty supper, made attendance extremely enjoyable for those partaking. Yet Addison's claims for the sheer transformative virtues of organised sociability, constantly echoed and emphatically endorsed by innumerable contemporaries, were also crucial. The pursuit of politeness provided an almost unanswerable moral case for exactly this sort of social engagement. And in promising to create a new and better kind of society, it had a very special allure for educated Scots in particular in the difficult years after 1707. After all, to people already beset by anxieties about their own country's backwardness and underdevelopment, the appeal of polite culture – a route to improvement that was agreeable, effective and, above all, quintessentially modern – may well have been almost irresistible.

Post-Union Scots found the problems and disputes of literature, philosophy and science an especially rich source of conversational material as well as the perfect excuse for organised debate and argument. This was true not only among the 'literati' (the collective name given to Edinburgh's leading academics and authors). It was also true for an ever-widening community of eighteenth-century Scottish students, lawyers, clergymen, merchants, lairds, noblemen and, in some cases, women, for whom intellectual discussion became an integral part of their social experience. Indeed, it says much about the ubiquity of such concerns that, when Alexander Hume Campbell, opposition MP for Berwickshire, had a chance encounter in Westminster Hall in 1747 with the 3rd Duke of Argyll, a fellow-countryman with whom he enjoyed a distinctly awkward political relationship, their discussion gravitated by tacit agreement towards the one important thing that united them: a confirmed interest in mathematics and the perusal of unusual scientific texts. In order to re-capture the contemporary culture which made such extraordinary personal exchanges feasible, and to see how the obsessive discussion of certain questions in particular came to represent the country's distinctive contribution to the Enlightenment, it is necessary to explore in detail the disparate fields in which the leading Scottish participants worked.

'Nature and nature's laws'

Natural philosophy (to use the standard eighteenth-century designation for scientific inquiries) occupied a central place in the Scottish Enlightenment. Partly this was because, in Scotland's physically small and close-knit intellectual community, it was inevitable that moralists and historians should rub shoulders with geologists and chemists. But it was also a result of a contemporary intellectual context in which many of the later distinctions between the human and the natural sciences were not yet fully formed. It was still widely assumed that the investigation of animal physiology, heat energy or the earth's original formation, inquiries which in any case were not so advanced as to be incomprehensible to the non-specialist, were logically inseparable from the study of linguistic development, political behaviour or the Emperor Charles V's place in European history. It was also taken for granted that all departments of knowledge were related because they were ultimately concerned with a single natural world – God's Creation, as virtually everyone still believed – of which mankind was at once an integral and by far the most ingenious part.

The unchallenged cultural centrality of science goes a long way towards explaining why even the Duke of Argyll was both able and willing to present himself on occasion as a serious student of geometry. Yet it was nonetheless on major original contributions to scientific inquiry, discovery and popularisation that Scotland's reputation mainly came to rest. One early contributor was Sir Robert Moray, soldier and servant of Charles II, eminent freemason and founder-member of the Royal Society in London in the 1660s. Important too was the natural historian and antiquarian Sir Robert Sibbald, who was appointed first professor of medicine at Edinburgh in 1685 and founded the city's Physic Garden for medicinal botany. Several members of the Gregory family also made disproportionate early contributions in the decades before 1700. James Gregory, professor of mathematics at St Andrews and Edinburgh in the 1660s, had interests in trigonometry and the theory of calculus. His nephew David, who lived until 1708, was professor of mathematics at both Edinburgh and Oxford, and noteworthy for his part in introducing Newton's startling recent discoveries into the university curriculum.

This pattern of closely related individuals playing the major roles was to be a distinctive feature of the Scottish Enlightenment, both in science and in other areas. Nowhere is its significance seen more clearly than in the long-running dominance of the Monro family. Three successive generations held the chair of anatomy at Edinburgh – and, as was then often the case, retained legal ownership of the subject's teaching collection – between 1719 and 1846. Each professor, confusingly, was christened Alexander (and so, in the humanistic culture of the time, they were known as *primus*, *secundus* and *tertius*). *Primus* and *secundus* promoted public inoculation against smallpox. *Secundus* popularised vaccination following Jenner's discovery of the technique in 1798, while also finding time to conduct pioneering work on the brain and nervous system. Both father and son helped develop the reputation of Edinburgh's new Faculty of Medicine, established in 1726, and tried to improve Scotland's scientific infrastructure: the first was involved in chartering Edinburgh's Royal Infirmary while the second assisted in the translation of the existing Philosophical Society into the Royal Society of Edinburgh in 1783. By this time a steady stream of foreign, and particularly American, medical students had been attracted to Edinburgh, not just by the Monros but by other key professors like the distinguished physiologist Robert Whytt.

It was, however, Newton's theories about light, motion and gravity, previously disseminated by David Gregory and Gershom Carmichael, that stimulated the outstanding scientific mind of the early Scottish Enlightenment. Colin Maclaurin was a child prodigy. A minister's son from Argyllshire, he entered the University of Glasgow at eleven, becoming professor at Marischal College at nineteen, Fellow of the Royal Society at twenty-two and professor at Edinburgh at twenty-eight. He was an influential teacher to the next generation of students and an important researcher in his own right, especially on tidal flows. But he also showed himself a lucid interpreter of Newton's achievements for the increasingly enthusiastic lay audience for scientific knowledge. Maclaurin's *Account of Sir Isaac Newton's Discoveries* (1748) was typical of many texts at this time which helped contemporaries come to terms with the far-reaching implications of the new natural philosophy.

The key feature of Maclaurin's popularisation of Newton was that it convincingly reinforced the conventional assumption that religious devotion and the systematic study of nature were complementary – a comforting view not fatally undermined until after Darwin's work more than a hundred years later. Maclaurin agreed that 'A strong curiosity has promoted men in all times to study nature; every useful art has some connection with this science; and the unexhausted beauty and variety of things makes it ever agreeable, new and surprizing.' Yet he was also at great pains to reassert the classic Argument to Design which saw in the awe-inspiring complexity of nature, as brilliantly laid bare by Newton, categorical assurance of God's existence and benevolence:

> . . . natural philosophy is subservient to purposes of a higher kind, and is chiefly to be valued as it lays a sure foundation for natural religion and moral philosophy; by leading us, in a satisfactory manner, to the knowledge of the Author and Governor of the universe. To study nature is to search into his workmanship: every new discovery opens to us a new part of his scheme.

Published only after his lamentably early death following his involvement in the defence of Edinburgh against the Jacobites in 1745, Maclaurin's text thus securely located the age's dominant system of natural philosophy in a Christian framework. It also eulogised Newton's famous method, insisting on being prepared to 'consult nature herself, to attend carefully to her manifest operations, and to extort her secrets from her by well chosen and repeated experiments'. The ability of empirical studies to shed new light on God's purposes was best seen, according to Maclaurin, in the study of those most visible yet mysterious products of Creation, the planets and the stars. Such expectations triggered the practical scientific activities of so many other educated contemporaries, whether humble rural clergymen like George Ridpath, practising telescopy in the Berwickshire countryside, or great potentates like James Douglas, 14th Earl of Morton: a Whig representative peer and grand master of England's grand masonic lodge, Morton was also a thoroughly competent astronomer and from 1764, as President of the Royal Society, effectively the leader of institutionalised British science.

Chemistry, always the most practical of studies and therefore very easy to reconcile with the faith in scientific empiricism preached by Maclaurin and the Gregorys, was another characteristic Scottish specialism. Not least this was also because the discipline had potentially profitable applications. Scotland was experiencing rapid economic growth, and inquiries into certain properties of compounds, such as into methods of enhancing soil fertility or improving bleaching, dyeing and fixing for the linen industry, related closely to agricultural and manufacturing developments. Yet applied research went hand-in-hand with pure academic science, the heroic quest for reliable natural knowledge. In chemistry this was led by William Cullen, first at Glasgow and then from 1756 at Edinburgh, and crowned by his younger colleague, Joseph Black, the French-born son of an Ulster Scot, who held the same two chairs of chemistry (receiving the more prestigious Edinburgh position in 1766). Black himself was a genial and gentle soul: a vegetarian, he eventually expired without disturbing the bowl of milk in his lap. But his lasting fame rests – apart, that is, from his walk-on part in encouraging the young Glasgow technician James Watt in his legendary experiments with steam condensers – on pioneering scientific investigations. These resulted in the isolation of carbon dioxide. Black also explained the capacity of ice to absorb heat without exhibiting any initial rise in its own temperature, a phenomenon known as 'latent heat' which he showed was the result of the energy transferred in the transition from a solid to a liquid state.

Similar habits of mind, of detailed practical investigation combined with awareness of a much wider intellectual framework, can be seen in the work of Black's younger friend James Hutton. Hutton began studying medicine and chemistry at Edinburgh, subsequently managing to extract sal ammoniac from soot. He then worked professionally in estate management and agricultural improvement. Yet Hutton eventually became an obsessive student of the landscape and, as a result, emerged as the effective founder of modern geology. Again the immediate inspiration was provided by unexplained phenomena: in this case apparently inexplicable fossil deposits, such as the remains of dead sea creatures found on hill tops. Hutton was also transfixed by the evidence of folding, classically observed at Siccar Point near St Abb's Head in Berwickshire. There, in a formation hinting strongly at a complex history of stratification, he discovered horizontal Devonian sandstones overlying vertical Silurian slates and grits. Hutton pondered deeply what these disparate phenomena implied about the combined formative potential of ice, water and vulcanism. In the process he developed an extensive critique of the rival contemporary schools of thought on the genesis of rock, each of which insisted that either volcanic or maritime forces were primarily responsible.

Hutton eventually concluded, as he announced to the Royal Society of Edinburgh in an audacious paper in 1785, that 'the greater part of our land, if not the whole, [has] been produced by operations natural to this globe'. The surface of the earth, he argued, is actually in a constant state of flux. It is locked into unending processes of rock formation and denudation powered by a full range of natural forces, including erosion, sedimentary deposit and uplift. Hutton, though a Deist, remained deferential towards the Argument to Design, suggesting that from future studies of geological dynamism 'an argument may be established for [the] wisdom and benevolence to be perceived in nature'. The philosophy of nature, 'rationally deduced from natural events' as Hutton insisted it must be, would again shed new light on the divine purpose, providing startling additional insights into the motives and intelligence of a Creator who had hitherto been known to mankind from biblical revelation alone. Yet with the immense later influence of Hutton's discoveries, geology had in fact moved decisively towards a mechanical and evolutionary and away from a metaphysical and scriptural explanation of the earth's history. Further employment of the same empirical procedures – though predecessors like Maclaurin could scarcely have imagined it – would eventually overwhelm the claims of Genesis to explain the natural world.

The limits of knowing

The first significant Scottish contribution to mental philosophy – and, significantly, yet another influential attempt to provide a convincing empirical alternative to metaphysics – came from Francis Hutcheson, in some ways the intellectual founding father of Scotland's Enlightenment. Like Black, he was an Ulster Scot. Having studied at Glasgow under Carmichael, Hutcheson spent many years in Dublin philosophical circles before returning in 1729 to succeed his old teacher as professor of moral philosophy. Even so, regarding him at least partly as a Scottish thinker has merits. First, it highlights his impact upon generations of educated Scots: when John Witherspoon satirised the Moderates in the 1750s, it was entirely natural for him to identify 'the late immortal Mr H——n' as the party's intellectual patron saint. Second, it directs attention to the way in which Hutcheson set the agenda for subsequent Scottish thinkers. To his successors he showed that a worthwhile modern philosophy needed to offer an epistemology, or theory of knowledge, plausibly explaining – against numerous sophisticated counter-arguments – the nature and extent of men's understanding of the world around them. Scottish philosophy after Hutcheson would also seek to confirm the social and communitarian instincts of mankind, demonstrating that individuals could be trusted to act benevolently because they possessed, at least in his initial formulation of this influential doctrine, a 'moral sense'.

In his Glasgow lectures, delivered in English, and in two seminal texts, the *Enquiry into the Original of our Ideas of Beauty and Virtue* (1725) and *An Essay on the Nature and Conduct of the Passions and Affections* (1728), Hutcheson developed an account of human morality which did not rely on metaphysical abstractions. It also confronted directly the challenges posed by recent scepticism. His immediate targets were two English works. One, Thomas Hobbes's *Leviathan* (1651), voiced the famous opinion that human existence was naturally 'nasty, brutish, and short', advancing an essentially egotistical theory of morality and interpreting all behaviour in terms of mere self-preservation: this grim deduction had unsurprisingly worried most orthodox opinion for more than seventy years. Bernard Mandeville's *Fable of the Bees* (1712) was a more recent but not much less disturbing intervention. It argued that people were indeed egotistical by nature. But it added that, supposedly like bees in a hive, this otherwise ignoble instinct actually resulted in the advancement of the wider community. In short, Mandeville, writing amid the burgeoning commercial wealth of Queen Anne's reign, had hit upon the convenient but extremely disturbing notion that the gratification of our innate selfishness is unintentionally productive of social benefit and, especially, of our collective material enrichment.

Hutcheson wished to rescue philosophy from these dangerous claims, and, above all, from Mandeville's provocative allegation that 'the moral Virtues are the political Offspring, which Flattery begot upon Pride, i.e. that they are all a Chimera, an idle Fancy, a mere Trick'. This he managed in part by drawing upon the work of Anthony Ashley Cooper, 3rd Earl of Shaftesbury. A cultivated English Whig nobleman, Shaftesbury had insisted that our capacity for moral judgement runs closely parallel with what seems the undeniably instinctive human capacity for the appreciation of beauty. If this equation of our ethical with our aesthetic judgement were merited (and, as we shall see, many contemporaries believed that it was), then an account of an innate human moral sense could be developed which would add immeasurably to Hutcheson's fundamental claim that benevolence is natural: that, as he triumphantly put it, 'the Moral Virtues have their Foundation in the Nature of Things'.

Hutcheson's commitment to the reality of Lord Shaftesbury's moral sense was a considerable boon in the wider endeavour to instil reverence for both theology and morality (though his willingness to employ secular philosophy in the defence of Christianity led Witherspoon to mock the apparent belief in 'the divinity of L. S——'). Yet like a growing number of his Scottish contemporaries – such as Andrew Baxter, a much-underrated non-academic philosophical author from Whittinghame in Berwickshire, who wrote in support of both Newton and Maclaurin – Hutcheson's researches were also inspired in methodological terms by the empiricism influentially advanced by John Locke, another late seventeenth-century English scholar. Locke's *Essay Concerning Human Understanding* (1690) counselled a commitment to inquiries based exclusively upon known facts and experience. It thus appeared to offer techniques by which mental philosophy could begin at last to emulate the physical sciences, where, particularly to Newton's growing number of admirers, experimental data seemed capable of unlocking the secrets of nature. This empiricism, in which observation and experiment are the only reliable guides, shaped Hutcheson's own works, which he loaded with appeals to the apparently incontrovertible evidence of his own and his readers' everyday experiences. But, crucially, his philosophy also went further and embraced Locke's key technical deduction. This was an epistemology in which the human mind is held to have direct contact not with the external world itself but only with mental phenomena such as perceptions and sensations. The ultimate results of accepting this conclusion were, however, surprising, as the century's greatest original mind, Hume, soon showed.

Hume as a philosopher was in the Scottish Enlightenment but never entirely of it. He was centrally involved in Edinburgh's intellectual life as socialite, essayist and historian. Yet his devastating originality as a thinker largely transcended his time, the mirthful attacks on a whole host of comforting assumptions proving too much for his non-plussed contemporaries either to understand or to bear. Hume's work nevertheless represents the very foundation of modern philosophy. It is useful, as well as customary, to cite Kant's claim that the Scot's troubling work had provoked his own lifetime of speculative labour. For Hume's *Treatise of Human Nature* (1739–40), while falling 'still-born from the press', as the disappointed young thinker famously lamented, marked a revolution in the study of the mind, taking his successors to the brink of what would now be called psychology. Fusing Locke's empirical method with Hutcheson's theory of ideas, but pushing both in a direction which neither had remotely foreseen, Hume arrived at a scepticism about the real basis of our knowledge. Brilliantly innovative and also powerfully compelling, no other thinker, from his horrified contemporaries to the present day, has entirely managed to refute his arguments.

For Hume, the 'association of ideas' – the peculiar way in which the mind integrates separate mental phenomena into a seamless web – was indeed demonstrable on empirical principles. But once this was accepted as the foundation of epistemology, as Locke and Hutcheson had urged, he showed that several other much less palatable conclusions ought also to be conceded. First, the mind is forever denied direct contact with the external world. Trading only in what Hume called 'impressions and ideas', it can have no independent knowledge of the existence of anything beyond its own confines. Second, any relationships which arise between those perceptions, and especially the ways in which they build into complex ideas, are not determined by the actual structure of the external world. They are formed only by habits of mind – mere operations, sorting processes integral to our own mental apparatus which reveal nothing about the reality of the world outside. Third, Hume argued that certain crucial and apparently intuitive forms of knowledge, such as the connection between cause and effect, are similarly no more than products of the mind's habit of associating specific ideas, otherwise 'entirely loose and separate', in particular ways. As he therefore reasoned, 'The falling of a pebble may, for ought we know, extinguish the Sun, or the wish of man control the planets in their orbits.' The result was a comprehensive undermining of virtually all claims to certain knowledge about the world around us, even of apparently the most elementary kind.

Elsewhere in the *Treatise*, and particularly in the more successful reworkings published as the *Inquiry Concerning Human Understanding* (1748) and the *Inquiry Concerning the Principles of Morals* (1752), as well as in the more focused and provocative *Dialogues Concerning Natural Religion* (1777), which appeared posthumously, Hume fleshed out the consequences of these sceptical arguments for both moral and religious knowledge. Hutcheson's moral sense, inevitably, was abandoned to its fate. In its place stood an inclination towards certain kinds of behaviour founded neither in reason nor in a benevolent sense but in mere appetite and passion. For Hume, moral conduct is the outcome of a hunger for love and approval. Virtue, in his own words, is not a fixed quality but only 'whatever mental action or quality gives to the spectator the pleasing sentiment of approbation': in short, it is a social construct and not a divinely ordained constant. Equally, religious knowledge – not just traditional Christian revelation but even, and perhaps especially, the comforting Deism or natural religion to which many contemporaries subscribed – can have no reliable basis either in logic or in experience. Hume privately acknowledged the difficulty of attempting to live by such uncompromising sceptical principles. Yet he nevertheless accepted the need to flesh out their many further implications.

The Argument to Design was subjected to particularly effective attack, all the more shatteringly because it was so central to the mental furniture of contemporaries like Maclaurin and Kames. Hume pointed out that we have had no wider experience of the processes involved in manufacturing universes. Nor can we know how well or badly our own particular universe might compare with others. As a result, we cannot reasonably infer anything at all about how or by whom it was constructed, much less offer judgements about the relative skill (or, Hume wickedly suggested, even the basic competence) of any supposed Creator. Added to the outlandish claims made in other writings which were often published only after his death, such as the daring essays on suicide ('prudence and courage should engage us to rid ourselves at once of existence when it becomes a burden') and on the immortality of the soul ('What a daring theory is that! How lightly, not to say how rashly, entertained!'), these provocative arguments provide good grounds for accepting Hume's reputation as one of history's most subversive, challenging and inventive philosophical thinkers, much misunderstood and often feared by his contemporary Scots.

Chief among Hume's appalled countrymen were the Aberdonian trinity, Thomas Reid, George Campbell and James Beattie, the last a better poet than philosopher, for all Sir Joshua Reynold's then-famous portrayal of the author of the *Essay on Truth* (1770) as the triumphant victor in the war against infidel scepticism. The geographical location of this strong native reaction to the Edinburgh-based philosophy of Hume is significant. Aberdeen has produced many of Scotland's most conservative minds. It nurtured many lukewarm adherents to the Reformation, numerous unwilling subscribers to the Covenants, and more recently, as we have seen, a disproportionate number of Jacobites. Beattie's famous poem *The Minstrel* (1771–74), lauded by contemporaries for its conventional rusticity and blameless commonplaces in support of 'beauty, virtue, truth, and love, and melody', can be interpreted as merely the most enduring product of this Aberdonian philosophical assault on Edinburgh's slippery metropolitan artifice – even though it was in fact the work of a man who was himself an habitué of the Scottish capital's social institutions and a favourite drinking companion of Henry Dundas.

Reid, a relation of the scientific Gregorys, was much the greater philosopher. Accordingly he was meticulous in his unpicking of what he considered Hume's elaborate web of deceit. The circumspect Reid even sent his pre-publication proofs for correction by Hume, an action which, like Campbell's fondness for Hume as a man, says something about the relative cordiality possible within Scotland's incestuous intellectual community. The gesture was, however, underwritten by a justified confidence. Partly as a result of the failure of Hume's backers to finesse the complex patronage system determining university appointments, but also because of the obvious threat posed to tender young minds by his unrepentant heresies, the doubter failed to secure posts at Edinburgh in 1745 and later at Glasgow. By contrast, Reid's *Inquiry into the Human Mind on the Principles of Common Sense* (1764), published in the year he moved from Aberdeen to fill Glasgow's chair of moral philosophy, became a standard university textbook in nineteenth-century Britain, France, Germany and America. His reputation was further burnished by the *Essays on the Intellectual Powers of Man* (1785) and the *Essays on the Active Powers of the Human Mind* (1788). It would in fact remain secure so long as Hume's corrosive scepticism was deemed a threat within an education system designed primarily to inculcate moral propriety and religious belief through the teaching of philosophy.

Reid's peculiar contribution was that, unlike some, he fully recognised the strength of Hume's position. This led him to develop an unusually bold critique, rejecting the epistemologies not only of both Locke and Hutcheson but of other key modern thinkers like Descartes and Berkeley. Indeed, as he explained, he had eventually realised that the 'sceptical system . . . leans with its whole weight upon a hypothesis, which is ancient indeed, and hath been very generally received by philosophers, but of which I could find no solid proof'. Reid argued that the mind does after all have direct contact with external realities, just as most people presume. In other words, one of the chief tenets of British empiricism, the claim that 'we do not really perceive things that are external, but only certain images and pictures of them imprinted upon the mind, which are called impressions and ideas', was erroneous. Reid then wisely proceeded not so much with a frontal attack as with a mixture of terminological hair-splitting and loaded appeals to everyday occurrences. He claimed disingenuously to give 'great attention to the operations of my own mind and . . . what I conceive every man, who gives the same attention, will feel and perceive'. This accessible and agreeable 'common sense' Scottish riposte to Scottish scepticism, rather than Hume's difficult and disturbing thesis itself, formed the cornerstone of the curriculum in the coming generations.

By 1800, men like Dugald Stewart, Reid's greatest pupil, embodied all that had come to seem most valuable and enriching in Scotland's philosophical tradition, confidently commencing his lectures at Edinburgh in the early 1780s with 'some elegant general illustrations of the excellencies of science & the superiority acquir'd by the philosopher by means of its study . . .'. Reflecting warmly on his own undergraduate days, Cockburn would later accord Stewart one of the most fulsome tributes to a teacher ever uttered: 'To me his lectures were like the opening of the heavens. I felt I had a soul. His noble views, unfolded in glorious sentences, elevated me into a higher world. . . . They changed my whole nature.' Intellectual transformation of this sort was, of course, the very purpose of Scottish philosophy as it grew from obscurity to international pre-eminence. Initiated by Hutcheson, it was refined by Reid and popularised above all by Stewart in his lectures and in his seminal articles for the *Encyclopaedia Britannica* (the latter another typical product of Scottish commitment to breadth of knowledge, founded in Edinburgh in 1768 by a group including William Smellie, polymathic printer and former Newtonian Society member). Learning how to think and to discourse rationally had by this time become the overriding preoccupation of educated Scots and their teachers. It can also justly be regarded as one of the principal foundations of the Scottish Enlightenment.

'From savage to Scotchman'

The contribution of Scottish thought to the formation of the modern social sciences is widely recognised. Notwithstanding the competing claims of Hume in the essays and of the Jacobite scholar Sir James Steuart in his *Inquiry into the Principles of Political Economy* (1767), Adam Smith is usually seen as the founder of political economy; his associate Adam Ferguson has readily been assigned a roughly similar status in relation to sociology or social anthropology. Indeed, when added to Hume's audacious advances into the realms of psychology, and taken together with William Robertson's innovative historical works, it is sometimes assumed that there are grounds for seeing the Scottish Enlightenment as an intellectual revolution – a dramatic shift in European thought when a whole range of inquiries and academic disciplines were re-cast virtually overnight into a recognisably modern form. Yet this interpretation distorts what was really happening. As important, it does a great disservice to what men like Smith, Ferguson and Robertson were actually seeking to achieve, and how they conceived their own activities. It is, for example, exceptionally unlikely that Ferguson or Kames would remotely have understood, much less been comfortable with, the abstract theorisation and, particularly, the refusal to make moral judgements about human behaviour which have come to characterise so much of modern sociology.

This gulf between eighteenth-century conceptions and subsequent intellectual developments is most emphatically seen in the case of Smith, one of Scotland's most famous and most misunderstood sons. Born in Kirkcaldy in 1723, he was educated there and at Glasgow under Hutcheson, before heading to Oxford to complete his studies. Like his near-contemporary Gibbon, he found the indolence of the English dons unpalatable, and, as he would later relish pointing out, clinching evidence for the belief (partly reflecting the Scottish practice of supplementing salaries with fees) that professors should be paid according to the number of students their lectures could attract. On his return he lectured on rhetoric in Edinburgh, before being called back to the professorship of logic and metaphysics at Glasgow in 1751. The next year, leaving the vacancy for which Hume's name was canvassed, he moved sideways to fill Hutcheson's old chair in which he was in turn succeeded by Reid. He later spent many years in Kirkcaldy, before accepting from Dundas an Edinburgh customs commissionership. This position allowed him to maintain his close friendships with the leading literati, and particularly with Black and Hutton (his eventual executors). Yet it was in his Glasgow period – where he was also involved in both the Literary and the Political Economy Society – that Smith had first developed the comprehensive educational curriculum which underlay his intellectual achievements. This included some early elements of his economic thought. Crucially, however, it also situated them within a course in moral philosophy, jurisprudence and rhetoric. Student dictations of these lectures, which were long believed lost, were rediscovered in 1896 and subsequently published in a modern edition. These findings have simply confirmed much of what his first great published work, *The Theory of Moral Sentiments* (1759), always hinted about Smith's unfolding ideas.

Smith clearly envisaged a wide-ranging syllabus designed to provide a proper education in what he subsequently described as 'the science of a legislator': that is, he wished to disseminate the knowledge and techniques necessary to govern a rapidly commercialising modern society. Despite his later notoriety as a supposedly shameless proponent of selfish acquisitiveness, the *Moral Sentiments* reveals Smith as the admiring disciple of Hutcheson, at least in so far as the work, while denying the moral sense, paints man as essentially guided in his social concerns by a principle of 'sympathy' (a concept also found in Hume, who used it somewhat differently). A natural fellow-feeling, a deeply rooted desire to love and be loved, this leads one's every social action to be carried out with a view to winning the welcome approval of a hypothetical observer of one's own creation, whom Smith dubbed 'the impartial spectator'. By this means Smith provided not only a cogent explanation of human behaviour but, crucially, a theory of morality which, in swapping a crude instinct to inward-looking selfishness for a much more sophisticated mechanism of self-interest in social relations, to some extent split the difference between Mandeville and Hutcheson.

This profound concern for social and moral conduct needs to be understood as part of Smith's conception of a comprehensive modern philosophical curriculum. The *Lectures on Jurisprudence* illuminate several elements of this wider vision, emphasising such matters as political organisation, the origins of government and, critically for the future (since it was what Smith's Marxist successors profitably extracted from his writings), the significance of property in social advancement and organisation. But the *Inquiry into the Origins and Nature of the Wealth of Nations* (1776) remains by far Smith's best-known contribution and too often the work by which, in splendid isolation, he has been judged. Conceived as part of the same educational programme as the *Moral Sentiments*, it stands not least in the grand tradition of European natural law. In it Smith seeks to throw unprecedented historical light upon the motivational and material processes by which eighteenth-century Britons (and particularly the Scots) were enriching themselves, the better to identify for active statesmen, like his admirer and correspondent Dundas, the specific roles which they too might be required to take.

Sadly, it has proved difficult for later critics accurately to distinguish what Smith favoured from what he was merely attempting to explain. His treatment of the de-humanising consequences of the division of labour is in fact as effective a moral critique of the emerging patterns of industrial organisation as could be imagined. It was, moreover, astonishingly prescient, penned in the early 1770s and before production-line organisation had properly emerged in Britain's factories:

> The man whose whole life is spent performing a few simple operations, of which the effects too are, perhaps, always the same, or very nearly the same, has no occasion to exert his understanding, or to exercise his invention. . . . The torpor of his mind renders him, not only incapable of relishing or bearing a part in any rational conversation, but of conceiving any generous, noble, or tender sentiment, and consequently of forming any just judgment concerning many even of the ordinary duties of private life.

From this morbid account, a study in abject depravity for anyone steeped in the rich traditions of Addisonian polite sociability and concerned with the need to allow people to construct their own 'impartial spectator', stemmed Smith's insistence on the state's reponsibility for the proper education of the general population. In his judgement this was essential if society were to counteract the baleful human side-effects of commercial change.

Smith's greatest achievement in the *Wealth of Nations*, exhibiting an attention to psychological detail befitting a former professor of moral philosophy, was to identify that a form of self-interest on the part of individuals was indeed what lay behind commercial growth. Following Mandeville's controversial lead, he rejected as mere wishful thinking the frequently heard platitude, implicit in Shaftesbury and Hutcheson, that a concern for the common good might somehow be behind those of our actions which confer material benefits upon others. As he quipped, with a characteristic sense of the absurdity of some of his opponents' claims:

> It is not from the benevolence of the butcher, the brewer, or the baker, that we expect our dinner, but from their regard to their own interest. We address ourselves, not to their humanity but to their self-love, and never talk to them of our necessities but of their advantages.

Similarly his explanation for the moral and organisational mechanisms which had made possible the recent dramatic rise in wealth rested on a remarkable grasp of detail. His close examination of numerous examples, ranging from pin-factories to market traders, led him to the seminal insight that 'The greatest improvement in the productive powers of labour and the greater part of the skill, dexterity, and judgment with which it is any where directed, or applied, seems to have been the effects of the division of labour.' This, more than anything else, was the technical foundation for all future analyses of the modern economy.

Adam Ferguson, Smith's friend and Black's cousin, shared the characteristic intellectual preoccupations of the eighteenth-century Scottish elite, only occasionally managing to look convincingly like the model of a modern social scientist. Born at Logierait in Perthshire in the same year as Smith, he studied at St Andrews before becoming chaplain to the recently founded 43rd Foot, the Black Watch, the British army's first permanent Highland regiment. Although untrue, legend maintains that the young minister was conspicuous at the battle of Fontenoy in 1745, emboldening his men with a passionate Gaelic sermon on heroism and loyalty before leading them personally into the French guns. Like his clerical friends Home and Robertson, and no doubt further encouraged by his early patron Lord Milton, he combined the duties of the presbyterian ministry with staunch attachment to the Hanoverian British state and was a natural leader of the Poker Club. Subsequently, however, with his intellectual interests quickening, he became a private tutor. He then secured Edinburgh's vacant chair of natural philosophy (through blatant jobbery by Bute – Ferguson being no physicist and unable to deliver the lectures). It was only after his transfer to the much more congenial chair of moral philosophy, in which he was eventually succeeded in 1785 by Stewart, that he was able to cement his reputation as both an eloquent teacher and a daringly original thinker.

Nowhere more fluently than in the *Essay on the History of Civil Society* (1767), Ferguson tried to teach his readers that a set of fundamentally natural processes, analogous in some ways to Hutton's geological forces, had shaped and re-shaped human society through history: 'Not only the individual advances from infancy to manhood', he asserted in a lucid and wide-ranging preamble, 'but the species itself from rudeness to civilization.' Ferguson's argument drew upon a bewildering variety of empirical data. Culled from the writings of explorers, missionaries and traders, as well as from the more familiar histories of the European nations, including especially Rome (of whose republican period he also published a great history in 1783), his evidence encompassed the tribespeople of South America and the great civilisations of India and China, as well as acute observations on modern Scottish and English society. The result was a rich comparative framework, quasi-anthropological both in its breadth of vision and in its tendency towards the naturalistic explanation of human beings and their social environment. It was this which allowed Ferguson to account plausibly for the development of many phenomena whose historical origins he was among the first to attempt to chart – including marriage, poetry, property laws and the arts.

This constant emphasis on psychological and environmental rather than supernatural causes, partly deriving from his admiration for the great French scholar Montesquieu, crystallised in Ferguson's memorable image of man as an inventive, thrusting and restless creature, driven ceaselessly to seek his own advancement and self-improvement in all places and ages:

> He applies the same talents to a variety of purposes, and acts nearly the same part in very different scenes. He would be always improving on his subject, and he carries this intention where-ever he moves, through the streets of the populous city, or the wilds of the forest. While he appears equally fitted to every condition, he is upon this account unable to settle in any. At once obstinate and fickle, he complains of innovations, and is never sated with novelty. He is perpetually busied in reformations, and is continually wedded to his errors.

In this way, Ferguson offered a seductively familiar impression of active and ambitious Enlightenment man, perfectly suited to the expansive and rapidly developing post-Union Scottish society in which he was writing. But it was also, as things transpired, to be instrumental in succeeding generations in shaping European thinking about the essentially creative and progressive impulses of humankind.

The seminal importance of these historical concerns can hardly be overestimated. The contribution of Smith and Ferguson to what later became fully fledged social science disciplines was nothing less than to attempt for the first time to trace the history of the economy and society. Their colleagues and contemporaries – for example, Kames with his fascinating *Historical Law Tracts* (1757), Sir John Dalrymple with *An Essay Towards a General History of Feudal Property* (1758) and Gilbert Stuart with the *Historical Dissertation Concerning the English Constitution* (1764) (which incidentally popularised the notion of seeking out the origins of English liberties among their ancient Germanic ancestors) – were doing the same thing only a little less ambitiously for contemporary legal and political systems. The application of historical perspective to fundamental human phenomena also inspired John Millar at Glasgow, Smith's former student, whose *Origin of the Distinction of Ranks* (1771) and *Historical View of the English Constitution* (1787) explored the foundations of such things as social inequalities and the evolving structures of government, and William Alexander, a Scottish doctor whose *History of Women* (1779) essayed a pioneering study of changing gender relations down the centuries. On such evidence it does not seem to have been straining the point for Hume himself to describe his own era as 'the historical Age' and Scotland as 'the historical Nation'.

Hume's *History of England* (1754–62) was itself an engaging story, witty and ironic but also insightful, consummately stylish, and occasionally, to those who understood the elaborate sub-text, unashamedly provocative. That he outraged both Whig and Tory critics is, of course, testament to his matchless skill in the art of provoking responses. But it is also proof that his contemporaries could correctly decipher Hume's meaning, both in the *History* and in his numerous historically focused essays. Determined above all, like Addison, to teach his readers about the stabilising influence of polite conversation and the folly of believing the self-serving cant of party politicians of all kinds (which, in his sceptical view, promised only to increase instability and rancour), he set about slaughtering a whole herd of ideological sacred cows, historically baseless but rhetorically advantageous to Britain's competing political factions. The cruel tyranny for which Charles I had supposedly been justly punished in the Civil Wars was re-interpreted merely as a mixture of kingly misfortune and weakness; the alleged divine assistance and far-sighted wisdom which had made possible the 1688–89 Revolution against James VII and II was equally derided. Accident rather than design, misadventure rather than skill: these were to Hume the normal agencies of historical change, and the inflated claims of politicians to omnipotence and omniscience required puncturing in a way that only resolutely 'moderate opinions' could achieve.

For Hume, his star already rising with the popularity of the essays, historical writing gave him the ear of the wider public (and the substantial income) that his dense and difficult epistemological speculations had denied him. For William Robertson the study of the past similarly provided an accessible way of presenting to his large readership a range of philosophical concerns. Some of these were closely connected with the Enlightenment 'science of man'. Indeed, Robertson played a crucial role in popularising what became known, thanks again to Dugald Stewart's influential commentary, as 'theoretical' or 'conjectural' history. Cognate with contemporary European thinkers and particularly with the much-admired Montesquieu, this approach to the past insisted on the reality of fundamental principles of human nature and so the likelihood of common evolutionary processes across all known societies.

One of Robertson's key deductions from this set of assumptions was that the essential universality of human experience made it possible to speculate reasonably – to 'conjecture' – about the character of those historical peoples or individuals for whom surviving evidence was scant. Thus the native American tribespeople were not essentially inferior to Europeans. Rather, they happened currently to live in a society comparable with Europeans in the remote past, about whom the present conditions of the modern Iroquois or Apache also allowed plausible conclusions to be drawn. Robertson was convinced that the study of specific instances, such as the strikingly similar social customs found in primitive peoples on different continents, offered confirmation of the validity of general processes of historical change. These assumptions ultimately resulted in Robertson's acceptance of a 'stadial' theory of history, of the sort for which his friends Smith and Ferguson have become well-known. Within stadialism, human societies can be shown to evolve through a succession of identifiable stages, each marked by distinctive features: in Smith's version, the classic four-stage taxonomy, these were the economically defined phases of hunter-gathering ('savagery'), pastoralism ('barbarism'), agriculture and commerce.

Robertson's various philosophical convictions are best seen in the *History of the Reign of the Emperor Charles V* (1769), financially as well as intellectually a masterwork which netted him the colossal sum of £4,000 when he sold the copyright. Here the life of a sixteenth-century Habsburg prince not only incorporated a vast, sweeping perspective on European affairs amid what Robertson perceptively identified as the birth-pangs of the modern world. It even took the reader back to the barbarian tribespeople who had originally overrun the Roman empire. In the *History of America* (1777), published early and incomplete because of its topicality following the Declaration of

Independence, he was able both to subject pre-Columbian civilisation to conjectural treatment and to transform the story of the sixteenth-century conquest of the New World into a thought-provoking exploration of imperial over-stretch and maladministration. The inhabitants of George III's Britain, who bought Robertson's work in large numbers, found his purple prose irresistibly relevant during the bitter war with the Americans – as, to judge from its similar ubiquity in libraries, they did *The History of the Reign of Philip II, King of Spain* (1778), the work of Robert Watson, Blair's cousin and professor of rhetoric at St Andrews, which offered another fluent critique of authoritarian government in a colonial power.

Conjectural history was typical of enlightened Scottish scholarship at its most creative and intellectually expansive. But Robertson also had more obviously polemical concerns. As the leader of the Moderate clergy, he employed his majestic historical narratives to denounce not only Catholic 'superstition' but also Protestant 'enthusiasm'. In the *History of Scotland* (1759), Robertson judiciously cut his own presbyterian predecessors down to size: Knox was revealed as a bigoted rabble-rouser; Melville, similarly, 'often defeated laudable designs, by the impetuosity and imprudence with which he carried them on'; and Mary, Queen of Scots, since the sixteenth century a target of vicious presbyterian diatribe, was partially rehabilitated by Robertson as a sensitive and star-crossed woman. At the same time, his writings, like Hume's, reflected a strong faith in the Union, which was in any case, and certainly by the 1750s, the settled will of educated Scots.

The latter commitment was crucial, leading Robertson to view with undisguised disdain much of the history of pre-Union Scotland. Its material poverty and traditionally violent feudal politics – he claimed that 'the balance which ought to be preserved between a king and his nobles was almost entirely lost in Scotland' – were contrasted starkly with the blessings of the mixed Hanoverian constitution poured upon later generations by the happy transaction of 1707. In Robertson's interpretation, the treaty seemed even more clearly the ultimate good deal, bringing the Scots at last into fruitful partnership with England's historic wealth and much more robust parliamentary traditions. Such comforting opinions were widespread among the literati as among the political classes: Sir John Dalrymple, who played a prominent part in Montgomery's legislative assault on entail, even claimed in his *Memoirs of Great Britain and Ireland* (1771), with obvious significance for a calculation of the benefits of the Scots having accepted a full incorporating union with the southern kingdom, that 'the history of England is the history of liberty'. Yet friction also arose amid the scholarship. The Earl of Buchan, the radical nobleman and enthusiast for Scotland's own libertarian heritage – in other words, for the freedoms not of Westminster government but of Wallace and the Bruce – tried to re-orientate the historical obsessions of the age by founding the Society of Antiquaries of Scotland in 1780. This ruffled feathers among the other Edinburgh institutions, not only with Buchan's insensitive style but, by claiming a role in scientific inquiry, with its apparent challenge to the supposed intellectual prerogatives of the university and Philosophical Society: Robertson even attempted unsuccessfully to block its application for a royal charter.

The study of the past was clearly the means by which increasing numbers reflected on Scotland's own experiences: to borrow the nineteenth-century aphorism of Walter Bagehot, the literati were concerned, above all, to discover how 'from being a savage, man became a Scotchman'. The explanation of economic development or social advancement, the deflating of pompous political rhetoric, the elimination of religious prejudice and the reconciliation of the Scots with the English and the Treaty of Union: these were urgent priorities which historical analysis usually addressed. But the Scots also achieved more than just ostentatious self-examination when, as historians, they produced some of the age's best-selling books. They had greatly increased the range of possibilities available to other scholars. They were among the first to show how to build a bridge between history and other, different kinds of study. They greatly advanced the scope for comparative history. They sketched the outlines of a natural history of society. And they began the serious investigation of other human phenomena, many previously lacking a history to call their own. In these respects, as in the field of geological science, the Scottish Enlightenment was without precedent – even if eighteenth-century scholars can have had no notion of where their inquiries were eventually to lead.

Sense and sentiment

The Scottish Enlightenment was also fully reflected in creative endeavour. At all points from the age of Union to the dog days of the Napoleonic wars more than a century later, Scots approached poetry, drama, prose fiction and music as devotedly and as successfully as they approached their interests in science, philosophy and the study of the past. Indeed, in the baroque cantatas of the patrician aesthete and former Union commissioner Sir John Clerk of Penicuik (who had studied in Italy under Arcangelo Corelli), or the symphonies, overtures and sonatas of Thomas Erskine, 6th Earl of Kellie (himself a pupil of the elder Johann Stamitz of Mannheim), we hear very clearly how the Scots' aesthetic sensibilities were coming into even closer convergence with those of the great European cities. Yet it was in contributing to literature that they faced their greatest creative challenge. For Scottish authors grappled continually with the problem of how far a people, employing a tongue very similar to the English with whom they now also shared a government, could be said to possess, and should also seek to retain, a distinctive cultural identity of their own. As the antiquarian Sir John Dalyell put one of the opposing viewpoints at the end of the century, 'When a native of Scotland writes in English, he writes in fetters'. The different responses which emerged to this problem provide a useful way of thinking about the varied literature which eighteenth-century Scotland produced.

Around 1700 it might even have seemed that Scotland lacked a living literary tradition of its own. This was certainly a view widely shared by eighteenth-century Scottish commentators themselves, Dugald Stewart announcing to the world that the country had toiled through a 'long night of Gothic barbarism' and John Pinkerton claiming that his own century had proved itself 'as glorious for Scottish literature as the preceding had been adverse'. Such interpretations are not, however, endorsed by more recent scholarship, which confidently traces native literature back through the poems of Drummond of Hawthornden and the dramas of Sir William Alexander in the seventeenth century to the 'Castalian Band' patronised by James VI and the 'Makars' supported at the courts of his Stewart predecessors. Moreover, it is now clear that it was precisely this earlier tradition which gave real impetus to the eighteenth century's own literary revival. For in the years before and after the Treaty of Union, two scholars who shared a resentment of English indifference to Scottish letters and a professed desire to protect its core tradition from obliterative anglicisation took it upon themselves to publish celebratory editions of earlier Scottish poetry.

The first of these, James Watson, was an Edinburgh-based printer from Aberdeen. His three-volume *Choice Collection of Comic and Serious Scots Poems* (1706–11) was one of the most important texts for the preservation of older poems ever to appear in Scotland, containing such key earlier productions as 'Christ's Kirk on the Green', the reputed work of King James V himself. It was also patriotically inspired, or so Watson claimed, by 'the frequency of Publishing Collections of Miscellaneous Poems in our Neighbouring Kingdoms and States'. Watson's colleague was Allan Ramsay, born at Leadhills near Edinburgh. Perhaps a covert Jacobite and certainly a substantial man of letters, his *The Evergreen* (1724) and five-volume *Tea-Table Miscellany* (1724–37) built on Watson's achievement. For Ramsay presented once again to modern Scots a collection of poems in their own distinctive vernacular. These works seemed to confirm the existence, as well as to assist the survival, of a serious literary tradition in Scotland. Yet none was quite what it seemed. Watson, and to a greater extent Ramsay, had interpreted their editorial duties liberally. The latter had modified the poems' language, reconciling them with the refined Augustan tastes of his public. Both editors had also inserted a number of contemporary pieces (in Ramsay's case, some of his own), distorting and re-fashioning the national poetic tradition with pleasing compositions more appropriate to an age of politeness.

Contemporaries encountering what was long seen as Ramsay's masterpiece, *The Gentle Shepherd* (1725), may have believed that its Scots vernacular was what had attracted them. A play based on the couthy characters of a Lowland village, it offered a literary idealisation of Scotland's traditional rural life, couched in the tongue of its native people. Later readers, however, may notice different things. One is a tendency for Ramsay's supposedly unaffected rustic characters to drop into anglicised linguistic forms of a sort not usually found among Scotland's rural poor. Even more revealingly, *The Gentle Shepherd* portrays human interactions in which (unsurprisingly, given Ramsay's involvement in the Easy Club) the distinctive but artificial light of Addisonian sociability shines brightly through the enveloping bucolic haze. These tensions between rusticity and polite formality are even discernible in the opening salutations, one character hailing another with the distinctly un-vernacular exclamation 'This sunny Morning, Roger, chears my Blood,/And puts all Nature in a jovial Mood.' Like his and Watson's collections of Scots poetry, Ramsay's pastoral play, which ran to fully sixty-six editions before the end of the century, subverted the older literary forms even as it claimed to perpetuate them, artfully mingling archaisms with a more fashionable, increasingly polished style.

Ramsay's beguiling mixture of the old and the not-so-old was by no means the only option. Scottish authors also had available an alternative, which some assiduously followed: the open embracing of English literary fashion to the fullest extent. Of this tendency, quite the best-known contemporary example (though rather less well-regarded today) is James Thomson, a minister's son who left Roxburghshire for London when still young. In England he produced some of the most striking patriotic poetry of the age, including 'Rule, Britannia' (1740). He also produced the four-part pastoral cycle *The Seasons* (1726–30) – rapturously received, recited and subsequently to anthologise its way into the proto-Romantic consciousness. Another who placed at least four hundred miles between himself and his birthplace was Tobias Smollett, the product of a landowning family from the Vale of Leven in Dunbartonshire. After a medical education at Glasgow and a short naval career which included active service in the West Indies, he sought journalistic fame and fortune in London. He also spent many years travelling in Europe. Yet real literary success came only from his efforts as a novelist.

Progressing through *Roderick Random* (1748) and *Peregrine Pickle* (1751), Smollett's career was crowned by his best-known work, published as he lay dying at Livorno in Italy. *Humphry Clinker* (1771), an epistolary comedy, is in effect Smollett's homage to the blossoming achievements of his native land. The main protagonist, Matthew Bramble, leads a coach-ful of idiosyncratic characters on a breathless tour of Great Britain. It is, however, the party's visit to Scotland, where Edinburgh is fondly described and the merits of the Borders, Glasgow, Fife, Inveraray and Ayrshire are all advertised, which lingers longest in the memory. The recently founded medical school in Edinburgh was already 'famous all over Europe'; Scotland's established church, 'so long reproached with fanaticism and canting, abounds at present with ministers celebrated for their learning, and respectable for their moderation'; and there were 'many authors of the first distinction; such as the two Humes, Robertson, Smith, Wallace, Blair, Ferguson, Wilkie, &c. . . . as agreeable in conversation as they are instructive and entertaining in their writings'.

A more penetrating but also less enduring encounter with Scotland's Enlightenment was achieved by Henry Mackenzie. Educated in Edinburgh for the law, he was eventually hailed by Scott as 'the Scottish Addison' and ended his days the undisputed grand old man of Caledonian literature. He produced two polite periodicals, *The Mirror* (1779) and *The Lounger* (1785–87) in Spectatorial vein. His most famous work, *The Man of Feeling* (1771), similarly appears at first glance to absorb itself merely in the emulation of fashionable southern literature. Written in correct if slightly stilted English, it charts the successive social encounters of Harley, the eponymous hero. But Mackenzie had identified the fictional narrative as a vehicle for exploring human relationships and, in particular, for laying bare the affective sympathies which, as his friend Smith's *Moral Sentiments* had shown, bind people together. Harley's adventures in fact test many of the literati's fondest beliefs about sociability and moral judgement. His exquisite altruism and sensitivity ('There are some feelings which perhaps are too tender to be suffered by the world', he simpers before expiring) were hugely attractive to its original audience, even if their saccharine intensity tends to repel the modern reader. *The Man of Feeling* not only provided its creator with a best-seller, a volume Burns described as 'a book I prize next to the Bible'. It also gave the late eighteenth century a psychological novel perfectly reflecting the deepening sentimentalism of the mature Enlightenment. In effect, Mackenzie's triumph signalled the beginning of the end of Addison's strictly restrained and self-controlled model of politeness with its innate suspicion of strong human feelings. *The Man of Feeling*, a distillation of rarefied emotions, appears in retrospect as a landmark on the road towards Romanticism.

Despite his success, Mackenzie was bested as an influential author by the most enigmatic man of letters to emerge in eighteenth-century Scotland: James Macpherson. From Ruthven in Inverness-shire, Macpherson's name will forever be associated with a series of purported translations from the

Gaelic poems of the ancient bard Ossian. Much of the attention, then and since, has focused on doubts about their authenticity. Party lines were rapidly drawn. Scottish cultural patriots, notably Blair, who extravagantly praised the poetry's 'tenderness and sublimity', defended the productions of the brash young scholar as an accurate rendition of a newly rediscovered Celtic epic about the hero Fingal. Incurable sceptics and amused English observers (in this affair David Hume privately, and Samuel Johnson publicly, were unlikely bedfellows) loudly questioned both Macpherson's credibility and his competence. Doubters were particularly encouraged by the fact that some of Macpherson's ancient protagonists seemed suspiciously polite and sentimental, and their rugged environment sublime to a fault – almost as if tailored to appeal to the tastes prescribed by fashionable luminaries like Addison, Kames and Burke. A committee of inquiry chaired by Mackenzie duly raised more questions than it provided answers. For what it is worth, and while Gaelic scholars remain divided, current opinion credits Macpherson with the compilation of a single poem out of numerous fragments of genuine oral tradition, greatly altered and padded out with his own inventions. It is not today usually regarded as a continuous and authentic historical narrative.

Yet the cavills about Macpherson's techniques are secondary to the main historical point, which is the extraordinary contemporary reaction his works provoked. Quite how the cultural heights of late eighteenth-century Europe were stormed by a minor Highland poet of questionable probity – 'what I hear of your morals disposes me to pay regard not to what you say but to what you shall prove', snarled Johnson amid the controversy – will never be fully understood. For Ossian directly inspired countless imitators, particularly as the Romantic movement coalesced. Men as different as Goethe and Mendelssohn idolised the heroic figures of his tales. The empress Josephine even had Girodet bedeck Napoleon's palace at Malmaison with grandiose murals depicting episodes from Fingal's story. This was also done, only a little less bizarrely, by the painter Alexander Runciman for Sir James Clerk (3rd Baronet and Sir John's heir) at Penicuik. Ossian even stimulated a long overdue re-assessment of Scotland's Gaelic heritage. Scholars like John Macpherson, minister of Sleat on the Isle of Skye, and John Buchanan, who claimed (with good reason) that the Gaels had been 'illiberally insulted by the intemperate rage of an unprovoked enemy', were confronted by others like the eccentric Pinkerton. The last, a cantankerous journalist, historian and pioneer of racist stereotyping, was obsessed with proving that the ancient Pictish inhabitants of Scotland were not of backward Celtic stock but a Gothic people like their English and German cousins.

It is a bitter irony, of course, that a world obsessed with Macpherson's pale imitations of antique Celtic literature, and with the precise racial classification of the Gaels and Picts, should have been so blissfully ignorant of the fact that it also had in its presence some of the very finest exponents of a living Gaelic poetry. The great Donnchadh Bàn Mac an t-Saoir (Duncan Bàn Macintyre) passed much of his life in quiet obscurity in Glen Orchy. His predecessor Alasdair Mac Mhaighstir Alasdair (Alexander Macdonald), the searing Jacobite poet of Moidart, produced numerous masterpieces, memorably observing in one that 'The boar who's called King George,/son of the German sow,/his friendship and his love/is the raven's for the bone.' Such myopia, of course, was characteristic of the literati, simultaneously admirable in their intellectual breadth and frustratingly exclusive in their aesthetic preferences and ideological commitments. The relationship between eighteenth-century Scotland's two most original creative voices and the Enlightenment establishment was similarly unsatisfactory. For where Thomson took the high road to London and English literary celebrity, both of them, Robert Fergusson and Robert Burns, trod the more precarious low road through vernacular Scots expression.

In choosing to cast much of their work in Lowland Scots, and in developing literary careers which mingled remarkable inventiveness with deference to a wide repertoire of traditional songs and ballads, both poets set themselves apart, not only from the thoroughly British author of *Liberty*, not even just from the more equivocal creator of *The Gentle Shepherd*, but to a considerable extent from the literati and cultural arbiters of the day – men like Blair in Edinburgh, Watson in St Andrews and Alexander Gerard and his colleague Campbell in Aberdeen, university professors whose essentially anglocentric judgements of form and style could make or break fledgling Scottish literary careers. Fergusson, who studied at St Andrews before taking a clerkship in Edinburgh's commissary office, suffered from progressive mental disintegration before his tragic death in 1774 at the age of just twenty-four. But he had already shown an astonishing range, from satirically inventive Scots (notably the 'Elegy on the Death of Mr David Gregory, late Professor of Mathematics in the University of St Andrews') to formally correct English (Fergusson had, after all, been taught by William Wilkie, 'the Scottish Homer', whose *Epigoniad* (1757) was itself then regarded as the epitome of modern classicism). Fergusson also managed in his brief career to turn his native Edinburgh into the subject of an earthy yet fanciful poetry, best seen in the famous pieces 'Auld Reekie' and 'The Daft Days'.

Fergusson was even capable of the most pungent occasional verse. None were more acerbic than the mocking lines directed to the professoriate of his Alma Mater who had fawned before the visiting Dr Johnson, England's outrageous Scotophobe: 'Mind ye what Sam, the lyin loun!/Has in his Dictionar laid down?' Burns, the 'Heaven-taught ploughman' (in *The Lounger*'s eulogy), reckoned Fergusson his great inspiration and paid for a touching epitaph on his predecessor's tomb in Edinburgh's Canongate kirkyard. He himself had briefly flirted with Blair and literary Edinburgh, but found consolation (and, in truth, probably more sympathy) in bottle and bed, as well as in the production of incomparably boisterous, bawdy and passionate verse in the vernacular. No anthology of British literature is complete without at least one of Burns' compositions, perhaps 'O My Luve's Like a Red, Red Rose' or 'Tam O'Shanter'. It is worth remembering, however, that it was his very refusal to absorb himself fully in the prevalent literary and intellectual modes of the Scottish Enlightenment which made possible these peculiar achievements.

The Scot who most successfully negotiated the conflicting pressures towards cultural assimilation on the one hand and distinctiveness on the other was also the dominant force in Scottish – and European – literature by the third decade of the next century. Sir Walter Scott was very much a product of late Enlightenment Edinburgh. The grandson of an Edinburgh professor, he was educated at the High School and then the university under Stewart, where, like Cockburn, he joined the Speculative Society. Both through a sickly childhood and later as sheriff-depute of Selkirkshire, Scott immersed himself in the historical ballads of his beloved ancestral Borders. Setting out to preserve them, he eventually published them to critical acclaim in the first years of the new century as *Minstrelsy of the Scottish Border* (1802–3). This, however, was to be but the start of a glittering career. Scott subsequently produced the world's most significant early historical novels, beginning with *Waverley* (1814), a racy best-seller set during the 1745–46 rebellion which used a keen eye for period detail and a fascination with the interaction between individual personality and different social environments to consolidate, following Ossian, the nineteenth century's sentimental attachment to Scotland as a land of human heroism and natural beauty. Neither of these stupendous landmark works was published before 1800. Yet Scott's literary achievements rested centrally upon the distinctive intellectual heritage of the Scottish Enlightenment, with its rampant historical obsessions and deep interest in psychology.

In the mind's eye

No expression of Scotland's post-Union dynamism is more impressively tangible than its achievements in the graphic arts and architecture. Underplayed in many accounts of the Scottish Enlightenment, the work of William Aikman, the younger Allan Ramsay, Alexander Runciman and Henry Raeburn, like the Scots' achievements in urban planning and

Georgian architecture, can only properly be understood as an integral part of the eighteenth-century cultural experience. For they serve as a further necessary reminder that the ideas and aspirations so elegantly expressed by the literati also had life beyond the written page. There were vital connections between the Enlightenment philosophy of mind and contemporary aesthetics. An urgent striving for a psychological understanding of the human condition, which in a different way was mirrored in the experimentation of Smollett and Mackenzie with characters' behaviour in various social settings, could hardly help but inform the tradition of Scottish portraiture which reached its apogee in Raeburn, the great immortaliser of those who illuminated late Enlightenment Edinburgh.

Other factors linked enlightened thought with contemporary Scottish art. Firstly, there was no effective separation between practitioners. Aikman, the century's first great painter, was a friend of the poets Ramsay and Thomson and the nephew of the cultivated antiquarian and harpsichordist Sir John Clerk of Penicuik. Ramsay junior, a fast friend of Hume, was also supported by both Forbes and the 2nd and 3rd Dukes of Argyll, whose formal portraits are among his finest works. Hutton was accompanied on expeditions by his friend the senior John Clerk of Eldin, Penicuik's son, whose illustrations for *The Theory of the Earth* (1796) gave visual expression to the geologist's theories: Clerk himself, not coincidentally, became one of Scotland's most respected landscape engravers as well as, curiously, a once-famous author on naval tactics. Raeburn, a member of the Cape Club along with Fergusson and Runciman, was also a friend of Reid and Stewart, both of whom sat for him. Other acquaintances painted by Raeburn included Hutton and Scott, as well as numerous Dundases. His *Sir John and Lady Clerk of Penicuik* (1792), a stunning combination of portraiture and landscape which sets the 4th Baronet (the earlier Sir John's grandson) with his wife against the backdrop of their Midlothian estate, also serves as a reminder of the intermingling of wealth and creativity in eighteenth-century Scotland brought about by the close ties of patronage and friendship.

A further point of contact between art and wider intellectual culture was more precisely philosophical, arising in the assumptions characteristic of the leading Scottish thinkers. As we have seen, most Scottish moralists and educators, following Shaftesbury and Hutcheson, believed that, in apprehending virtue, the human moral sense operates in a manner analogous to the mind's intuitive identification of beauty. This psychological intertwining of ethics and aesthetics obviously has profound implications, many of them actually explored by Scottish contemporaries. An early and influential contribution came in the *Treatise on Ancient Painting* (1740) by George Turnbull, a friend of the younger Ramsay and himself Reid's teacher at Marischal College. Turnbull claimed that the appreciation of art, like the study of history and literature, inculcates politeness and refinement: 'the immediate Effect of good moral or historical Pictures upon the Mind', he claimed, 'is either directly virtuous, or at least exceedingly strengthening and assistant to Virtue'. Precisely because, as Turnbull echoed Hutcheson in concluding, 'We have . . . by nature a moral Sense', art was itself a valuable educational commodity, stimulating and succouring an acute and discriminating sensitivity to virtue and vice.

A final factor confirmed this synergy between art and philosophy which Turnbull had discerned. This was the Scottish Enlightenment's empirical preoccupation with human perception, and especially with the bewitching mechanism of sight. According to Hume (whose essays significantly also included ones on taste and the aesthetic senses), it is by this means that men receive the discrete and unconnected impressions of an external world which are then sorted and organised according to their own imaginations. Alternatively, on Reid's counter-argument, it is by the miracle of sight that they are provided with information about an external world which the mind is intuitively able to perceive in a way which is both reliable and accurate. A fascination with the subjective representation of an objective world, combined with a natural wish to keep profitably abreast of changing fashions in wider British art, consequently underlay much of the Scottish painting of this period.

Aikman's *Sir John Clerk of Penicuik* (*c.*1720) and *Sir Hew Dalrymple, Lord North Berwick* (1722), for example, sought an improved clarity and truthfulness of depiction. This aspiration had several roots but stemmed in part from a sympathy with the empiricism of Newton and Locke which Aikman shared with his contemporary Hutcheson. Ramsay, in turn, raised this attention to detail to new heights. His 1749 portrait of Argyll, his *Hew Dalrymple, Lord Drummore* (1754) and particularly his *Margaret Lindsay* (*c.*1757) each strove to capture something of the actuality of vision through meticulous brushwork. Raeburn, by contrast, was touched by the 'Common Sense' school of his friends Reid and Stewart. His broad and sweeping brush technique had an obvious affinity with their philosophical approach, seen to particular effect in mature works such as *Lord Newton* and *John Robison.* Here Raeburn's daringly approximate strokes resolve uncannily into an overall effect very similar to that achieved when our eyes perceive objects in real life.

On a much larger scale, this interest in human nature and particularly in perception, together with the inevitable affinities between the social elite and professional architects, produced an eighteenth-century revolution in the design of buildings and townscapes which similarly captured many of the key ideas of the Scottish Enlightenment. This was true both in the public and in the private realm and whether contemporaries were concerned to erect magnificent but singular country homes like Mavisbank and the frequently remodelled Hopetoun House or extensive and inter-linked developments like the progressive phases of Edinburgh's New Town. The last remains the most useful example of the relationship in enlightened Scotland between ideas and their physical realisation, with much to be gleaned about the intellectual agenda of those involved in manufacturing it. The aim of constructing an entirely new urban core for the Scottish capital on a greenfield site was not only indicative of the vaulting ambition of the social and intellectual elites of mid-century Edinburgh ('the genius of no people in the world is more devoted to architecture than that of the nobility and gentry of Scotland', claimed one commentator, William Guthrie, as the New Town finally began to rise). It was also testament to the extraordinary way in which Scotland's quickening post-Union commercial expansion and the accompanying Addisonian notions of polite society were able powerfully to reinforce one another in promoting an urban revolution.

In August 1752 the *Scots Magazine*, founded in 1739, printed the text of a proposal for the improvement of Edinburgh, previously endorsed by the Convention of Royal Burghs. No one could have guessed how dramatically the city's face would be changed in the space of just fifty years. The proposers, led by Lord Provost Drummond and the corporation, sketched out a visionary prospect of a modern capital city. Eyes seem in particular to have been beadily fixed on London's recent growth. It was intended that the Scots should enjoy a similar economic and cultural renaissance: they would abandon the squalid medieval confines of the Old Town, fashioning instead an Enlightenment metropolis, 'a centre of trade and commerce, of learning and the arts, of politeness, and of refinement of every kind'. In other words, this was to be a thoroughly contemporary setting. The full gamut of professional business would be more efficiently transacted. Aristocrats and the rapidly expanding middle classes would be accommodated. A social milieu of intellectual and moral cultivation – the reign of politeness – would be inaugurated. Appropriately, when Drummond and his colleagues paraded through the city to lay the foundation stones, they did so in their full masonic regalia, visibily declaring the links between Edinburgh's progressive re-fashioning and the contemporary concerns of clubbable sociability which had helped stimulate it.

From 1767 onwards, the implementation of the neo-classical grid-iron layout devised by James Craig, the twenty-seven-year-old nephew of the poet Thomson, allowed the New Town's creators to pay further homage to key Enlightenment principles. The public authorities provided the essential infrastructure, such as the roads, pavements and sewerage, and stipulated a standard roof line. But the original scheme left it to the developers – sometimes aspiring occupants, sometimes enterprising builders – to erect private properties along the thoroughfares. It thus combined intense civic pride with attractive opportunities for the expression of proprietorial individualism in a fashion which embodied some of the balances between liberty and order, between anarchic laissez-faire and intolerable dirigisme, which Smith and Hume in particular thought needed to be struck by a civilised commercial society.

Nor was the human interaction with the new urban quarter conceived in isolation from the intellectual vision that had recently enlivened the old. Purpose-built venues, notably the Assembly Rooms, provided an institutional framework within which a polite public might pursue beneficial social interaction. The civic self-assurance of late Enlightenment Edinburgh was also lent substance in several landmark constructions, such as the imposing neo-classical development of a new university building to the south of the Old Town, and Register House, to house Scotland's historic public records, the first building in the New Town. Similarly, the generously proportioned footpaths and two formal squares of the latter, named with deliberate Hanoverian loyalism (George Street, Charlotte Square, Hanover Street, Frederick Street, Princes Street and Queen Street), could not have been better designed to facilitate the respectable Addisonian taste for leisurely conversation and – as many Georgian engravings of the streetscapes confirm – for the enjoyment of sociable perambulation.

Edinburgh was thus transformed into the heavenly city of the enlightened intelligentsia and of the rest of the political, legal and mercantile elites: emblematically, David Hume and Sir Lawrence Dundas both moved early to the New Town, while Glasgow, Aberdeen, Perth and St Andrews each in their different ways tried to emulate the capital. The nobility and landed classes simultaneously imposed a related order upon the rural landscape. The planned villages characteristic of improved agriculture, such as Newcastleton and Tyninghame, and other examples like Inverary in Argyllshire (laid out by the 3rd Duke of Argyll from the 1740s), Fochabers in Moray (laid out after 1776 by the 4th Duke of Gordon) and Charlestown in Fife (established in the 1770s by the 5th Earl of Elgin), were intended to kindle commerce, while providing the domestic and social amenities a prosperous tenantry and industrious workforce would require. Grid-iron layouts, squares, ample thoroughfares and monumental public buildings were all ubiquitous. Rational and orderly yet also fundamentally utilitarian, such designs confirmed the subjection of both the surrounding countryside and the community to the firm but enterprising and benign proprietorship of which Enlightenment thought generally so wholeheartedly approved.

Equivalent symbolism was also found in a domestic setting, expressing the same familiar intellectual assumptions. For this was the great age of the Scottish country house. The roll-call of talented contributors begins with

Colen Campbell, who trained as a lawyer in Edinburgh. Through his *Vitruvius Britannicus* (1715), he was responsible for advancing neo-Palladianism throughout Britain. He not only designed Scottish properties like the home of Daniel Campbell of Shawfield, which was sacked by the Glaswegian rioters in 1725; he also worked on Houghton Hall in Norfolk, the residence of Walpole himself. His older associate, James Smith, who remodelled Dalkeith Palace for the Buccleuchs and built Drumlanrig for the 1st Duke of Queensberry, probably did more to develop neo-Palladianism in practice. Seeking to re-capture the austere purity of ancient Roman styles, and explicitly rejecting the overbearing grandeur and excessive formalism of the French and Italian Baroques, this distinctively British architectural movement was widely applauded by influential commentators like Addison, Shaftesbury and Lord Burlington.

Essentially reformist in its search for a simpler and more authentic neo-classicism, and chiming particularly well with Scotland's contemporary experiences of growing cultural self-confidence and urgent national re-definition in the wake of Union, this movement soon produced the greatest architectural dynasty in British history, founded by William Adam, a Kirkcaldy builder. In the mid-1720s he completed a landmark neo-Palladian property, Mavisbank near Loanhead, as a retreat for Sir John Clerk of Penicuik. As a versatile thinker in his own right, whose unpublished poem 'The Country Seat' (1725) explored the purpose of the modern proprietorial residence, Clerk was actively involved in the design (as his heir Sir James also helped design Penicuik House in due course). A staunch Whig presbyterian, Adam was a favoured contractor with those in authority: Fort George in Inverness-shire, the gargantuan post-Culloden complex, was his most striking government project, the plans of Inverary town for the Argylls the largest private commission. But his residential works also contributed greatly to the mature realisation of the Palladian style in Scotland: a partly executed near-contemporary plan for the remodelling of Hopetoun House for Clerk's friend the 1st Earl of Hopetoun; Haddo House in Aberdeenshire, built in the 1730s for the 2nd Earl of Aberdeen; and particularly the exuberant Duff House in Banffshire, constructed before 1743 for one of Scotland's coming generation of parvenu proprietors, William Duff of Braco, subsequently 1st Earl of Fife, who ultimately refused to meet the full expenses, embroiling Adam in protracted and ruinous litigation.

The later Adams – John, James and above all his second son Robert – were able to benefit from the accelerating confidence and commercial success of Scotland's propertied elite (and, increasingly, from ambitious town councils such as Edinburgh's) as they sought to push neo-classicism further towards its conceptual limits. Hopetoun was an early and successful project for the partnership, a further remodelling for the 2nd Earl during the 1750s which finally completed Scotland's grandest eighteenth-century aristocratic palace (fittingly for the post-Union age, it was the home of a family whose roots lay not in the warrior medieval nobility but among ferociously competent Scots lawyers). Robert was himself an Edinburgh graduate who subsequently designed the university's majestic new precinct on the South Bridge. He was a friend of Hume, Smith and the younger Ramsay, as well as, like Burns and Scott, an active freemason. He also became the intellectual driving force behind the 'Adam Revolution'. Using his experiences on the Grand Tour, from which emerged what is effectively his manifesto, *The Ruins of the Palace of the Emperor Diocletian at Spalato* (1764), he added greatly to the innovative character of British neo-classicism, thereafter selling it successfully to English as much as to Scottish patrons.

Robert's architectural vision encompassed a range of residential features suited to the emphasis on politeness and sociability which characterised the mature Scottish Enlightenment. Differentiated and increasingly imaginative room designs were pursued to better serve distinct social functions. Airy but cleverly equipped libraries allowed clients to flaunt their intellectual interests – notably at Harewood House in Yorkshire. Carefully designed drawing-rooms and stunningly decorated dining-rooms, in which Adam co-ordinated work by famous associates such as Angelica Kauffmann and Thomas Chippendale, facilitated the sort of structured exchanges which modern people, their expectations moulded by Addisonian precepts, considered so necessary. Gosford House in East Lothian, built in the 1790s for the 7th Earl of Wemyss, was the consummation of an unparalleled career in country-house building, with its extensive social facilities and distinctive classical touches (notably a Venetian window echoing its designer's youthful visit to Split). Rivals like Robert Mylne, whose works included Pitlour House in Fife for the soldier Philip Skene in the 1770s, could scarcely compete with this winning combination of business acumen, strong connections, design ingenuity and deep awareness of the social and cultural environment in which his physical structures would be situated.

By the end of the century the Adams, still closely in touch with wider intellectual developments, were participating in the perceptible shift in late Enlightenment aesthetic preferences. A more imaginative way of thinking about national identity through a close appreciation of history had gradually emerged. In creative writing this was marked by the Ossian phenomenon and later by Scott's evocative balladry. But sentimentalised historicism as a cultural mode also produced two major architectural developments. First, it stimulated even more inventive gestures towards classical models, culminating eventually in the Greek Revival, replete with fluted Ionic and majestic Doric columns, which would make Edinburgh truly 'the Modern Athens' by the 1820s. Opposing the Grecian, though stemming from the same tendency towards exaggerated historical referencing, was the increasing immersion in pseudo-medieval Gothicism, what Mark Twain subsequently derided as 'the Walter Scott Middle-Age sham civilization', supposedly the authentic re-creation of Scotland's own distinctive physical heritage.

Neither fashion should be dismissed as merely superficial. The Grecian, typified by properties such as Broomhall in Fife, built in the late 1790s by Thomas Harrison for the 7th Earl of Elgin (whose subsequent notoriety rests on his purchase of the Parthenon frieze), was closely related to the flowering of serious Greek historiography in Scotland at the hands of men like Walter Anderson, minister of Chirnside in Berwickshire, and John Gillies, a private scholar and Fellow of the Society of Antiquaries of Scotland, whose *History of Greece* (1786) earned him the coveted title of Historiographer Royal after Robertson's death. Such studies fuelled the burgeoning conceit that the intellectual achievements of Edinburgh and their political triumphs within Great Britain meant that the Scots were indeed entering their own glorious Athenian age: as Robert Mudie, an early nineteenth-century cynic, scoffed, it had seemed for a time that Dundas himself was 'the express image of Pericles'.

The Gothic, conversely, was the realisation in battlements and turrets of the growing fascination of scholars like Pinkerton and Stuart with Scotland's medieval history and putatively Germanic origins. Inveraray, begun in 1744 for the 3rd Duke of Argyll, turned out to be the first of many castellated modern residences. Others eventually included Douglas Castle in Lanarkshire, an Adam production for the 1st Duke of Douglas; Oxenfoord Castle in Midlothian, his project for the lawyer and historian Sir John Dalrymple; and the superbly situated Culzean Castle, a substantial Adam rebuilding for the 10th Earl of Cassillis. Eclectic in composition, and often skilfully mingling neo-classical with Gothic, they articulated the yearning for a distinctive national cultural identity, securely rooted in the historical past, which was so fundamental to the last phase of the Scottish Enlightenment.

There are, as Twain wryly observed, many ironies about this excessive fondness among Scotland's late eighteenth-century elite for manifest heritage, fashionably if implausibly rendered as an ivy-covered mock-baronial fastness or pristine Athenian portico. It came as, seventy years after the Union, an independent Scottish polity was finally passing out of living memory; as the elite's own culture was being transformed by connections with England and with the European Enlightenment; as the onset of full-blown industrialisation was altering the very fabric of Scottish society. Most interestingly, the Gothic and the Grecian, striving desperately to re-attach modern Scotland to recognisably medieval or ancient European antecedents, emerged just as the country's links with the non-European world were attaining a scale and sophistication of which, before 1707, few could even have dreamed. Scotland's architectural vocabulary may have been becoming increasingly ersatz. Yet nothing at this time was more real or more immediate than the Scots' deep immersion in the cultures, societies and economies of North America and India. It is to that remarkable eighteenth-century experience of empire that we must now turn.

CHAPTER FIVE

Empire

By the end of the century Scotland's place in the wider world had been transformed. Closely involved in Britain's commercial and military empire in North America and India, and in its post-1763 dominance over other European powers, the Scots were prominent as soldiers, traders, administrators, adventurers and settlers; they were doomed also to play a prominent role in the debacle of 1775–83 when the American empire disintegrated. At all times the Scots' relationship with imperialism was reciprocal. They helped make and mar the British empire (and significantly, from the time when Sir John Oldmixon published his *The British Empire in North America* the year after the Treaty of Union, it was rarely described merely as an English empire). Yet their politics, society and economy, their very identity and self-perceptions, were also affected by worldwide commerce and conquest. Nor was this all. The Scots' contribution to the empire after 1707 was truly distinctive, not least because their earlier experiences had been so very different from those of the English.

Migrants, mercenaries and the will to empire

Since the later middle ages, overseas knowledge had been relatively extensive in Scottish society. Ambitious individuals had been a constant export to France and Italy and, since the Reformation, to the Low Countries and Germany; many had returned home familiar with foreign lands. Others, by professional choice or deterred by the threat of religious persecution in Scotland, remained overseas, carving out successful careers as part of

Europe's educational and intellectual establishment. Scottish merchants also participated actively in international trading networks. In France, Flanders and Holland, and as far into the Baltic region as the coastal plains of northern Germany, the Scandinavian kingdoms, Poland and Estonia, traders from ports like Leith, Dundee and Aberdeen had for centuries been regular visitors and, sometimes, settlers. Less glamorously, the Scots had also experienced the brutal migratory pressure of famine, especially in the 1690s, when there had been a mass flight from the south-west to Ulster.

A further long-term factor which similarly underlay the Scots' distinctive post-Union role in the British empire was their military heritage. Like other poor European countries such as Switzerland, Scotland was traditionally an exporter of soldiers. Early-modern states depended heavily upon mercenaries, preferred often to native subjects, who in any case could not usually be conscripted. The resulting Continental market for Scots troops survived even after James VI's accession to the English and Irish thrones ended the substantial career opportunities for Highland soldiers (the famous 'Redshanks') in Ireland. Certainly they had ample opportunity to embellish their military fame across the blood-stained battlefields of seventeenth-century Europe. Sir Robert Moray, who raised soldiers for Louis XIII's French armies, and both Alexander Leslie, 1st Earl of Leven, and David Leslie, Lord Newark, who graduated from service under Gustavus Adolphus of Sweden to leadership of Covenanting armies against Charles I, exemplified this integral Scottish involvement in the major international conflicts of the pre-Union era.

After 1688 the Scots were also effectively drawn into the great Continental wars in which their English neighbours were engaged. King William presided over a huge expansion of both the English and the Scottish military establishments, mainly to fight Louis XIV's armies in Flanders. In the process William practically invented the British army, employing those forces which were his by right of the Scottish crown as part of a single royal army (and also fighting alongside the long-standing Scots brigade in the Dutch service). By 1707, many thousands of officers and men had therefore had experience of service abroad in forces controlled from London: regiments of future distinction such as the 1st Regiment of Foot (Royal Scots), the Earl of Mar's Regiment (Royal Scots Fusiliers), the Earl of Leven's Regiment (King's Own Scottish Borderers), the Cameronians, the Scots Guards and the Royal Scots Greys, some with a prior history in the French service or in the conflict between the presbyterians and the Stuart monarchy, all came under the authority of the crown and its English ministers during this period. In this respect as in several others, the Treaty of Union, by granting Scottish politicians at least some say in the disposition of Scotland's own military manpower, seemed likely merely to set matters to rights.

The seventeenth-century crown had also helped introduce the Scots to the experience of colonisation. It was to his fellow-countrymen as well as the English that James VI turned for migrants whose Protestantism and civilised manners might provide a bulwark against native Catholic barbarity in northern Ireland. In practice there was more effective settlement by Scots in the implanted counties of Down and Antrim than in the formal plantations now being established elsewhere: indeed, it is from the famine migrants of the 1690s that most of the Ulster-Scots language and Lowland surnames of the modern Loyalist community come. Similarly halting efforts by James also saw Lowlanders employed in a process of internal colonisation to assist in the subordination and development of the Gaelic-speaking Western Isles: the 'Men of Fife' or 'Fife Adventurers', unlikely merchant–colonists from central Scotland, were transplanted to the Isle of Lewis in 1599 from where they were swiftly expelled by MacLeod clansmen. Their claims ultimately fell to the more efficient Gaelic imperialists of clan Mackenzie.

The Stuart monarchy also patronised, though neither enthusiastically nor successfully, various extra-European enterprises mounted by its subjects. Here the famous project of Sir William Alexander, 1st Earl of Stirling, might be noted: though essentially a money-making exercise purveying nominal title to land in what was imaginatively called Nova Scotia (but which, under the name of Acadia, was already claimed by France), this was an abortive Scots plantation designed to match English ones in Virginia and Irish ones on the Amazon – the latter also still-born. Lord Ochiltree's similarly short-lived New Galloway venture led in 1629 to his embarrassing expulsion from Cape Breton by French forces. Ironically, the territories involved in both of these schemes were finally subjected to successful Scottish colonisation only under the aegis of the eighteenth-century British state.

Yet these largely speculative ventures are only part of the story. For from the 1680s the Scots tried with more success to penetrate the English colonies directly. The settlement of East New Jersey, of which Robert Barclay of Urie became Governor, comprised mainly Quakers and episcopalians from Aberdeenshire: this de facto Scottish colony survived until 1702 when the proprietors sold out to English interests. In the Carolinas in the 1680s, Lord Cardross and William Dunlop, later Principal of the University of Glasgow, promoted Stuart's Town, a colony peopled by a mixture of Ulster Scots and presbyterian refugees and distinguished by a Scottish landholding system: this was soon extinguished by Spanish attacks from Florida. More sporadic emigrations also occurred. Expatriate Scots and their families cropped up in places as distant as Antigua and Rhode Island, while Covenanters, beggars and gypsies were among the other arrivals. The Cromwellian regime even used England's colonies, notably Virginia and Barbados, as dumping grounds for Scottish prisoners of war.

Throughout this period, moreover, the word 'empire' had deeply ambiguous connotations for those contemplating its desirability for Scotland. It was undoubtedly a matter of being able to exploit overseas possessions for material profit. But it was simultaneously about the successful assertion of national sovereignty against the competing claims of would-be overlords: this crucial resonance, reflected in the fascination with the 'closing' of crowns to signify imperial status (i.e. acknowledging no earthly superior), is particularly well seen in the lawyer James Anderson's *Historical Essay Shewing that the Crown and Kingdom of Scotland is Imperial and Independent* (1705), published in the wake of the nation's final disastrous attempt at overseas colonisation. Anderson strenuously maintained his country's sovereign status, rejecting English allegations that Scotland was not even a properly imperial kingdom. The importance of vindicating the Scots' political equality with other nations, especially at a time when they were actually considering a new partnership with England, was duly recognised when the Edinburgh Parliament voted Anderson a cash prize.

In this light the Darien scheme can be understood not only as a crucial economic venture designed to kick-start Scotland's commercialisation but also as an ideological enterprise of some importance. While emulating Dutch-style trading entrepôts, it simultaneously demonstrated the Scots' independent power through assertive international activity. The ensuing rebuff by Spain, blatant English scorn and the subsequent unravelling of the entire project were therefore immensely damaging to Scotland's self-confidence, as well as to its financial position. They signalled to many Scots that their vaunted aspirations to equality with other nations were built on sand. Compensation for Darien's material losses was inevitably an important consideration in the resulting Union. But so too was the opportunity that it presented to re-cast the Scots' frustrated ambitions in a much more promising imperial framework. And, of course, even the most optimistic calculations in the years around 1707 barely did justice to what eventually proved possible.

North America and settlement

The Union dramatically increased the potential for Scottish involvement in North America in particular. Shortage of capital remained a significant early hurdle, while anxiety about English competition even led some who would subequently benefit most from imperial trade – notably the royal burgh of Glasgow – initially to oppose the draft treaty. Yet within a generation the British Atlantic commercial networks, prospering under the protection of

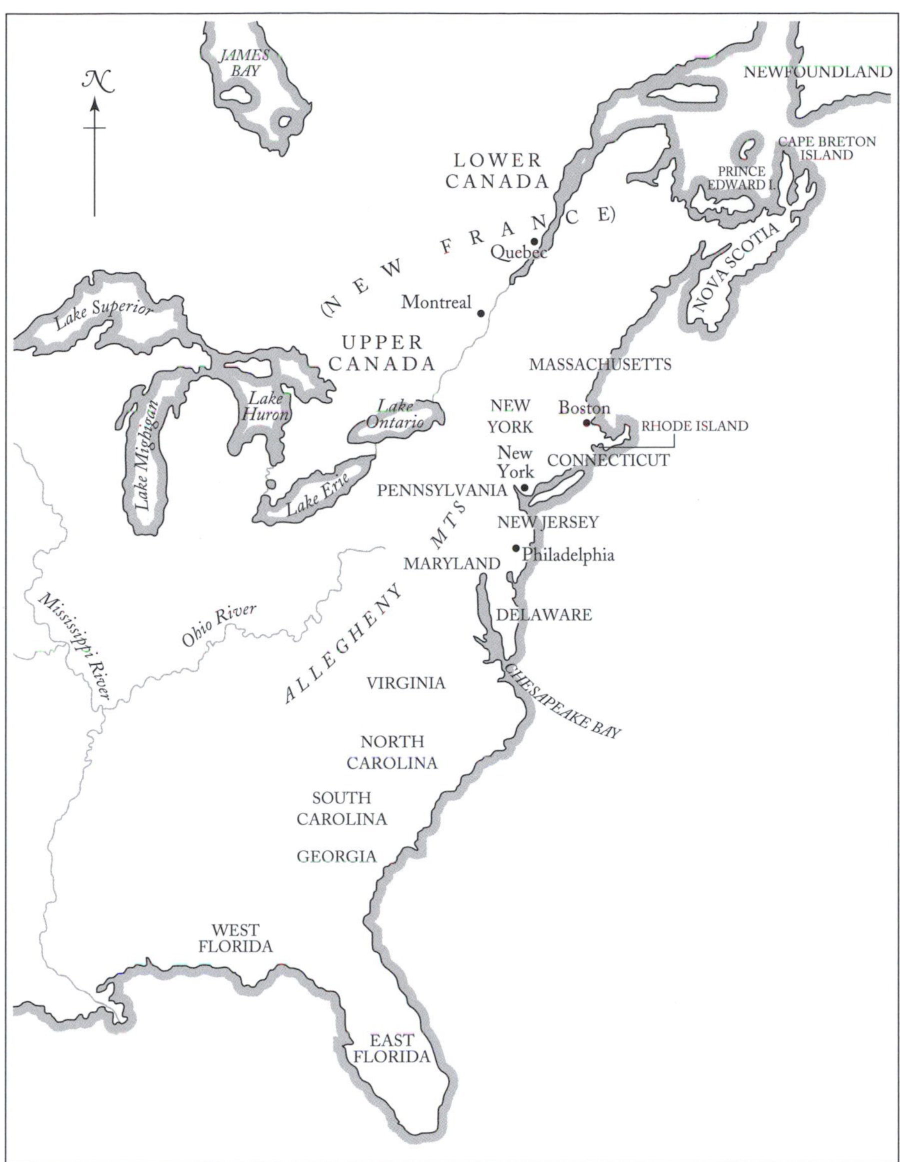

Map 3 North America in the eighteenth century

the Navigation Acts, had incorporated substantial numbers of enterprising Scots. High office and real influence also beckoned: some Scots were as prominent, though happily few were quite as corrupt, as the execrable Andrew Cochrane Johnstone, the younger son of the 8th Earl of Dundonald, who at the end of the century accumulated a harem as Governor of Dominica and was shortly afterwards court-martialled for peculation. Moreover, amid the French and Indian Wars of the late 1750s and early 1760s, and then again after 1775, members of the Scottish elite and many thousands of others from Scotland fought and not infrequently died on American soil: Peter Halkett of Pitfirrane, whom we first encountered as MP for the Dunfermline Burghs, was actually killed in 1755 during the failed assault on Fort Duquesne (later Pittsburgh); Cochrane's more reputable elder brother Charles was among the fallen at Yorktown. Nor did their high visibility in the British colonies always make the Scots popular. Anxiety about Scottish ambitions was probably as common among American Englishmen as it was among resentful metropolitans back in London: it says much that the original draft of the Declaration of Independence chose explicitly to denounce the Scots along with the other 'foreign mercenaries' who had supposedly oppressed the colonists

Individual Scots certainly made many signal contributions to the remarkable eighteenth-century extension of British North America. Robert Dinwiddie from Germiston near Glasgow, appointed Lieutenant-Governor of Virginia, became involved in the early 1750s in land companies with claims on the uncolonised trans-Appalachian interior – claims challenged by French positions along the Mississippi, the crucial link between New France and Louisiana. Realising that the strategic future of the entire continent lay in the balance, Dinwiddie sent the young Colonel George Washington to attempt to prevent the French advance down the Allegheny River into the disputed Ohio Valley. As the conflict inevitably escalated, Scots once again took the lead in advancing British interests. John Campbell, 4th Earl of Loudoun, a zealous Whig and one of Ayrshire's principal landowners, became Commander-in-Chief in North America. James Abercrombie from Glasslaw in Banffshire also secured for himself a deserved reputation for military incompetence at Ticonderoga in New York: many Highlanders died there, including Campbell of Inverawe, although the unflinching conduct of the Black Watch under intense fire contributed much to the rapidly increasing respect outside Scotland in which the country's kilted warriors were held.

On the Heights of Abraham beside Quebec City in 1759, General James Wolfe, who had commanded a regiment in Cumberland's army at Culloden, had the richly ironic experience of leading to victory an army in which the 78th Highlanders, raised by Simon Fraser, 12th Lord Lovat, veteran of the rebel army at Falkirk and son of the most slippery Jacobite of them all, distinguished themselves. Wolfe's ambivalence towards his Highlanders – his *obiter dictum* that they were 'hardy, intrepid, accustomed to a rough country, and no great mischief if they fall' is frequently quoted against him – was, however, to be expected in an officer whose career had largely been devoted to counter-insurgency operations against Jacobite clansmen. By the time of the Peace of Paris in 1763, which Wolfe, of course, did not live to see, such older attitudes were in rapid decline. They were being superseded by a new admiration for Highland soldiers generated by their performance in wars from Flanders to Canada. In retrospect, the dramatic expulsion of France from North America appears only the prelude to the irreversible fragmentation of the British Atlantic empire a dozen years later. Yet stirring memories of Fontenoy and the Heights of Abraham proved much more enduring.

In measuring the rapid assimilation of the formerly dissident into the British fold, and the role of empire as a context in which this transition to respectability often occurred, it is particularly significant that Quebec's first post-conquest Governor was yet another Scot whose own father and brothers had been Jacobites: even this handicap had not stopped James Murray of Elibank from rising to brigadier under Wolfe. A second Murray, John, 4th Earl of Dunmore, similarly attained the highest rank despite parental implication in the 'Forty-five: he became Governor of New York in 1770 and of Virginia the following year. Such easy accommodation, facilitated by George III's policy of ceasing the proscription of Tories and former Jacobites, provoked mystification at the time and continues to exercise historians. One view – understandably popular with contemporary English critics – held that high colonial office presented opportunities for unaccountable executive action that were especially attractive to Scottish proprietors accustomed to the exercise of feudal jurisdiction and steeped in family commitment to divine-right kingship. More likely, however, the expanding number of colonial opportunities after 1763 simply provided the Scottish elite, unable to break into the English professions (particularly since the Union had preserved so many separate Scottish and English institutions), with the chance to claim a fair share of the spoils in what was a genuinely British enterprise. Some Scots, indeed, positively flaunted their humbler backgrounds, implying that this had given them a vital competitive edge in the scramble for imperial rewards: 'I was born a Scotsman and a bare one', claimed Walter Scott later, 'Therefore I was born to fight my way in the world.'

A less frequently remembered aspect of the Scots' contribution to the extension of the empire was the work of traders, trappers and explorers in the service of the Hudson's Bay Company, the chartered company responsible since the 1670s for opening up the vast territories to the north and west of New France. With notional claims to as much as one-quarter of the North American land mass, the Company's posts and men in reality clung close to James Bay. But it rapidly acquired an unmistakable Caledonian tincture. By the 1750s more than two-thirds of the traders were Scots – many from Orkney, the immediate British port of call for Company ships. In the 1780s, when the rival North-West Company was established in Montreal, it too was dominated by Scots eager to break the monopolistic grip of their own countrymen on the lucrative fur trade: it was led by the domineering Simon McTavish (known as the 'Marquis'), and others like Alexander Henry, Thomas Curry and James Finlay, who explored Saskatchewan.

Fittingly, the very greatest contributor to the eighteenth-century exploration of the continent was also a Scot. In 1789 Sir Alexander Mackenzie, from Inverness, canoed with native companions across the Great Slave Lake and down what is now the Mackenzie River to reach the Arctic coastline. He led another intrepid party across the Rockies to the Pacific Ocean by Vancouver Island in 1792–93, becoming the first white man to traverse North America from coast to coast. The existence of modern Canada owes much to the work of eighteenth-century Scots pioneers such as these, subsequently continued by figures like the Lowland peer Thomas Douglas, 5th Earl of Selkirk, who tried to settle Highlanders in Canada both as a way of improving the lot of an exploited people and as a defence screen against American aggression.

Almost all who crossed the Atlantic were, of course, seeking in some sense to better themselves. Scottish professionals usually returned to Scotland or to England after a spell as 'sojourners in the sun' making money in the West Indies or on the Chesapeake. The patrician speculators or glory-hunters, if they lived, always went home. But steady absorption into settler society was the mundane reality for the vast majority of Scots who chose to traverse the ocean. Much emigration involved individuals and single families, commonly arriving as indentured servants whose labour on arrival repaid the cost of their passage. Yet it could also entail the transplanting of entire communities. Some were religious dissenters, like Robert Sandeman, son of a Perth merchant and prominent in the Glasite church, who, with a community of fellow-believers, ended his days in Connecticut. A few groups comprised genuine political refugees, leaving Scotland because of their anti-Hanoverian beliefs or radical aspirations. Others were unwilling emigrants – transported convicts, including those found guilty of insurgency. Notable shiploads of the latter arrived in North America following both major Jacobite risings: the *Friendship* and *God Speed* docked in Maryland in 1717 with defeated Scottish rebels taken at Preston, the *Johnson* also arriving there from Liverpool thirty years later with the chastened followers of Charles Edward Stuart.

Each emigrant community had its distinctive Scottish origins as well as its preferred North American destination. And it is worth remembering in this regard that tens of thousands of ethnic Scots actually left Britain not from Scotland itself but from Ireland: in 1718, not an untypical year, five ships carrying over seven hundred 'Scots Irish' arrived in Boston. These Ulster Scots settled in particularly large numbers in the Appalachian mountains of Kentucky and Tennessee, as well as in Pennsylvania – a region robustly presbyterian in the colonial era, though in the nineteenth century a tidal wave of Baptism swept over them, as over most of the upper South. In rather different circumstances, Gaelic-speaking communities also emigrated en masse from Scotland, often led by clan gentry or tacksmen. One especially popular destination for Highlanders from the 1720s was the Cape Fear River in the Carolinas: here the early Scottish settlers came most frequently from Argyllshire, among the first Highland districts to experience the pressures introduced by tenurial reform.

By 1776, as many as 12,000 Scottish emigrants had settled in this region alone. Perhaps the best-known were the tacksman Allan MacDonald of Kingsburgh and his wife Flora, who in 1746 had helped the Young Pretender evade capture by the redcoats. In the north of New York, which until the 1760s remained part of a buffer zone between New France north of the St Lawrence and the British colonies to the south and east of the Great Lakes, the Scots were again particularly welcome: the Superintendent of the Northern Indian Department had long been Sir William Johnson, an Irishman who encouraged Highland ex-officers to settle with their dependants in territories he controlled in the Mohawk Valley. Not infrequently, once inured to American pioneer life, the Scots would then head west. Setting out from Georgia (with its evocatively named settlement of New Inverness in the Darien district, established in the 1730s, mainly by Mackintosh clansmen) and from the other southern territories where Scottish traders and settlers had played a disproportionate part in establishing and stabilising the more recent British colonies, they would also be among the earliest Europeans to set out across the Alleghenies and into the unclaimed lands bisected by the Ohio River.

Given these patterns of extensive but also diverse Scottish involvement throughout the colonies of the Atlantic seaboard, it is hardly surprising that the outbreak of the American Revolution in the 1770s should have been so deeply perplexing. After all, some of the very latest arrivals were grizzled veterans of Scottish regiments such as the 77th (Montgomery's) Highlanders, who had recently helped expel France from North America. Ex-soldiers and their families now found themselves in a divided colonial community seeking to break away from the empire for which they had just fought so doggedly. In Georgia, in the Carolinas and in New York, the majority instinctively followed their social superiors and once more took up arms for the crown. Numerous ex-Jacobites were among these Loyalists, and were apparently comfortable in their new roles as die-hard partisans for the Hanoverian dynasty. MacDonald of Kingsburgh found himself first a major-general, then imprisoned by his erstwhile American neighbours, before deciding, perhaps understandably, to re-emigrate back to Skye. The North Carolina Highlanders were actually a six-hundred-strong regiment formed from Scots Loyalists. Such people fought for a British empire in which they genuinely believed, and in whose continued success and stability, with favourable tenures and tangible interests in colonial property, they often had a significant personal investment.

Other Scots, meanwhile, participated actively on the Patriot side. Thomas Leiper, a tobacco merchant from Lanarkshire, was a prominent Philadelphian who fought in several of the war's early engagements. James Swann, an emigrant clerk from Fife, took part in the 'Boston Tea Party' and was twice wounded at Bunker Hill. John Paul Jones from Arbigland in Kirkcudbrightshire, lately resident in Virginia, fought his way into the pantheon of the United States Navy. James Wilson from Ceres in Fife was, with John Witherspoon, one of two Scottish-born signatories of the Declaration of Independence and a vocal early advocate of armed resistance to the British government. Ultimately there were four Patriot major-generals and twenty-two brigadier-generals of discernible Scottish extraction – including first-generation settlers like Alexander MacDougall, a New York merchant who had left Islay with his parents in the 1720s, and Arthur St Clair from Thurso in Caithness, an Edinburgh medical graduate and veteran of Quebec who had settled in Pennsylvania.

The Scots therefore were necessarily divided by the Revolution, not least because of their own varied circumstances. Many of the resident merchants in the colonial ports, like the factors of the tobacco companies, had never intended to settle permanently and thus failed utterly to identify with the American cause. Scots were also predictably unpopular with the indebted planters in particular, while the instinctive Loyalism of the majority of the more recent Scottish arrivals again made them automatic bogey-figures to active Patriots. Yet others from Scotland did feel a natural affinity with the aggrieved colonists. Indeed, some had already contributed substantially to colonial life and to the development of a distinctive American identity and culture. The inspirational Witherspoon at Princeton, and both William Smith and Francis Alison, who with Franklin founded what became the University of Pennslyvania, played key roles in building the peculiar institutional fabric of what was now emerging as a new nation. Earlier, the remarkable James Blair, former episcopalian minister of Cranston in Midlothian, had established the College of William and Mary at

Williamsburg in Virginia. Many clergymen and doctors of the late colonial period were emigrant Scots of this kind, and were natural pillars of their American communities. Hundreds of American-born professionals had also travelled in the opposite direction, graduating from Scotland's increasingly prestigious universities where often they had imbibed the liberal thinking which was so evident among some of the Scottish professoriate. Their education, their social position and their political inclinations again made such people effective leaders of the American resistance to the imperial government.

Substantial settlements by Scots, and an active part in community leadership, also characterised the early history of Canada, a trend greatly reinforced in the years immediately before and especially following the American Revolution. Prince Edward Island received a mixed party of Catholic Highlanders and Dumfries-shire presbyterians in 1767. More came to the island in the next few years, notably John MacDonald, a laird from Glenaladale in Inverness-shire, who in 1773 settled there with people from both South Uist and his native Moidart. Subsequently MacDonald formed the 84th Royal Highland Emigrant Regiment, a two-battalion unit, for government service against the American rebels. In 1773 a group of Highland families from Wester Ross, Inverness-shire and Sutherland settled in Nova Scotia, displacing the native Micmac Indians: by an irony too often overlooked, though it was repeated again and again in North America and later in Australasia, Scots who nursed righteous grievances about the tenurial revolution at home consoled themselves by dispossessing indigenous peoples of their own lands. Others established what remains to this day the Gaelic-speaking community of Cape Breton.

That same year McDonell clansmen, led by their tacksmen, escaped from tenurial changes in Inverness-shire first by emigrating to upper New York and then, as United Empire Loyalists, moving north after 1776 into what became Glengarry County on the border between Upper and Lower Canada (the modern provinces of Ontario and Quebec). Here they were joined by a further party of newly emigrated MacDonells from Glenelg led by their Catholic priest. New Brunswick, meanwhile, received two regiments of disbanded Loyalists after the Revolution. Thus by the time that emigrations, removals and evictions peaked in the early nineteenth-century Scottish Highlands, Canada had already emerged as a favoured destination for whole communities of emigrants looking to put down roots in a familiar but more promising environment already peopled by kinsfolk who could provide information, guidance, shelter and cultural integration for new arrivals from Scotland.

While we have so far emphasised the impact of the Scots on North America, we would do well to note the reciprocal effect of imperial ties on

Scotland itself. For the country was undoubtedly altered by its increasing contact with the Americas. As we have seen, although the Scottish population grew rapidly through the eighteenth century, by 1800 it was clearly growing less dramatically than England's or, especially, Ireland's. Emigration, overwhelmingly to North America, was perhaps the most obvious limiting factor. Exact figures will never be known, but present estimates put trans-Atlantic emigration from Scotland at around 75,000 people between 1700 and 1780, of whom 80 per cent were from the Lowlands. By 1800 perhaps a further 15,000 had crossed the ocean, now preponderantly Highlanders heading for the Maritime Provinces or eastern Upper Canada. Even taking no account of the children and grandchildren of emigrants, who were also irretrievably lost to Scottish society, emigration on such a scale – with the century's likely total number of departures equivalent to at least 15 per cent of the actual population increase experienced in Scotland over the same period – can only have depressed significantly the rate of domestic demographic expansion.

Similarly Glasgow's prodigious growth can in part be attributed to its proximity to the imperial trading routes converging in the Firth of Clyde. The blessings of American and West Indian commerce, bringing wealth to the Speirs and Glassfords as well as elegant townhouses, docks, retail developments and an enhanced civic infrastructure to the city, were also widely felt. They underwrote the emerging provincial banking system in the west, while the Atlantic trade directly stimulated other enterprises as diverse as rope manufacturing, sugar refining and textile production. Indeed, vertical integration of this sort was essential, and was particularly significant in the tobacco trade – allowing the Scottish syndicates to procure export cargoes for their ships and goods for their stores concentrated at the head of the navigable rivers draining the Chesapeake plantations. It was those goods which in turn helped the Scots keep colonial planters enmeshed in the web of credit that sustained their lifestyles. Although current research has not yet permitted accurate quantification, it seems unlikely that industrialisation in west-central Scotland, by the 1770s requiring capital on an unprecedented scale, did not also benefit directly from the profits remitted by the Atlantic economy.

The political impact of the American empire on Scotland must likewise have been significant, however difficult this also is to enumerate. As we have seen, members of Jacobite families in particular reintegrated with the British state through active service, troop-raising and settlement-sponsorship. But the same was true of the hitherto problematical Highlands as a whole: the energies and ambitions of Gaelic-speaking Scots were channelled into regimental heroism and pioneering, which, in the minds of admiring non-Gaels, quickly became their special contribution to the realisation of

Britain's imperial destiny. In general terms, the military and administrative openings across the Atlantic simultaneously increased the patronage openings available to Scotland's politicians and their managers. At the same time, personal involvement in America also played a part in furthering the domestic influence of many individuals: James Abercrombie from Stirlingshire, sometime attorney-general of South Carolina and a colonial plantation owner, had by the mid-1760s become MP for Clackmannanshire, while several Scottish participants in the West Indian trade subsequently secured seats in the Commons – for English as well as Scottish constituencies. It therefore seems likely that Scotland's politics were at least given greater richness and, perhaps, an increased fluidity as a direct result of the opportunities presented by the North American empire.

India and the East

Before 1707 the Scots were virtually unknown in India – despite it having been part of the Darien Company's original intention to open up trade between Scotland and the East Indies. It is therefore difficult to interpret their subsequent heavy involvement in colonisation and commerce in Asia as anything other than a seminal consequence of Union. Most of the subcontinent, of course, remained independent even in 1780. But by the end of that decade the East India Company's increasing holdings in India in the three Presidencies of Bengal, Madras and Bombay had been taken over by the crown. Scots, like Irishmen, were disproportionately active in the Company's armies (where commissions were cheap, a real consideration for the penniless younger son of a laird or a squireen). Just as the Irishman Laurence Sulivan rose to be the principal Company man of business by the 1750s, so did a Scot, Henry Dundas, dominate the new era of government control after 1784.

Walpole may have been bribing Scots with Company patronage in the 1730s, and a growing number of Scottish doctors had certainly begun to penetrate the Indian medical service from an early date. But Scottish soldiers and administrators saw their major achievements largely concentrated in the period following Clive's victory at Plassey in 1757, which initially won Bengal for the Company, and especially the years of Warren Hastings's terms as Governor of Bengal and later Governor-General of India. It was, for example, not Clive but Sir Hector Munro of Novar who won the really conclusive engagement in Bengal, at Buxar in 1764, where he overcome the Nawab's forces and decisively confirmed Company control in the north-east. Munro, it should be added, also lost the less well-known battle of Pollilur in 1780: his use of Gaelic in communication was a measure of the

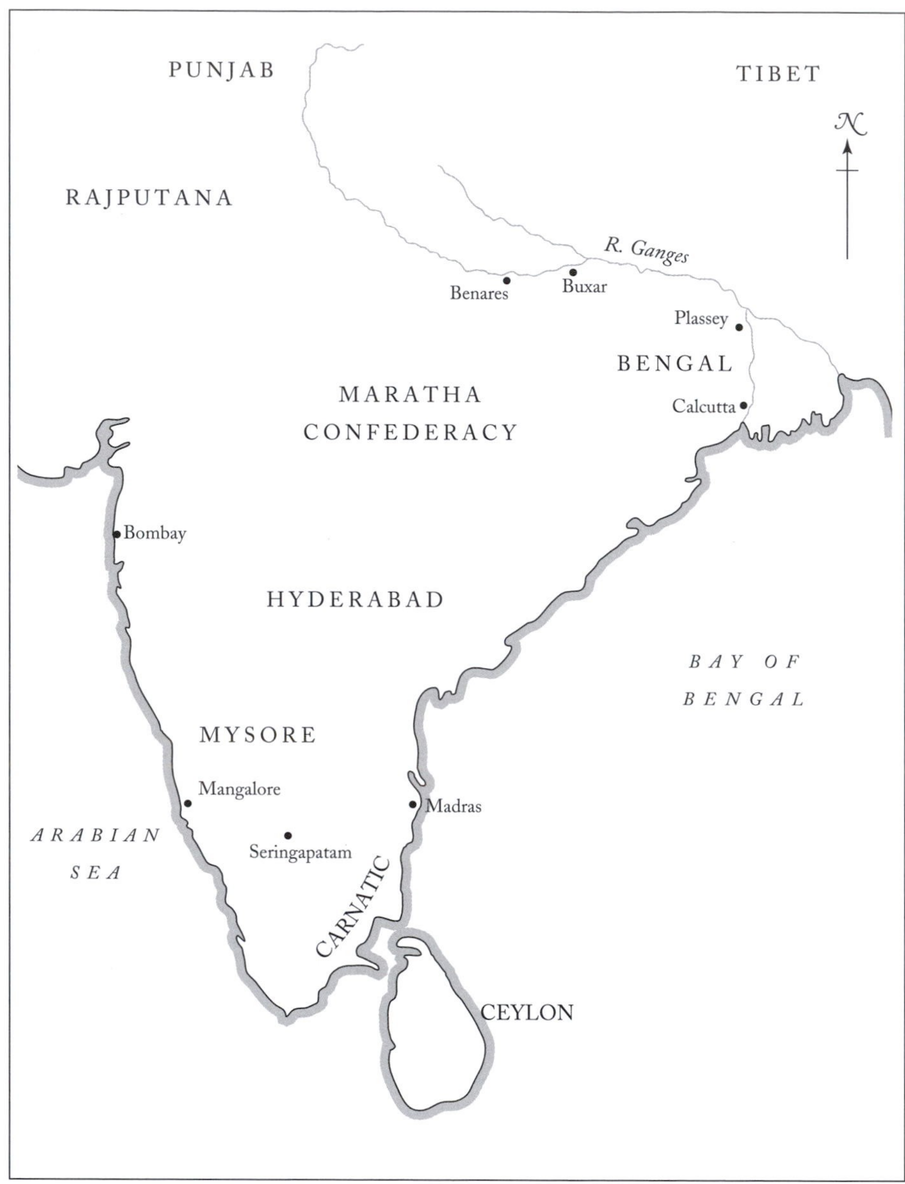

Map 4 India in the eighteenth century

Madras Presidency's lack of basic preparation for war, including military cyphers, yet the expedient also hints at the preponderance of Scots, and Highlanders in particular, among Munro's colleagues. Others were prominent in the conflicts against Haider Ali, Raja of Mysore, and his celebrated son Tipu Sahib, the next obstacles in the Company's path: William Fullarton and John Campbell (who led the desperate defence of Mangalore in 1783–84) were only among the most noteworthy. When at Seringapatam in 1799 Tipu was finally killed, fittingly it was another Scot, Sir David Baird, from Newbyth in East Lothian, who secured a victory which finally secured the Company's grip on southern India.

Scots were also involved in rather more cerebral strategies for the extension of British power. None was more spectacularly successful than the unlikely Hugh Cleghorn, sometime professor of civil history at St Andrews, who, tiring of hum-drum academic life (he had made, it has to be said, little original contribution to the Scottish Enlightenment), conceived for himself an unusual role in the exotic world of Asian imperialism. Exploiting his chance acquaintance with the brother of the owner of Swiss mercenaries garrisoning the Dutch possession of Ceylon, which was in serious danger of being ceded to Revolutionary France, he bought them from their erstwhile employers in 1795 and then reached Ceylon after a hazardous journey down the Red Sea to assert his proprietory rights. This allowed British forces from Madras to take the island almost unopposed the following year.

Other Scots put their education to good use, learning Persian, the universal language of empire in India, as well as the local vernaculars. Sir Thomas Munro, the son of a tobacco merchant and a Glasgow graduate, earned his spurs as a subaltern in the Mysore wars but also picked up both Persian and Hindustani along the way. By the 1790s Munro had developed an effective system of public revenue, levying land dues directly from peasant *ryots* rather than through a tax-farming class of *zemindars*. His conviction, unfashionable and disastrously ignored by his successors, was that British officials should work with and not against the grain of Indian conditions: 'We make laws for them as though they were Englishmen', he observed, 'and are surprised that they should have no operation. A law might be a very good one in England, and useless here.' He also concluded that, once the native peoples had 'become sufficiently enlightened to frame a regular Government for themselves, and to conduct and preserve it . . . it will probably be best for both countries that the British control of India should be gradually withdrawn'. Such precocious insights made Munro one of the age's most admired administrators, the recipient of a knighthood and in due course Governor of Madras.

The intellectual skills honed by a Scottish education could also be turned to advantage in other ways. Alexander Dalrymple, Lord Hailes's brother and Adam Smith's friend, was a brilliant polymath, the first hydrographer to the Company and the father of the Admiralty chart. His failure to secure the leadership of the Australasian voyage subsequently undertaken by Cook was owing to a prohibition on non-Royal Navy commanders, but it pushed Dalrymple towards a career in cartography at a time when the extent of the southern continent and the existence of the fabled North-West Passage were still matters of contention. Others were plainly enchanted by Asia. George Bogle, from a Lanarkshire family prominently involved in the tobacco trade, led a pioneering embassy to the Teshu Lama in 1774, becoming the first Briton to cross the Himalayas to Tibet. Bogle even took a local wife and was deeply attracted by Tibetan culture: 'Farewell ye honest and simple people', was his moving valediction, 'May ye long enjoy that happiness which is denied to more polished nations.' John Gilchrist produced the first English–Hindustani dictionary and became a seminal Asian grammarian: his pious hope, characteristically Scottish in its assumption that in education lies the key to worldly success, was that all Company employees might be 'in future obliged first to qualify themselves as linguists'.

Intellectual gifts were clearly no bar to Indian achievement. Yet it was more usual to proceed by steady promotion through the Company's ranks. Scots who took this more orthodox route to high office included Jonathan Duncan from Wardhouse in Angus, at first a writer in Calcutta but by 1795 Governor of Bombay: he became greatly interested in native education, establishing the first Sanskrit university at Benares in 1788. Sir John 'Boy' Malcolm, from a Dumfries-shire farming family of seventeen children, went out to India at the tender age of thirteen, impressing the appointing committee with the boast that, if he should meet Haider Ali, he would 'Take out my sword and cut off his heid'. Becoming an expert in Persian affairs and a trusted aide of the young Arthur Wellesley, he too eventually became Governor of Bombay, and, like Munro and Duncan, shared the fascination with Indian society and culture shown by many British men in India prior to 1800. Sir John Macpherson, son of the scholarly Gaelic minister from Sleat on Skye and cousin of Ossian's translator, rose from a clerkship to become Hastings's successor as Governor-General in 1785–86 (though allegations of dubious business practices earned him the amusing soubriquet 'Johnny MacShuffle' and early replacement after a period in office for which in fact much may be said).

Such successes were never solely the result of undue Scottish influence in London: conspicuous talent, brashness and good fortune all catapulted individuals, often from relatively unprepossessing backgrounds, to success in the dynamic, expansive and essentially opportunistic career environment that was eighteenth-century India. Yet under Hastings in the 1770s, who advanced his 'Scotch guardians' on meritocratic principles, their share of appointments in Bengal, the richest Presidency, rose inexorably from a generous one-third to at least one-half. By the late 1780s a growing number of domestic critics readily placed all of the blame for manifest Scottish pre-eminence in India where they wanted to believe that it lay: specifically, with Dundas, who, from 1781 when he chaired a parliamentary investigation into alleged Company malpractice under Hastings and particularly after 1793 when he became President of the government's new Board of Control, was the greatest single source of Asian patronage in the British Isles.

Untangling the precise relationship between Scotland and India by this stage has never been easy: the aphorism of a later Scottish Prime Minister, the Earl of Rosebery, that Dundas had 'Scotticised India, and Orientalised Scotland' expresses well the exaggeration which has flourished in this area though also capturing an important reciprocity. How far Asian opportunities were merely a tradable currency for the furtherance of domestic political ambitions, and how far his grip on Scottish public life was actually the means by which Dundas leveraged himself into a position from which to impose his vision of British imperialism, is unclear. Certainly Dundas had strong views about the emerging Indian empire. He favoured a less rapacious policy by the crown than that pursued by the Company. He also saw the subcontinent as a strong geopolitical counterpoise to the lost American colonies: it was this assessment of Asia's potential to be the new focal point of Britain's global power, setting him at odds with his Eurocentric cabinet colleague Grenville, the Foreign Secretary, that helped bring about in 1801 the summary ejection of Napoleon from Egypt, also allowing Dundas's countryman Sir Ralph Abercromby, the leader of the expedition, a hero's death at Alexandria.

Scott's observation in 1821 that 'India is the corn chest for Scotland, where we poor gentry must send our younger sons as we send our black cattle to the south', the inevitable overstatement of a phrase-mongering literary man, also contains the nub of reality. We have already seen how the 'nabobs' were enriched by their Indian activities: to those mentioned earlier might be added entrepreneurs like Alexander Brodie, the Madras merchant who became MP for the Elgin Burghs, Sir Alexander MacLeod, who repatriated sufficient funds to purchase Harris in 1778 and to attempt the improvement of the local fisheries, or John Farquhar from Crimond in Aberdeenshire, a Company chemist and subsequently an explosives manufacturer in Bombay, who amassed rather more than £1,000,000 at eighteenth-century values before returning home to an English mansion. Scotland's soldiers were not far behind. The victor of Buxar held the Inverness Burghs for thirty-four years from 1768. Fullarton was MP for the Haddington Burghs in 1787 and for Ayrshire in 1796: an opposition Whig, he actually led the parliamentary assault on Hastings. Robert Abercromby, former Commander-in-Chief of Indian Forces, followed his brother Sir Ralph as MP for Clackmannanshire in the 1790s. Sir Alexander Campbell of Inverneil, formerly governor of both Jamaica and Madras and the major-general who in 1787 raised the 74th Highlanders for Indian service, similarly found himself at Westminster representing the same Stirling (or Dunfermline) Burghs which in the 1730s had been squabbled over by the Erskines and Halkett of Pitfirrane and which had subsequently also been represented for a time by Cochrane, the future Governor of Dominica: married to a grand-daughter of the poet Ramsay, who had once been so profoundly sceptical about the Union's supposed benefits, Campbell's career nicely illustrates the immense opportunities for advancement that empire had in fact opened up. Even James Campbell of Succoth, rising from humble subaltern in the Madras army in 1771 to the modest seniority of colonel by 1797, returned to Scotland and a house in Edinburgh's New Town with a fortune of £25,000.

Other effects of Scottish contact with Asia can also be clearly identified. Imported Asian goods were, of course, inevitable even without the Union: they would simply have been bought from the Dutch. But the peculiar obsession with Eastern tastes and styles which increasingly gripped Scottish consumers, like those in eighteenth-century England, was reinforced by appreciation of the patriotic achievements in commerce and colonisation which lay behind the products now available in Stirling, Aberdeen or Edinburgh. Widening access to Asian commodities was nevertheless double-edged. Unfamiliar foodstuffs imported by the Company, some from within its Indian territorial empire but others from its trading stations at Mocha on the Red Sea or Canton in China, created a whole new social environment for Scots: ultimately neither Addison's coffee-house culture nor the polite tea-drinking of the Rev. Ridpath in rural Berwickshire were conceivable without Britain's global commercial extension. Yet the same novelties attracted suspicion in equal proportions. In the 1720s Mackintosh of Borlum, the venerable Jacobite, was complaining that 'Formerly I had been served with two or three substantial dishes of beef, mutton, and fowl, garnished with their own wholesome gravy . . . [but] I am now served up little expensive ashets with English pickles, Indian mangoes, and anchovy sauces.' By century's end Ramsay of Ochtertyre could reflect quizzically on his countrymen's early prejudice that tea was simply 'an expensive, unpleasant drug'.

More pertinently, the taste for Chinese porcelain and silks, for new beverages and exotic spices, gave Scotland's visionary political thinkers further ammunition for troubling comparisons between the burgeoning British empire and ancient Rome. Fears of fatal exposure to the luxurious material culture and absolutist political traditions of Asia co-existed uneasily with the high-flown imperial bombast. John Logan's *A Dissertation on the Government,*

Manners and Spirit of Asia (1787) deployed a variant on the Enlightenment's characteristic theory of natural social evolution to argue that because of their stifling climate, their mild-mannered religion and their sheer physical openness, 'the plains of Asia form the seat of despotism'. William Robertson, too, surveying early European history in the glorious aftermath of Plassey and Buxar, dwelled at length upon the deadly entanglement of imperial Rome with the East, hinting darkly that a similar fate might yet befall his British readers through their blind infatuation with India.

Yet Asia also produced less pessimistic responses from some Scottish thinkers. Robertson is again a good example, the *Historical Disquisition Concerning the Knowledge Which the Ancients Had of India* (1791) proving that the shafts of insight obtained by first-hand visitors like Bogle and Malcolm were steadily percolating through to growing numbers back home who devoured vicariously the bewildering but incomparably stimulating experience of the East. For Robertson, indeed, Indian religion proved conclusively that certain features of human religiosity are common to other cultures – in short, that the same processes of development are truly at work in all societies. John Williamson, the curious quasi-mystical figure from Moffat in the Dumfries-shire hills who befriended the young Boswell, managed to acquire for himself the exotic soubriquet 'Brachman' and wrote an extensive manuscript tract, Scotland's first essay in philosophical vegetarianism, praising the abstinence of the Hindu priesthood. Even Farquhar, the explosives magnate, was reputedly influenced in his personal life by the Indian propensity for asceticism.

The consequences of the Scots' fascination with India were therefore diverse. For the Haldane brothers it helped make them by 1800 among the greatest dissenting preachers in Scotland, converting whole communities to evangelical Christianity in otherwise unpropitious regions such as the Small Isles. It was in India that their consciences had first been pricked by the problem of mass ignorance: opposition from the Company and Dundas to his plan for missionary work in Bengal was almost certainly what had led Robert to conceive the significantly titled Society for Propagating of the Gospel at Home. In genteel Perth, meanwhile, the Literary and Antiquarian Society, originally preoccupied with narrow concerns like the Pictish standing stones of Strathearn and the economic history of Scotland's provincial towns, was by the late 1780s hankering enthusiastically after more extensive knowledge of Asia, urgently requesting a copy of 'the Asiatic Miscellany by a Society in India' and collecting botanical and zoological artefacts brought back from the tropics. Plainly, the reality of global empire in the first century of Union had begun to stimulate the Scots' imaginations in myriad different ways. But how far had it also changed their image of themselves?

An imperial Union

Empire was in fact integral to eighteenth-century assessments of the Anglo-Scottish state's position in the contemporary world. Indeed, it became increasingly common for Hanoverian Scots themselves, much more plausibly than it could ever have been for their predecessors who had vainly coveted Darien, to regard commercial and territorial success overseas not only as economically beneficial but as a just reflection of their own destiny as a free and Protestant people. This imperial dimension, as Dundas once declared in the Commons, clearly demonstrated how much the Scots in particular had gained by the treaty: 'The Union has increased the privilege of the Scotch members', he argued in 1799, 'for, instead of confining their deliberations to the affairs of Scotland, they are empowered to take part in discussions respecting the affairs . . . of the whole British empire.' Evidently a Scot, at least as much as an Englishman, could bask in the dignity and the power conferred by empire.

Yet different conclusions about the imperial experience could still emerge, carrying with them important further implications for the Scots' self-image. For, by accustoming men to the absolute power characteristic of alien societies, empire was also perfectly capable of diminishing rather than vindicating the rights of 'free-born Britons' at home. Robert Watson, Cleghorn's erstwhile St Andrews colleague and the age's definitive historian of Philip II, dwelled morbidly upon the temptations to which the sixteenth-century Spaniards had supposedly succumbed: empire had made them 'a nation noted for their violent use of power in the Netherlands and Italy, infamous for the barbarities which they had exercised over the natives of America . . .'. Watson's nervousness about the potential consequences of empire, shared by Scots as different as the younger Ramsay and Dempster (the latter railed in the Commons against the 'rapines and cruelties' of the 'eastern species of government'), were natural in classically trained men for whom Rome presented the obvious parallel: this ancient precedent appeared to prove conclusively that colonial success, especially in Asia, had always been politically threatening as well as economically rewarding, morally sapping as well as irresistibly alluring.

Empire, indispensable to any realistic evaluation of their nation's place in the eighteenth-century world, may at the same time have helped suppress any vestigial Scottish tendencies towards renewed independence. It certainly contributed to weakening what had remained for longer a much more widely shared aspiration: the continuation of that substantial semi-autonomy which had initially survived the Union. The Hanoverian state had, after all, successfully weathered the Jacobite threat, the American debacle, and even, for most of the century, the severe menace periodically presented by France. Its winning combination of political durability, relative internal tolerance and an ability to generate impressive economic growth exerted an increasingly powerful pull on Scottish loyalties. And the seemingly limitless fruits of empire further encouraged among those with significant political and economic interests a generally positive evaluation of the Anglo-Scottish state's credentials. Along with the related commercial acceleration which overtook Scotland from the 1740s, burgeoning global opportunities were among the most conspicuous merits of a Union which had initially disappointed the forecasts of its most ardent supporters.

With regard to the perennially delicate question of their relative access to the patronage networks central to the Hanoverian polity, it is likely that overseas jobs were of disproportionate importance to the formation of political identity among those Scots who sought or secured them. As we have seen, in North America, especially Canada, and in late eighteenth-century India above all, Scots reaped after the 1750s not merely a reasonable but a quite indecent share of the spoils. Every holder of a British office or commission, meanwhile, especially one who had seen a wider world from the perspective of Bengal or New Brunswick, was also a man less likely to oppose robustly the further erosion of those many exclusively Scottish domestic institutions and practices, indispensable only when regarded from Aberdeenshire or East Lothian, which had at first been left untouched by the Union. In striking contrast with the 1720s and 1730s, when the treaty had still to deliver substantial benefits and resistance to anglicisation even saw popular rioting winked at by elements within Scotland's own elite, the generation of the early nineteenth century, their attitudes and expectations moulded by successful experience within the wider British imperial state, proved far less willing to object.

The Scots' admission to the empire had, of course, one further long-term implication. For emigration and settlement, which first became significant during the eighteenth century and expanded further in the nineteenth with the opening-up of the Australasian colonies, not only underlined their own investment in imperialism. It also established living links between Scotland and other British territories around the globe. Especially in the colonies of settlement, emigration stimulated a heavy stress on Scottish ethnicity, still echoed today in the far-flung Burns Suppers, St Andrew's Balls and Highland Games of the diaspora. Conversely, so long as the empire remained an important reality, it also contributed to a sense of joint enterprise with other British peoples. It therefore seems likely that the enduring strength of British identity deep into the twentieth century, despite its coalescence only in the last three hundred years, owes more than a little to the successful eighteenth-century activities of a thrusting Anglo-Scottish state on the world stage.

CHAPTER SIX

Endings

By 1800, many of the currents shaping Scottish life through much of the previous hundred years had begun perceptibly to ebb. This was a matter for agreement among otherwise discordant commentators. Cockburn, looking back wistfully to this period, claimed that his own early adulthood (he turned twenty-one at the dawn of the new century) had in fact been the 'last purely Scotch age' – indeed that 'the eighteenth was the final Scotch century'. John Gibson Lockhart, Scott's son-in-law, judged that, compared with the expansiveness once characterising the life of the mind in Scotland, people had begun mentally to batten down the hatches: 'The circle within which men's thoughts move', he wrote in 1819, 'becomes every day a narrower one. . . .' Even the erudition and civility of the Scottish church, a commonplace for eighteenth-century observers like Smollett and Pennant, was no longer widely accepted. Sir William Hamilton, holder of the chairs of civil history at Edinburgh from 1821 and then of logic and metaphysics after 1836, considered presbyterianism in retrospect almost a regrettable commitment on the part of the Scots, their national religious heritage merely 'the choice of an unlearned people'. A less likely slur could not have been imagined by Hamilton's proud, cultivated and patriotic Moderate predecessors of the 1770s.

While one might disagree with the details of each of these undeniably polemical nineteenth-century statements, there remain grounds for accepting the contemporary consensus that, shortly before or after 1800, Scotland had entered a new era. This was, of course, partly a simple question of overwhelming economic *force majeure.* Urbanisation was accelerating dramatically, as the inaugural UK census, conducted in the first year of the new century, revealed. Industrialisation, and especially mechanisation, was also becoming more widespread and more deep-seated. The timeless resources of men's hands and muscles, the labour of their animals and their exploitation of naturally flowing water were being replaced as the foundation of society's material existence by complex machinery powered by steam engines and capable of hitherto unimaginable productivity. By the 1830s both Scots and English alike accepted that a recognisably different kind of society had emerged, with consequences for the way in which people thought about their own place in the world. 'Men have grown mechanical in hand and heart', Thomas Carlyle, Scotland's first definitively post-Enlightenment philosopher, was able to lament by 1829: 'They have lost faith in individual endeavour, and in natural force, of any kind.'

The quickening pace of economic development also had social and political implications. Something very close to class relations had begun to coalesce, first of all in Scotland's industrial workplaces. By the 1820s the experience of proletarianisation among manual workers had produced the first modern trade unions. Indeed, political sentiments were increasingly capable of uniting a disparate and geographically dispersed population throughout Britain, whether of reformers or of radicals. Meanwhile, economic change was having drastic consequences for whole communities. In 1806 the most notorious tenant evictions of all, those on the Sutherland estates overseen by Patrick Sellar and James Loch, got underway, initiating the great age of forced removal. In the Lowland towns, too, the sudden narrowing of the price–income gap during the 1790s was for many Scottish workers, now accustomed to steadily improving living standards, a rude shock and an early taste of the characteristic vagaries of industrial capitalism. After 1810 the urban experience of growing numbers of migrants was yet further darkened by the onset of epidemic fevers: typhus, and later cholera, actually produced in places like Edinburgh and Glasgow a rising death rate, a malevolent reversal of eighteenth-century trends. It was therefore clear that a new and difficult period in Scotland's demographic history had dawned: towns, once simply the benign markers of a society's prosperity and sophistication – literally of its 'civility' and 'urbanity' – were seen also to bring intractable social ills in their wake.

The French Revolution, in sweeping away France's *ancien régime* and creating unprecedented tensions in the relationship between governors and governed in Britain, also contributed both to the changing political realities and to the perceptible mood of *fin de siècle*. In the late 1790s the political elite was forced to close ranks. But the failure of the radical movement merely stored up problems for the future. Dundas himself soon left office, at first the victim of Pitt's unexpected resignation following the failure to achieve Catholic Emancipation in the wake of the Irish Act of Union, then impeached (though ultimately acquitted) on charges of malversation involving naval funds. Scottish contemporaries were shocked and amazed at the spectacular fall of a figure who to them epitomised Scotland's mature post-Union politics. Even his opponent Brougham, Edinburgh reformer and future Lord Chancellor of England, noted how 'men awaited in trembling the uncertain event, as all living things quail during the solemn pause that precedes an earthquake'. As things transpired, Dundas's countrymen were right to be nervous: Scotland would never again possess a colossus at the heart of the Westminster system so adept at protecting the country's semi-autonomous structures and making the Union work to the Scots' advantage. By the 1830s, the triumph of progressive Scottish Whiggism, led by Cockburn, Jeffrey and Brougham, would bring modernisation to Scotland's legal, educational and political systems, which, to its native opponents, looked suspiciously like anglicisation by another name.

At the same time, the general souring of the political atmosphere in the decades following the French Revolution had other unforeseen and unwelcome side-effects. Not least of these was the ideological polarisation of Scotland's academic and literary communities – symbolised by competing journals, the waspishly Whiggish *Edinburgh Review* (from 1802) and later the abrasively Tory *Quarterly Review* (from 1809: London-based but with a strong Scottish input) and *Blackwood's Magazine* (from 1817). Clubs and societies also began to suffer: in the 1820s, for example, the historian of the Perth Literary and Antiquarian Society, trying to explain its unaccustomed inactivity during the last years of the eighteenth century, observed that 'in the troubled state of the political world in 1792, and for some years after, they might not have found it convenient to call the members together'. Such crippling anxiety was a far cry from the clubbable age of Hume and Smith in the 1760s, when ideological partisanship – reviled by most right-thinking men as the antithesis of Addisonian politeness and propriety – had seemed distasteful. Disturbing organisations such as the United Scotsmen, dangerous phenomena such as the 'Pike Plot' was presumed to be, and the general rancour which attended any explicit discussion of progressive political aspirations by 1793, all belonged to a different world created primarily by the shattering events across the English Channel.

The Scottish Enlightenment itself, if it survived at all, had also entered into a new phase by 1800. Aesthetically, Scottish culture had since the 1760s been drifting away from the cool classicism and self-restraint counselled by *The Spectator*, first towards the sickly-sweet sentimentalism of *The Man of Feeling* and then on to the ragingly popular Gothicism and historical romanticism of Scott. Indeed, the latter's novels were such a success because they tapped into a growing understanding by 1814 that the mid-eighteenth-century world of 'sixty years since' (as *Waverley*'s subtitle evocatively put it) had finally passed from living memory. At the same time, the new aesthetic obsessions – Gothic, Grecian and Celtic – seemed to offer an imaginative re-connection with antiquity in which might be found the stability and solace necessary for many Scots in a period of unparalleled and disorientating change. The values of which this architectural vocabulary spoke, such as community, kin, piety, chivalry, honour, self-sacrifice and human dignity, also explain much about the popularity achieved by Scott's novels. Rooted in an impregnable historical past, they seemed to provide an uplifting antidote to the worship of utility, profit and materialism which Carlyle influentially condemned: 'Practically considered, our creed is Fatalism', he wailed in the 1820s, '. . . free in hand and foot, we are shackled in heart and soul.'

Nor, as a coherent critique of recent developments in Scotland, was Hamilton's side-swipe at the national church entirely unfair. The increasing strength of the evangelical party by 1800 meant that Hill's Moderate establishment was under threat from within, even as the continued growth of the dissenting presbyterian churches among the labourers, skilled workers and prosperous middle classes was making a mockery of the Church of Scotland's historic claim to represent the whole nation at prayer. A generation later, events proved even more fatal to its pretensions. The evangelicals, led by the formidable Thomas Chalmers, finally marched out of the General Assembly in 1843, enacting the Disruption which produced two rival institutions, the rump Church of Scotland and the new Free Church of Scotland. Even during the Ten Years' War of legal and political conflict which preceded this cataclysm, there were grounds for thinking that the golden age of powerful, respected and cultivated individuals like Robertson, Blair, Home and Carlyle, whose consummate manipulation of the established church ended with their own deaths in the 1790s and early 1800s, had decisively passed away. At the same time, the increasing denominational diversity within Scottish Protestantism, added to the social and economic transformation of the country, was steadily undermining the remaining credibility of those ecclesiastically based structures in education, moral control and welfare provision which had long characterised Scotland's distinctive civil society.

It is therefore possible to agree with the next generation that the beginning of the nineteenth century did represent a natural ending to an important phase of Scotland's history. Yet we are entitled to ask what the enduring legacies of the preceding century nevertheless were. Above all, the age had created the Union. As importantly, it also made it work. For the forging of the British state and of a British identity was to be profoundly significant for generations after 1800. The Scots' successful and profitable incorporation into the Westminster political system shaped their own future national development. It also ensured that Great Britain would play a leading part in world affairs. As a focus of patriotic loyalty and a stable basis for effective political action, the fledgling state which emerged from the Union was to reveal a resilience far beyond what the cantankerous years prior to 1707 might have suggested. Reinforced rather than weakened by a succession of stresses and strains – empire and industrialisation in the eighteenth century, social and political change in the nineteenth, total war in the twentieth – the Anglo-Scottish partnership would for the best part of three hundred years not be found seriously wanting.

The Union, particularly under Dundas, its most articulate contemporary product and defender, also had other implications specifically for the Scots. Oceanic commerce and emigration within a British imperial framework helped re-shape Scotland's internal demography. Imperial trade reinforced the country's shift to the west, with Glasgow centre-stage: even by the 1760s this trend was obvious, underwritten by the Atlantic economy on which the first British empire was built and in which the Union had securely embedded Scottish merchants and Scottish workers. Emigration, meanwhile, also contributed to the distinctive demographic profile of modern Scotland. Almost certainly blunting the effects of overall natural population increase, and having a dramatic localised impact in certain parts of the country, emigration to North America, which began on a large scale between the 1730s and 1790s, ensured that the Scots steadily shrank in proportion to other parts of the British population, while at the same time further reducing the proportion of Scots living in the Highlands, islands and Borders. Yet immersion in the British empire had more positive effects. The clear benefits included the enrichment of the landed elite, the growth of a prosperous middle class, the stimulation of urbanisation and an important part in triggering industrialisation, which itself facilitated unparalleled long-term improvements in living standards across most of society.

Apart from the Union, the eighteenth century also brought other pointers to the future. Certainly this was the last age in which the Scots could seriously claim to be a Protestant nation: Irish Catholic immigration, increasing exponentially after 1800, would destroy forever Scotland's much-vaunted religious homogeneity, simultaneously throwing into further doubt the long-term viability of social institutions overseen by an established presbyterian church. The reign of the Moderates from mid-century had also given an influential airing to the novel proposition that religious affiliation was purely a personal rather than a public matter: although the populace at large remained unconvinced, wide intellectual and political credence was being given to arguments for toleration by 1770. These changing perceptions among Scotland's educated elite at the same time helped create the congenial social and institutional climate in which a Scottish Enlightenment could flourish by the middle of the century. Scotland may today be known as widely for the political economy of Adam Smith, the philosophy of David Hume, the poetry of Burns and the novels of Scott, as it is for Watt's steam condenser or for Dale's cotton mills. This is not inappropriate. For they were not the least of the achievements which made the age of Union and Enlightenment so central to the creation of modern Scotland.

BIBLIOGRAPHICAL ESSAY

It is obviously necessary to strike some sort of balance between the full-length general studies more likely to be available in public and college libraries and the fact that so much of the most interesting and innovative work on eighteenth-century Scotland is consigned to the specialist academic periodicals. My suggestions therefore start with a presumption in favour of writings which the reader is more likely to be able to obtain; but mention has also been made of individual essays or papers from which particular benefit would derive.

General

Among general histories, Michael Lynch's *Scotland: A New History* (London, 1991) contains much good sense on this period, and is pointed as well as pithy. R.H. Campbell's older *Scotland since 1707: The Rise of an Industrial Society* (Oxford, 1965) is also sound, especially on social and economic developments. Both Rosalind Mitchison's *Lordship to Patronage: Scotland 1603–1745* (London, 1983) and Bruce Lenman's *Integration and Enlightenment: Scotland 1746–1832* (London, 1981) are excellent, although they split the century in two and, taken back-to-back, reveal the different pre-occupations of their authors. T.M. Devine and J.R. Young's *Eighteenth-Century Scotland: New Perspectives* (East Linton, 1999) contains several essays worth reading, particularly on Highland history. Devine's *The Scottish Nation, 1700–2000* (London, 1999) is a fluent overview of the modern period from an acknowledged eighteenth-century master. Widely seen as the greatest work of recent early-modern Scottish scholarship, T.C. Smout's *History of the Scottish People, 1560–1830* (repr. London, 1985) also deserves its reputation, particularly in relation to social and economic developments. *People and Society in Scotland*, Volume I: *1760–1830* (Edinburgh, 1988), edited by Devine and Mitchison, is a valuable introduction to eighteenth-century Scotland pitched particularly at undergraduates. The historiography of the period is surveyed in Rab Houston's 'Eighteenth-Century Scottish Studies: Out of the Laager?', *Scottish Historical Review*, 73 (1994), 64–81.

Chapter 1: Nation

On the background to the Treaty of Union, the literature is dense and often spikey. The finest (and fairest) recent summary is Christopher Whatley's short work *'Bought and Sold for English Gold'? Explaining the Union of 1707* (Glasgow, 1994), while works expressing the case for the prosecution include P.H. Scott's *Andrew Fletcher and the Treaty of Union* (Edinburgh, 1994) and William Ferguson's 'The Making of the Treaty of Union of 1707', *Scottish Historical Review*, 43 (1964), 89–110. The grubby political background is still best explained in P.W.J. Riley's classic full-length study *The Union of England and Scotland: A Study in Anglo-Scottish Politics of the Eighteenth Century* (Manchester, 1978), while, providing necessary balance, John Robertson's collection *A Union for Empire: the Union of 1707 in the History of Political Thought* (Cambridge, 1995) contains several contributions which scotch the insidious myth that the contemporary analysis of the treaty's merits lacked theoretical depth.

Post-Union politics remain largely shrouded in obscurity, though several studies offer insights into certain aspects. Alexander Murdoch's *The People Above: Politics and Administration in Mid-Eighteenth-Century Scotland* (Edinburgh, 1980) is indispensable on the structures of Scottish administration before the 1760s. John Shaw's *The Management of Scottish Society, 1707–1764: Power, Nobles, Lawyers, Edinburgh Agents and English Influence* (Edinburgh, 1983) is also useful for its analysis of the Argathelian dominance, while Michael Fry's *Dundas Despotism* (Edinburgh, 1992) is the best study of the later decades. Ronald Sunter's *Patronage and Politics in Scotland, 1707–1832* (Edinburgh, 1986) is an underrated but fascinating series of case studies of Scotland's electoral processes and domestic politics. Information on local administration, of much greater interest to contemporaries than it appears to be to modern scholars, is available from Ann E. Whetstone's *Scottish County Government in the Eighteenth and Nineteenth Centuries* (Edinburgh, 1981).

Radicalism and popular politics are explored in T.M. Devine's 'The Failure of Radical Reform in Scotland in the Late Eighteenth Century: the Social and Economic Context', in his *Conflict and Stability in Scottish Society, 1700–1850* (Edinburgh, 1990), as well as in John Brims's essay in the same collection, 'From Reformers to "Jacobins": the Scottish Association of the Friends of the People'. Kenneth Logue's *Popular Disturbances in Scotland, 1780–1815* (Edinburgh, 1979) is especially strong on the later age of political radicalism. The relationship between Scottish politics and events in Europe after 1789 is the subject of H.W. Meikle's classic study *Scotland and the French Revolution* (Glasgow, 1912), while Hamish Fraser's *Conflict and Class: Scottish Workers, 1700–1838* (Edinburgh, 1988) is essential reading for an understanding of the mass experience of industrialisation.

Scottish identity has attracted intense recent interest. Important considerations include Smout's 'Problems of Nationalism, Identity and Improvement in Later Eighteenth-Century Scotland', in Devine's collection *Improvement and Enlightenment* (Edinburgh, 1989), which advanced the useful concept of concentric multiple identities for post-Union Scots; his 'Perspectives on the Scottish Identity', *Scottish Affairs*, 6 (1994), 101–13, is a valuable overview; and Colin Kidd's 'North Britishness and the Nature of Eighteenth-Century British Patriotisms', *Historical Journal*, 39 (1996), 361–82 is an insightful discussion of contemporary loyalties. John Robertson's *The Scottish Enlightenment and the Militia Issue* (Edinburgh, 1985) is a convincing study of a distinctive national cause with deep roots in Scotland's intellectual and political culture. For a wider perspective on the Scots' integration into a British polity in which Protestantism and successful commerce and warfare were the crucial building-blocks, the outstanding account is Linda Colley's recently influential *Britons: Forging the Nation, 1707–1837* (New Haven, 1992).

Chapter 2: Belief

Recent years have also seen a growing body of sophisticated scholarship on eighteenth-century religion, though some of its achievements are as yet reflected only in shorter essays. The key full-length study is Callum Brown's impressive *The Social History of Religion in Scotland since 1730* (London, 1987), revised as *Religion and Society in Scotland since 1707* (Edinburgh, 1997), which correctly emphasises the depth of popular religious commitment far into the modern period. An unusual but remarkably perceptive study of evangelical presbyterian piety is Leigh Eric Schmidt's *Holy Fairs: Scottish Communions and American Revivals in the Early Modern Period* (Princeton, 1989). Formal ecclesiastical history is still reliant upon older and drier works such as Andrew L. Drummond and James Bulloch's *The Scottish Church, 1688–1843: The Age of the Moderates* (Edinburgh, 1973). Two very different studies in a more modern vein give purchase on the established church's internal tensions: *Church and Theology in Enlightenment Scotland: the Popular Party, 1740–1800* (East Linton, 1998) by John R. McIntosh, which begins the task of exploring the evangelical clergy; and *Church and University in the Scottish Enlightenment* (Edinburgh, 1985) by Richard B. Sher, which rather more convincingly investigates the cultural activities and religious and political commitments of Edinburgh's clerical elite.

Developments within the established church through an age of social and cultural change have also been illuminated by several shorter studies, including Ned Landsman's 'Presbyterians and Provincial Society: the

Evangelical Enlightenment in the West of Scotland, 1740–1775', in *Eighteenth Century Life*, 15 (1991),194–209, emphasising the cultural sophistication of evangelicalism, and Callum Brown's 'Protest in the Pews: Interpreting Presbyterianism and Society in Fracture During the Scottish Economic Revolution', in Devine's *Conflict and Stability*. Moderatism, aside from Sher's seminal *Church and University*, is explored in Ian Clark's 'From Protest to Reaction: the Moderate Regime in the Church of Scotland, 1752–1805', in *Scotland in the Age of Improvement* (repr. Edinburgh, 1996), edited by Nicholas Phillipson and Rosalind Mitchison and a highly influential collection since its initial publication in 1970: Clark's is an important essay that condenses his path-breaking Cambridge doctoral thesis which first confirmed the numerical weakness of Robertson and his allies. The key short study of popular piety as experienced in the communion seasons is Smout's 'Born Again at Cambuslang: New Evidence on Popular Religion and Literacy in Eighteenth-Century Scotland', *Past and Present*, 97 (1982), 114–27.

Particular aspects of ecclesiastical affairs covered in other essays include Daniel Szechi's 'Defending the True Faith: Kirk, State and Catholic Missioners in Scotland, 1653–1755', in *Catholic Historical Review*, 82 (1996), 397–411; Fiona Macdonald's 'Irish Priests in the Highlands: Judicial Evidence from Argyll', in *Innes Review*, 66 (1995), 15–33; and Emma Vincent's 'The Responses of Scottish Churchmen to the French Revolution, 1789–1802', *Scottish Historical Review*, 73 (1994), 191–215. Monograph studies worth consulting on specific features of contemporary church history are David Lachman's *The Marrow Controversy, 1718–1723: An Historical and Theological Analysis* (Edinburgh, 1988) on the doctrinal convulsions of the early eighteenth century, and Robert Kent Donovan's *No Popery and Radicalism: Opposition to Roman Catholic Relief in Scotland, 1778–1782* (New York, 1987), a timely reminder of the contemporary limitations of Moderation and Enlightenment.

A mass of material, not all of it reputable, caters to the abiding fascination with Jacobitism among the general public. Among the serious contributions are *The Jacobite Challenge* (Edinburgh, 1988), edited by Eveline Cruickshanks and Jeremy Black; *The Jacobites, Britain, and Europe, 1688–1788* (Manchester, 1994) by Daniel Szechi; *The Jacobites* (London, 1988) by Frank McLynn; and *The Jacobite Cause* (Glasgow, 1986) by Bruce Lenman. The latter has been responsible for several important studies, including *The Jacobite Clans of the Great Glen 1650–1784* (repr. Aberdeen, 1995), which brilliantly connects the economic and dynastic concerns of leading chieftains with their Jacobite activities. *Lochiel of the '45: the Jacobite Chief and the Prince* (Edinburgh, 1994) by John Gibson is the key study of reluctant involvement in the 'Forty-five, while the motivation of the clans in an age of economic and social change is the principal focus of Allan Macinnes's thought-provoking *Clanship, Commerce and the House of Stuart, 1603–1788* (East Linton, 1996).

Other investigations of particular phases of Jacobite activity include Gibson's *Playing the Scottish Card: the Franco-Jacobite Invasion of 1708* (Edinburgh, 1988); *Jacobitism and the '45* (London, 1995), edited by Michael Lynch; and *The Stuart Court in Exile and the Jacobites* (London, 1995), edited by Eveline Cruickshanks and Edward Corp. *The Myth of the Jacobite Clans* (Edinburgh, 1995) by Murray Pittock makes controversial claims for the viability and strength of Charles Edward Stuart's cause, while Jeremy Black's *Culloden and the '45* (Stroud, 1990) and Stuart Reid's *1745: A Military History of the Last Jacobite Rising* (Staplehurst, 1996) give detailed accounts of the final campaign. W.A. Speck's *The Butcher: the Duke of Cumberland and the Suppression of the '45* (Oxford, 1981) is devoted to the victor of Culloden and the battle's harsh aftermath.

On non-Christian beliefs the literature remains patchy and of inconsistent quality. Of some use will be *Folk Lore in Lowland Scotland* (repr. Wakefield, 1976) by Eve Blantyre Simpson; *History of British Folklore* (repr. London, 1999) by Richard M. Dorson; *Scottish Folklore* (Edinburgh, 1991) by Isobel E. Williams; and Raymond Lamont-Brown's work of the same title (Edinburgh, 1996). Specific treatment of Gaelic popular beliefs is given in Francis Thompson's *The Supernatural Highlands* (London, 1976), and *The Seer in Celtic and Other Traditions* (Edinburgh, 1989) edited by Hilda Ellis Davidson. The standard study of Scottish witchcraft remains Christina Larner's *Enemies of God: The Witch-Hunt in Scotland* (London, 1981), although much interesting research is currently in progress.

Chapter 3: Lives

Scottish demography possesses an obvious foundation-text in M.W. Flinn's *Scottish Population History from the Seventeenth Century to the 1930s* (Cambridge, 1977), minor revisions to whose findings constitute the main occupation of recent scholars: Rab Houston's 'The Demographic Regime', in Devine and Mitchison's *People and Society*, and Robert Tyson's 'Demographic Change', in Devine and Young's *Eighteenth-Century Scotland*, are important instances. Knowledge of contemporary illegitimacy rates relies heavily upon the work of Mitchison and Leah Leneman, notably *Sexuality and Social Control: Scotland 1660–1780* (Oxford, 1989) and its sequels *Girls in Trouble: Sexuality and Social Control in Rural Scotland, 1660–1780* (Edinburgh, 1998) and *Sin in the City: Sexuality and Social Control in Urban Scotland, 1660–1780* (Edinburgh, 1998). Other relevant shorter studies include Houston's 'Age at Marriage of Scottish Women, *c.*1660–1760', *Local Population Studies*, 43 (1989), 63–6, and Ian Whyte's 'Population Mobility in Early Modern Scotland', in his and Houston's *Scottish Society, 1500–1800* (Cambridge, 1989).

A variety of useful insights into general processes of economic development are found in several collections: *Industry, Business and Society in Scotland since 1700* (Edinburgh, 1994), edited by Devine and A.J.G. Cummings; *Conflict, Identity and Economic Development: Ireland and Scotland, 1600–1939* (Preston, 1995), edited by S.J. Connolly, Rab Houston and R.J. Morris; and *Scottish Society, 1500–1800* (Cambridge, 1989), edited by Houston and Whyte. An important survey of the longer perspective is the latter's recent *Scotland Before the Industrial Revolution: An Economic and Social History, c.1050–c.1750* (London, 1995), which also serves as a critical analysis of the technical debates. Germane to an old chestnut among economic historians of this period are Christopher Whatley's excellent 'Economic Causes and Consequences of the Union of 1707: A Survey', in *Scottish Historical Review*, 68 (1989), 150–81, and T.C. Smout's brave attempt at definitive quantification, 'Where Had the Scottish Economy Got To by 1776?', in István Hont and Michael Ignatieff's collection *Wealth and Virtue: The Shaping of Political Economy in the Scottish Enlightenment* (Cambridge, 1983) – the answer being, not as far as pro-Unionists might have expected. Whatley's *Scottish Society 1707–1830: Beyond Jacobitism, Towards Industrialisation* (Manchester, 2000), which appeared just as this bibliography was being compiled, argues with great skill and conviction for the benefits ultimately delivered by the treaty.

The study of eighteenth-century Scottish agriculture has been marked in recent years by a difference of emphasis between those historians who believe that the pre-Union era saw important changes and those who consider that the period after 1750 was the definitive 'Age of Improvement'. The latter view has been most ably presented by Devine in *The Transformation of Rural Scotland: Social Change and the Agrarian Economy, 1660–1815* (Edinburgh, 1994), utilising new evidence from several estates across central Scotland; older accounts in the same vein include two works by J.E. Handley, *Scottish Farming in the Eighteenth Century* (London, 1953) and *The Agricultural Revolution in Scotland* (London, 1963). The revisionist view is closely associated with Ian Whyte, whose 'Before the Improvers: Agricultural and Landscape Change in Lowland Scotland, *c.*1660–*c.*1750', in *Scottish Archives*, 1 (1995), 31–42, is the most accessible summary of his case. Whyte's widely influential monograph *Agriculture and Society in Seventeenth-Century Scotland* (Edinburgh, 1979) is the key text arguing for a pre-Union phase of improvement. On rural life an interesting evocation is David Kerr Cameron's *The Ballad and the Plough: A Portrait of the Life of the Old Scottish Farmtouns* (Edinburgh, 1997), while the social implications of agrarian change are explored in Devine's essay 'The Making of a Farming Elite? Lowland Scotland, 1750–1850', in his collection *Scottish Elites* (Edinburgh, 1994); more extensively in his collection *Farm Servants and Labour in Lowland Scotland, 1770–1914* (Edinburgh, 1984); in his monograph *The Transformation of Rural*

Scotland (Edinburgh, 1994); and in R.H. Campbell's 'The Landed Classes', in Devine and Mitchison's *People and Society*.

The Highlands have, of course, attracted immense interest, the historiography skewed by continuing controversies over the character and timing of structural change in Gaelic Scotland and the nature and motivation of population movements. Macinnes's *Clanship, Commerce and the House of Stuart*, taken together with Devine's *Clanship to Crofters' War: the Social Transformation of the Scottish Highlands* (Manchester, 1994) and supplemented by the outstandingly coherent analysis of R.A. Dodgshon in *From Chiefs to Landlords: Social and Economic Change in the Western Highlands and Islands* (Edinburgh, 1998), currently provide the best single-volume overviews of a technically difficult subject, and generally support the view that commercialisation and social change were already underway substantially before Culloden.

The growth of trade and the consequent restructuring of the Scottish economy are key topics to which Devine has again been the outstanding modern contributor. His *The Tobacco Lords: A Study of the Tobacco Merchants of Glasgow and their Trading Activities, c.1740–90* (Edinburgh, 1975) remains definitive. Other essays, such as his 'The Colonial Trades and Industrial Investment in Scotland, *c.*1700–1815', in *The Organization of Interoceanic Trade in European Expansion, 1450–1800* (Aldershot, 1996), edited by Pieter Emmer and Femme Gaastra, have fleshed out some of the implications. Infrastructural developments have also received much attention, including, on the financial sector, Sidney Checkland's *Scottish Banking: A History, 1695–1973* (Glasgow, 1975), and the relevant parts of the recent study by Richard Saville, *The Bank of Scotland: A History, 1695–1995* (Edinburgh, 1996).

The finest overview of Scottish industrialisation, particularly with respect to its timing, is Christopher Whatley's *The Industrial Revolution in Scotland* (Cambridge, 1997), which should be read in conjunction with older and larger studies such as the still-popular Henry Hamilton, *The Industrial Revolution in Scotland* (repr. London, 1996). Specific aspects of industrialisation have been subjected to intense scrutiny. Whatley's 'New Light on Nef's Numbers: Coal Mining and the First Phase of Scottish Industrialisation, *c.*1700–1830', in Devine and Cummings's *Industry, Business and Society* is particularly interesting on the impact of coal-mining on the wider economy, as are the same author's monograph *The Scottish Salt Industry 1570–1850* (Aberdeen, 1987) and A.J. Durie's *The Scottish Linen Trade in the Eighteenth Century* (Edinburgh, 1979). The key industry is perhaps best reviewed in John Butt's 'The Scottish Cotton Industry During the Industrial Revolution, 1780–1840', in *Comparative Aspects of Scottish and Irish Economic and Social History, 1600–1900* (Edinburgh, 1977) edited by L.M. Cullen and T.C. Smout.

On Scottish urban growth in this period, see Ian Adams's *The Making of Urban Scotland* (London, 1978), Michael Lynch's edited collection *The Early*

Modern Town in Scotland (London, 1987), Whyte's 'Urbanization in Early Modern Scotland: A Preliminary Analysis', *Scottish Economic and Social History*, 9 (1989), 21–35, and Devine's 'Urbanisation', in his and Mitchison's *People and Society*. The best monograph study of an eighteenth-century Scottish city is Rab Houston's *Social Change in the Age of Enlightenment: Edinburgh, 1660–1760* (Oxford, 1994), which is especially strong on occupational structure. The social and material dimensions of urbanisation have also been illuminated by Stana Nenadic, notably in her essays 'The Rise of the Urban Middle Class', in *People and Society*, and in 'Middle Rank Consumers and Domestic Culture in Edinburgh and Glasgow, 1720–1840', *Past and Present*, 145 (1994), 122–56. Women's importance in early Scottish industrialisation has been emphasised in important studies such as Whatley's 'Women and the Economic Transformation of Scotland, *c.*1740–1830', in *Scottish Economic and Social History*, 14 (1994), 19–40.

Socio-economic protest, for which the literature on contemporary England is substantial, has received less attention in Scotland, not least because of the presumption that the Scots were less prone to resistance. But for recent scepticism of this traditional interpretation see Whatley's 'How Tame were the Scottish Lowlanders During the Eighteenth Century?', in Devine's *Conflict and Stability*; his 'An Uninflammable People?', in *The Manufacture of Scottish History* (Edinburgh, 1992), edited by himself and Ian Donnachie; and Ian Whyte's 'A Relatively Orderly, Authoritarian, Society?', *Scottish Economic and Social History*, 12 (1992). Whatley's new *Scottish Society* is the finest and utterly convincing exposition of this emerging new consensus. Questions of living standards are explored by J.H. Treble, in 'The Standard of Living of the Working Class', in Devine and Mitchison's *People and Society*, and in A.J. Gibson and Smout's fascinating *Prices, Food and Wages in Scotland, 1550–1780* (Cambridge, 1995). The problems of class formation are discussed in T. Clarke and T. Dickson's 'The Birth of Class', also in *People and Society*, though a more cautious note, and one which continues to be very influential, is struck in Smout's *History of the Scottish People*.

Ecclesiastical welfare provision has recently been greatly illuminated by Mitchison's *The Old Poor Law in Scotland* (Edinburgh, 1999). Education is explored in Robert Anderson's outstanding *Education and the Scottish People, 1750–1918* (Oxford, 1995), as well as in specific studies such as Alexander Law's *Education in Edinburgh in the Eighteenth Century* (London, 1965); its impact is investigated (and somewhat doubted) in Rab Houston's *Scottish Literacy and the Scottish Identity: Illiteracy and Society in Scotland and Northern England 1600–1800* (Cambridge, 1985). For the universities the best short summary of developments is Roger Emerson's 'Scottish Universities in the Eighteenth Century, 1690–1800', *Studies on Voltaire and the Eighteenth Century*, 167 (1977), 453–74. Aside from Sher's *Church and University* with its unapologetic

Edinburgh focus, and Emerson's *Professors, Patronage and Politics: The Aberdeen Universities in the Eighteenth Century* (Aberdeen, 1991), detailed institutional studies are lacking.

Leah Leneman's study of marital breakdown, *Alienated Affections: the Scottish Experience of Divorce and Separation, 1684–1830* (Edinburgh, 1998), provides an unusual insight into eighteenth-century Scottish family life and the pressures to which it was subjected. Social dissonance remains relatively poorly served by existing work. Criminality in particular is very largely unconsidered: useful preliminary case studies include Marion M. Stewart, '"In Durance Vile": Crime and Punishment in Seventeenth- and Eighteenth-Century Records of Dumfries', in *Scottish Archives*, 1 (1995), and, especially for the complex administration of justice before the Heritable Jurisdictions Act, Stephen Davies's 'The Courts and the Scottish Legal System, 1600–1747: The Case of Stirlingshire', in *Crime and the Law: the Social History of Crime in Western Europe since 1500* (London, 1980), edited by Victor Gatrell, Bruce Lenman and Geoffrey Parker. On insanity Rab Houston's new monograph *Madness and Society in Eighteenth-Century Scotland* (Oxford, 2000) offers an original and highly provoking analysis of increasing mental ill-health in this period.

Chapter 4: Ideas

Modern interest in the Scottish Enlightenment is conventionally dated to Hugh Trevor-Roper's provocative essay of that title in *Studies on Voltaire and the Eighteenth Century*, 58 (1967), 1635–58. Subsequent overviews include the outstanding illustrated volume *A Hotbed of Genius: The Scottish Enlightenment, 1730–1790* (Edinburgh, 1986), edited by Peter and Jean Jones and David Daiches; George Davie's brief *The Scottish Enlightenment* (London, 1981); and Alexander Broadie's recent *The Scottish Enlightenment: An Anthology* (Edinburgh, 1997), a convenient way into the original literature of the period. Edited collections, however, have proved dominant in this multi-disciplinary field, the more significant examples being *Origins and Nature of the Scottish Enlightenment* (Edinburgh, 1982) by R.H. Campbell and A.S. Skinner, and *Wealth and Virtue* by Hont and Ignatieff. A range of information on the regional dimension has also been afforded by the same route in Joan Pittock and Jennifer Carter's *Aberdeen and the Enlightenment* (Aberdeen, 1987), and *Glasgow and the Enlightenment* (East Linton, 1995), edited by Andrew Hook and Richard Sher.

The cultural and institutional environment is examined in key works such as Sher's *Church and University*, which charts the academic and clerical grip on Scotland's Enlightenment (and contains an outstanding bibliography to 1985), and David D. McElroy's *Scotland's Age of Improvement: A Survey of Eighteenth-Century Literary Clubs and Societies* (Washington, 1969), an encyclopaedic account of enlightened Scottish learned institutions. Roger Emerson has also contributed several studies of the intelligentsia's activities, notably 'The Social Composition of Enlightened Scotland: The "Select Society of Edinburgh", 1754–1764', *Studies on Voltaire and the Eighteenth Century*, 114 (1973), 291–330, and 'The Philosophical Society of Edinburgh, 1737–1747', *British Journal for the History of Science*, 12 (1979), 154–91, which was followed by further essays for the succeeding periods in the same journal over the next ten years.

Several essays by Nicholas Phillipson have exerted considerable influence, particularly in emphasising Addison's role in the formation of Scotland's enlightened culture. These include 'Politics, Politeness and the Anglicisation of Early Eighteenth-Century Scottish Culture', in *Scotland and England: 1286–1815* (Edinburgh, 1987) edited by Roger Mason; 'Politics and Politeness in the Reigns of Queen Anne and the Early Hanoverians', in *Varieties of British Political Thought, 1500–1800* (Cambridge, 1993), edited by John Pocock; 'Culture and Society in the Eighteenth-Century Province: The Case of Edinburgh and the Scottish Enlightenment', in Lawrence Stone's *The University in Society* (Princeton, 1974); and 'Towards a Definition of the Scottish Enlightenment', in P. Fritz and D. Williams's *City and Society in the Eighteenth Century* (Toronto, 1973). Other studies have continued to develop Phillipson's theme, not least John Dwyer's *Virtuous Discourse: Sensibility and Community in Late Eighteenth-Century Scotland* (Edinburgh, 1987), an invaluable study of moral thought in the era of Adam Smith and Henry Mackenzie.

Scottish natural science and mental philosophy have each been subjected to extensive technical examination. An overall impression might be gained from Peter Jones's edited collection *Philosophy and Science in the Scottish Enlightenment* (Edinburgh, 1988), but most of the literature is buried deep in specialist academic journals: perhaps the most approachable is J.R.R. Christie's 'The Origins and Development of the Scottish Scientific Community, 1680–1760', *History of Science*, 7 (1974), 122–41. Among the more accessible monographs remains Arthur L. Donovan's *Philosophical Chemistry in the Scottish Enlightenment: the Doctrines and Discoveries of William Cullen and Joseph Black* (Edinburgh, 1975). Donald W. Livingston's *Hume's Philosophy of Common Life* (Chicago, 1984) is a useful study of Hume's moral and epistemological ideas. Scotland's two greatest philosophers have journals all to themselves, providing a regular outlet for new research: *Hume Studies* and *Reid Studies*.

The view that Scottish moral philosophy and historical thought slipped imperceptibly into the idiom of modern social science was influentially advanced by Ronald Meek in his *Social Science and the Ignoble Savage* (Cambridge, 1976). A more sensitive reading of the evidence is found in Christopher Berry's *Social Theory of the Scottish Enlightenment* (Edinburgh, 1997), together with a very useful thematic analysis. The historical thought of the period is discussed in my *Virtue, Learning and the Scottish Enlightenment: Ideas of Scholarship in Early Modern History* (Edinburgh, 1993); Colin Kidd's *Subverting Scotland's Past: Scottish Whig Historians and the Creation of an Anglo-British Identity, 1689–c.1830* (Cambridge, 1993); and, with characteristic originality, in John Pocock's *Barbarism and Religion*, Volume 2: *Narratives of Civil Government* (Cambridge, 1999).

Important works on individual historians include Stewart J. Brown's edited collection *William Robertson and the Expansion of Empire* (Cambridge, 1997) and Phillipson's lucid short work *Hume* (London, 1989), which might be read in conjunction with Duncan Forbes's older *Hume's Philosophical Politics* (Cambridge, 1975), still the best study of Hume as historical and social thinker. Scotland's intellectual impact overseas has been another growth area, recently producing collections such as Richard Sher and Jeffrey Smitten's *Scotland and America in the Age of the Enlightenment* (Edinburgh, 1990) and monographs such as Fania Oz-Salzberger's *Translating the Enlightenment: Scottish Civic Discourse in Eighteenth-Century Germany* (Oxford, 1995) and Manfred Kuehn's *Scottish Common Sense in Germany, 1768–1800: A Contribution to the History of Critical Philosophy* (Kingston, 1987).

Post-Union literary lives, and the problems posed by anglicisation in particular, are best initially approached through such general studies as David Daiches's classic work *The Paradox of Scottish Culture: The Eighteenth-Century Experience* (London, 1964); Kenneth Simpson's *The Protean Scot: The Crisis of Identity in Eighteenth-Century Scottish Literature* (Aberdeen, 1988); and the earlier parts of Robert Crawford's *The Scottish Invention of English Literature* (Cambridge, 1991), which gives special attention to the involvement of Scotland's rhetoric professors in the formation of an English literary canon. On individual authors the literature is inevitably vast but the following are especially useful: A. Smart's *The Life and Art of Allan Ramsay* (London, 1952); L.M. Knapp's *Tobias Smollett* (Princeton, 1949); H.W. Thompson's *A Scottish Man of Feeling* (London, 1931), on Henry Mackenzie; several of the essays in Howard Gaskill's collection *Ossian Revisited* (Edinburgh, 1991); Fiona Stafford's *The Sublime Savage: A Study of James Macpherson and the Poems of Ossian* (Edinburgh, 1988); Daiches's *Robert Fergusson* (Edinburgh, 1982); Thomas Crawford's *Burns: A Study of Poems and Songs* (Edinburgh, 1960); and P.H. Scott's *Walter Scott and Scotland* (Edinburgh,1981). For art the definitive source is Duncan Macmillan's magisterial *Painting in Scotland: The Golden Age, 1707–1843* (Oxford, 1986), supplemented by his sumptuous *Scottish Art, 1460–1960* (Edinburgh, 1990), both of which contain useful bibliographies:

Macmillan's views are not uncontroversial but their integration of art with wider cultural and social currents usually makes sense. Architecture is covered in J.G. Dunbar, *The Architecture of Scotland* (London, 1978); in the outstanding recent *A History of Scottish Architecture: From the Renaissance to the Present Day* (Edinburgh, 1996) by Miles Glendinning, Ranald MacInnes and Aonghus MacKechnie; and, for the construction of the capital's New Town, A.J. Youngson's recently re-printed and extensively illustrated *The Making of Classical Edinburgh, 1750–1840* (Edinburgh, 1966).

Chapter 5: Empire

After many years of being regarded as politically incorrect, Scottish and British imperialism is now attracting more interest, though again chiefly in short essays. Indeed, the subject is still most expansively treated in Andrew Dewar Gibb's terminally dated *Scottish Empire* (London, 1937), a discernibly Nationalist account of patriotic achievement curiously intercut with what turned out to be prescient unease about the empire's future. The starting-point for modern analysis is *The Oxford History of the British Empire*, Volume II: *The Eighteenth Century* (Oxford, 1998), edited by Peter Marshall. The process of Scottish engagement with a previously English empire is also illuminated in several recent essays, including H.V. Bowen, 'The End of the English Empire', in his *Elites, Enterprise and the Making of the British Overseas Empire, 1688–1775* (London, 1996); John Robertson's 'Union, State and Empire: the Britain of 1707 in its European Setting', in *An Imperial State at War: Britain from 1689 to 1815* (London, 1994), edited by Lawrence Stone; John Mackenzie's 'Essay and Reflection: on Scotland and the Empire', in *International History Review*, 15 (1993), 714–39; Eric Richards's 'Scotland and the Uses of the Atlantic Empire', in *Strangers Within the Realm: Cultural Margins of the First British Empire* (Chapel Hill, 1991), edited by Bernard Bailyn and Philip D. Morgan; and Alexander Murdoch's 'Review Article: The Rise and Fall of the Scottish Empire', *Scotlands*, 2 (1995), 123–31, which explores the historiography. The pre-Union background is examined in David Armitage's 'Making the Empire British: Scotland in the Atlantic World, 1542–1707', in *Past and Present*, 155 (1997), 34–63. Armitage's 'The Scottish Vision of Empire: Intellectual Origins of the Darien Venture', in Robertson's *Union for Empire*, is also valuable, emphasising that empire satisfied ideological as well as material needs.

Emigration and overseas Scottish settlement have generated a welter of material, among the most pertinent of which are Ned Landsman's 'Border Cultures, the Backcountry and "North British" Emigration to America', in

William and Mary Quarterly, 163 (1991), 253–9; *Cargoes of Despair and Hope: Scottish Emigration to North America 1603–1803* (Edinburgh, 1993) by Ian Adams and Meredyth Somerville; *The Original Scots Colonists of Early America, 1612–1783* (Baltimore, 1989) by David Dobson; Anthony W. Parker's *Scottish Highlanders in Colonial Georgia: the Recruitment, Emigration and Settlement at Darien, 1735–1748* (Athens, 1997); Alan L. Karras's *Sojourners in the Sun: Scottish Migrants in Jamaica and the Chesapeake, 1740–1800* (Ithaca, 1992); and Stephen Hornsby, 'Patterns of Scottish Emigration to Canada, 1750–1870', in *Journal of Historical Geography*, 18 (1992), 397–416. Crucial studies for an understanding of relations between Highland economic change and North American emigration are Marianne McLean's *The People of Glengarry: Highlanders in Transition, 1745–1820* (Montreal, 1991), which needs to be read alongside John Bumsted's *The People's Clearance: Highland Emigration to British North America, 1770–1815* (Edinburgh, 1982). The even-handed and immensely erudite survey by Eric Richards, *A History of the Highland Clearances: Agrarian Transformation and the Evictions 1746–1886* (London, 1982), has now been usefully condensed as *The Highland Clearances* (Edinburgh, 2000). Michael Vance's 'Scottish Emigration to North America: A Review Essay', in *Scottish Tradition*, 20 (1995), 65–80, is also a helpful overview of a deeply contentious subject: the journal in which his essay appears, managed by a Canadian university richly endowed with Scottish settler connections, has a good record of publishing new research in the field.

The relationship between empire and domestic Scottish affairs has by contrast received little attention, but a start on the crude mechanics has been made with George McGilvary's 'Post-Union Scotland and the Indian Connection: Patronage and Political Management', in *Cencrastus*, 37 (1990), 30–3, and George Riddy's 'Warren Hastings: Scotland's Benefactor?', in *The Impeachment of Warren Hastings* (Edinburgh, 1989), edited by Geoffrey Carnall and Colin Nicholson. A sobering reminder of a key aspect of the Scots' imperial experience is found in Victor Kiernan's 'Scottish Soldiers and the Conquest of India', in Grant Simpson's *The Scottish Soldier Abroad, 1247–1967* (Edinburgh, 1992). A useful overview of the Asian empire with a keen eye for Scottish participation is Lawrence James, *Raj: The Making and Unmaking of British India* (London, 1997).

INDEX

Abercrombie, James, 170, 177
Abercromby, Sir Ralph, 181, 182
Abercromby, Robert, 181–2
Aberdeen,
  royal burgh, 59, 98, 129, 140–1, 151, 160, 166, 182
  King's College, 30, 49, 122, 155
  Marischal College, 49, 122, 134, 155, 157
Aberdeen, Earls of, 109
  William Gordon, 2nd Earl, 161
Aberdeenshire, 15, 16, 19, 45, 75, 90, 91, 98, 109, 161, 167, 181, 183
Aberfoyle, 77
academics, 44, 46, 49, 65, 76–7, 111–12, 128–9, 132–6, 137–8, 140–2, 143, 145–6, 155, 156, 175, 179, 188
accommodation, 84, 109, 110, 115, 118, 132, 158–64, 176
Achnacarry, 56
Acts
  Alien (1705), 9, 86, 98, 99
  Anent Peace and War (1703), 9
  Anent Witchcraft (1604), 79
  Anent Wrangous Imprisonment (1701), 32
  Annexing (1752), 60
  Combination (1799 and 1800), 126
  County Franchise (1661 and 1681), 16
  Disannexing (1784), 62
  Disarming (1716), 54
  Disarming (1725), 56
  Education (1696), 119
  Heritable Jurisdictions (1747), 26–7, 61
  Montgomery (1770), 92, 119
  Navigation (1660), 101, 170
  Patronage (1712), 48, 63–5, 68, 72
  poor law (1672), 123
  Proscription (1747), 61
  Reform (1832), 15
  Security (1704), 9
  Security (1707), 10, 47
  Settlement (1701), 8, 9
  Toleration (1712), 47–8, 63, 124
Adam, James, 161
Adam, John, 105, 161
Adam, Robert, 161–3
Addison, Joseph, 130–2, 147, 152, 153, 154, 160, 161, 162, 182, 188
Advocates, Faculty of, 21, 110
agriculture,
  commercialisation, 88, 90–6
  crofting, 95–6, 105, 121
  enclosure, 89–90, 91, 92, 93, 116
  farmers and farming, 74, 81, 87, 88–9, 90–2, 93–6, 103, 108, 110, 112, 114, 115, 116, 117, 180
  harvests, 7, 31, 87–8, 97, 108–9, 117
  improvement and innovation, 7, 84, 85–96, 100, 105, 114–15, 123, 135, 136, 160
  problems, 11, 86, 87–8, 125
  tenants and tenancy, 90, 92, 94–6, 114–15, 160, 175
Aikenhead, Thomas, 46, 67
Aikman, William, 156, 157, 158
Alexander, William, 147
Alexandria, 181
Alison, Francis, 174
Alva House, 112
America, 6, 34, 53, 69–70, 72, 77, 83, 94–5, 100–1, 106, 111, 112, 127, 130, 134, 141, 146, 148–9, 164, 165, 167–77, 184, 185, 190
anatomy, 133
Anderson, James, 168
Anderson, Walter, 163
Anglicanism, *see* Church of England
Angus (or Forfarshire), 24, 90, 98, 180
Annan, 17
Annandale, George Johnston, 3rd Marquis of, 121
Anne, Queen of Great Britain, 8, 9, 10, 11, 12, 47, 48, 51, 53, 131, 137
Anstruther-Wester, 99
Anti-Burghers, 73, 74–5
Antigua, 167

antinomianism, 46
antiquarianism, 133, 149–50, 183, 188–9
Antrim, county, 167
Appin murder case, 18
Arbigland, 174
Arbroath, Declaration of, 13
architecture and building, 109–10, 115, 156, 157, 158–64, 188–9
Argathelians, 22–3, 24, 25, 26–9, 35, 56
Argyllshire, 33, 75, 93, 134, 160, 173
Arianism, 46
Arkwright, Richard, 106
army and soldiers, 6, 7, 24, 26, 28, 32–3, 41, 52, 55–6, 57–60, 61, 62, 110–11, 112, 117, 145, 165, 166, 170–1, 173–4, 175, 176, 177–9, 181–2
Arniston, 110
Arnot, Thomas, of Chapel, 34, 37
art and aesthetics, 109, 110, 127, 138, 140, 146, 154, 156–64, 188–9
Articles of Grievances (1690), 43
assembly rooms, 131, 160
Associate Presbytery, *see* Secession Church
Assurance, Oath of, 47
astronomy and cosmology, 129, 134–5
atheism, 45, 78
Athelstaneford, 60
Atholl, John Murray, 4th Duke of, 21, 91
Auchinleck, 71
Auchtermuchty, 17, 44
Australia, 32, 175, 185
Austria, 56
Ayr, 15, 99, 121
Ayrshire, 65, 75, 88, 89, 106, 115, 153, 170, 181

Bagehot, Walter, 150
Baillie, George, of Jerviswood, 35
Baird, Sir David, 179
Balfour, John, of Balbirnie, 34
Baltic, 98, 102, 166
Banffshire, 15, 75, 83, 161, 170
Bank of England, 58
Bank of Scotland, 98–9
banks and banking, 7, 92, 98–9, 101, 112, 126, 176
Barbados, 167
Barclay of Urie, family, 18
  Robert Barclay, 167
Barron, William, 91
Bathgate, 32
Baxter, Andrew, 138
beans, 89
Beattie, James, 38, 140–1
Beith, 65
Belfour, John, 37, 38
Belhaven, John Hamilton, 2nd Lord, 11–12, 90
Bell, Andrew, 113
Benares, 180
Bengal, 130, 177, 180, 181, 183, 185
bere (or barley), 88, 89
Berkeley, George, 141
Berwick, 93
Berwickshire, 25, 46, 64, 75, 84, 86, 88, 89, 111, 132, 135, 136, 138, 167, 182
Black, Joseph, 135–6, 137, 143, 145
Blackwood's Magazine, 188
Blair Drummond, 110
Blair, Hugh, 66, 67, 71, 149, 153, 154, 155, 156, 189
Blair, James, 174–5
bleaching, 60, 107, 135
Blenheim, 52
bloodwite, 18
Bo'ness, 105
Board of Trustees for Manufacturing and Fisheries, 102
Boerhaave, Herman, 122, 123
Bogle, George, 180, 183
Bohemia, 4
Bombay, 177, 180, 181
bonnet lairds, 110, 114
bookkeeping, 121
Borders, 82–3, 84, 88, 95, 111, 153, 156, 190
Boston, 173, 174
Boston, Thomas, the elder, 46
Boston, Thomas, the younger, 74
Boswell, James, 21, 66, 71, 77, 183
botany, 133, 183
Braemar, 53
Braxfield, Robert MacQueen, Lord, 31, 62
Breadalbane, Earls of, 93
  John Campbell, 3rd Earl, 94
  John Campbell, 4th Earl, 95
Bremen, 102
brewing, 86, 113
bridges, 19, 88, 93
British Fisheries Society, 102–3
British Linen Company, 101
Broadie, Alexander, 107
Brodie, Alexander, 181
Broomhall, 163
Brougham and Vaux, Henry, Lord, 188
Bruce, Robert, King of Scots, 13, 149
Buccleuch, Dukes of, 109, 114, 161
  Henry Scott, 3rd Duke, 23, 91–2, 121

Buchan, James, 100
Buchan, David Steuart, 11th Earl of, 29, 36, 149–50
Buchanan, John, 154
Bunker Hill, 174
burgesses, 16–17, 29–30, 86, 87, 119
Burghers, 73, 74
burghs, 16–18, 48, 53, 63, 83, 85, 87, 113, 118, 119, 120, 121, 123, 158, 187
  of barony, 16–17, 18
  royal, 13, 14, 14, 16, 17, 18, 20–1, 28–9, 98
Burke, Edmund, 30, 154
Burlington, Richard Boyle, 3rd Earl of, 161
Burns, Robert, 13, 36, 153, 155–6, 162, 185, 191
Burntisland, 52
Bute, 16, 106
Bute, James Stuart, 3rd Earl of, 22, 24, 146
Buxar, 177, 181, 183
Byng, Sir George, 52

Caithness, 20, 29, 103, 174
Calcutta, 180
Callander, 60, 114
Calton weavers' strike, 117
Cambuslang, 45, 69, 73
Cameron, Catherine, 78
Cameronians, 72
Camerons, clan, 57, 58, 62
  Donald, of Lochiel, 56, 57, 60, 93
Campbell, Colen, 161
Campbell, Sir Alexander, of Inverneil, 182
Campbell, Daniel, of Shawfield, 28, 161
Campbell, Duncan, of Inverawe, 77, 170
Campbell, George, 140, 141, 155
Campbell, Sir James, of Ardkinglas, 24
Campbell, James, of Succoth, 182
Campbell, John, 179
Campbeltown, 15
Canada, 94, 167, 170–2, 175, 176, 185
Canton, 182
Cape Breton, 167, 175
Cape Fear, 173
Cardross, Henry Erskine, 3rd Lord, 167
Carlisle, 58
Carlops, 107
Carlyle, Alexander, 37–8, 71, 127, 129, 189
Carlyle, Thomas, 189
Carmichael, Gershom, 122, 134, 137
Carnock, 46, 73
Carolinas, 167, 173, 176
Caroline of Brandenburg, Queen of Great Britain, 28
Carron, 105, 106, 107
Carstares, William, 43, 47
cartography, 180
Cassillis, David Kennedy, 10th Earl of, 163
Castalian Band, 151
Castle Huntly, 112
catechism, 119
Catholicism, 8, 9, 41–3, 45, 49, 56, 58, 67–8, 69, 74, 75–6, 77, 149, 167, 175, 190
Catrine, 106
cattle and beef, 9, 86, 93, 100, 102, 115, 116
Ceres, 174
Ceylon, 179
Chalmers, Thomas, 189
Charles I, King of Scotland and England, 4, 5, 40, 147, 166
Charles II, King of Scotland and England, 4, 5, 40, 43, 79, 133
Charles V, Emperor, 133, 148
Charles XII, King of Sweden, 55
Charlestown, 160
cheese, 115
chemistry and chemists, 121, 133, 135–6, 181
Chesapeake, river, 100, 172, 176
Chester, 58
China, 146, 182
Chippendale, Thomas, 162
Chirnside, 163
Church of England, 5, 42, 43, 47, 63
Church of Scotland, 10, 26, 34, 35, 40–8, 63–75, 111, 118–25, 128, 153, 189
Clackmannanshire, 26, 177, 182
Claim of Right (1690), 43
clans and clansmen, 41, 43, 49–51, 54, 55–6, 57–63, 93–4
class, 112–13, 114
Cleghorn, Hugh, 179, 184
clergy and clergymen, 10, 24, 32, 35, 40, 43, 44, 45–8, 63–76, 77, 78, 82, 95, 96, 97, 98, 99, 100, 111, 113, 115, 119, 120, 124–5, 132, 145, 149, 152, 153, 175
Clerk of Penicuik, family,
  Sir James, 3rd Baronet, 154, 161
  Sir John, 2nd Baronet, 9, 10, 150, 154, 157, 158, 161
  Sir John, 4th Baronet, 157
  John Clerk of Eldin, 157
Clifton, 59
climate, 87, 108–9
Clive, Robert, 177
clothing, 84, 102, 107, 110, 113
clover, 91
Clyde, river, 100, 101, 105

coal and coalmining, 9, 76, 89, 105, 107–8, 110
Coatbridge, 15
Cochrane Johnstone, Andrew, 170, 182
Cochrane, Charles, 170
Cockburn, Henry, Lord, 17, 30–1, 129, 142, 156, 186, 188
Cockburn, John, of Ormiston, 91
cod, 103
coffee and coffee-houses, 97, 130, 132, 182
Coldingham, 84, 85
Coldstream, 93
colonisation and settlement, 165–76, 185
commission of supply, 19–20, 29
commission of the peace (JPs), 19, 116, 117, 125
Committee for Forfeited Estates, 61
Connecticut, 172
Constable, Archibald, 113
contraception, 84, 124
Convention of Royal Burghs, 17, 59
Cook, James, 180
Cope, Sir John, 57
Corelli, Arcangelo, 150
Cornfoot, Janet, 79
cotton, 106, 108, 117, 176, 191
counties, 14–16, 18–20, 21
Country party, 10, 12, 20
Court party, 12, 20
courts,
  of Exchequer, 23, 116–17
  of Justiciary, 19, 23, 110, 125
  of Session, 23, 29, 110, 126
  burgh, 17
  church, 40, 47–8, 64–5, 66, 124–5
  commissary, 125–6, 155
  franchise, 18, 26–7, 124, 125
  sheriff, 18–19, 126
craftsmen, 31, 113, 115–16, 119
Craig, James, 159
Crail, 99
Cramond, 71
Cranston, 174
Crawfurd, George, 97
Crieff, 60, 93
crime and criminal activity, 18, 19, 27–9, 31–2, 78–9, 116–17, 124–5
Crimond, 181
crofting and crofters, 95–6, 105, 121
Cromartie, Earls of, 15, 60
Cromartyshire, 15
Crompton, Samuel, 104
Cromwell, Oliver, 4, 5, 167
Cuba, 34
Cullen, 15
Cullen, William, 128, 135
Culloden, 59, 61, 93, 161, 170
Culzean Castle, 163
Cumberland, William Augustus, Duke of, 58–60, 61, 170
Cuming, Patrick, 64, 65
Cupar, 17, 20
Curry, Thomas, 172

Dale, David, 74, 106, 112, 191
Dalkeith, 109, 161
Dalrymples, family, 110
  Alexander, 179–80
  Sir David, *see* Lord Hailes
  Sir John, 147, 149, 164
Dalyell, Sir John, 151
Darien scheme, 6, 7, 9, 10, 97, 167, 177, 184
Darwin, Charles, 134
Deanston, 106
dearth, 87, 97, 108–9, 117
debt and credit, 54, 99
Deism, 45, 136, 140
demography, *see* population
Dempster, George, of Dunnichen, 20, 24, 112, 160
Denina, Carlo, 127
Derby, 58
Descartes, René, 141
Devon, 41, 54
Devonshire, Dukes of, 109
diet, 9, 84, 95–6, 97, 99, 110, 114–15, 132, 135, 182
Dingwall, 17, 20
Dinwiddie, Robert, 170
disease,
  cholera, 118, 187
  measles, 118
  plague, 85
  smallpox, 134
  tuberculosis, 118
  typhus, 85, 118, 187
dissent, 66–7, 72–5
division of labour, 144–5
divorce, 126
doctors and medical professionals, 24, 45, 46, 85, 105, 152, 174, 175, 177
Doddridge, Philip, 74
Dominica, 170, 182
dominies, *see* schoolteachers
Dornoch Firth, 106
Dornoch, 15, 20, 79
Douglas Castle, 163

Douglas, Dukes of, 126
Archibald Douglas, 1st Duke, 126, 163
Archibald, 1st Baron, 126
Douglas, Heron & Co., 99
Down, county, 167
drama and theatre, 45, 67, 132, 150
Drumlanrig, 161
Drummond of Hawthornden, William, 151
Drummond, family, 60, 75
Drummond, George, 65, 159
Dublin, 137
Duff House, 161
Duich, Loch, 55
Dumfries, 110, 123
Dumfries-shire, 69, 84, 116, 175, 180, 183
Dun, John, 71
Dunbartonshire, 61, 152
Dunblane, 54
Duncan, Jonathan, 180
Dundas, family, 110, 157
Henry, 1st Viscount Melville, 23, 24, 25, 27, 30, 31, 32, 33, 62, 64, 67, 71, 76, 116, 117, 141, 143, 144, 163, 180, 183, 184 187–8, 190
Sir Lawrence, 21, 24, 112, 160
Robert, 28
Sir Thomas, 24, 25
Dunning, 88
Dundee, 20, 24, 32, 72, 74, 98, 99, 112, 118, 121, 166
Dundee, John Graham of Claverhouse, 1st Viscount, 43, 52
Dundonald, Earls of, 89
Thomas Cochrane, 8th Earl, 170
Dunfermline, 26, 29, 72, 73, 170, 182
Dunira, 110
Dunkeld, 43
Dunkirk, 52
Dunlop, William, 167
Dunmore, James Murray, 4th Earl of, 171
dyeing, 107, 134

East India Company, 6, 24, 177–83
East Lothian (or Haddingtonshire), 7, 32, 88, 89, 162, 179, 185
Easter Ross, 116
Eastwood, 47
Eddrachillis, 96
Edinburgh,
royal burgh, 13, 15, 16, 17, 28–9, 31, 32, 33, 35, 38, 40, 42, 43, 45, 46, 47, 53, 54, 56, 57, 58, 64, 65, 66, 67, 70, 71, 83, 84, 86, 93, 94, 101, 106, 107, 108, 110, 113, 114, 116, 118, 119, 120, 121, 123, 125, 126, 127, 128, 129, 131, 132, 135, 138, 140, 141, 143, 150, 151, 153, 155, 156, 157, 159–60, 161, 182, 187
University, 43, 46, 64, 122, 123, 133, 134, 135, 136, 141, 142, 146, 150, 153, 162, 174, 186
Edinburgh Review, 188
education,
schooling, 34, 60, 118–22, 146, 189
university, 44, 45, 48, 118, 122–3, 129, 133–6, 141–4, 175
Egypt, 181
elders, 48, 124
elections and electorate, 16–17, 19, 20–5, 26, 29–33, 34
Elgin, Earls of, 89
Charles Bruce, 5th Earl, 160
Thomas Bruce, 7th Earl, 163
Elibank Plot, 61
Elizabeth, Queen of England, 3, 81
Elliot, Gilbert, of Minto, 64–5
Elphinstone, family, 24
emigration, *see* migration
empire and imperialism, 6, 7, 85, 97–8, 164, 165–85
enclosure, 89–90, 91, 92, 93, 116
Encyclopaedia Britannica, 142
England, 1, 2, 5–6, 7, 8, 9, 10, 19, 29, 32, 34, 35, 36, 37, 38, 39, 45, 47, 53, 55, 57–8, 63, 81, 82, 83, 84, 85, 86, 87, 88, 90–1, 93, 96, 97, 98, 100, 104, 105, 107, 111, 117, 119, 120, 122, 125, 126, 129, 131, 138, 146, 147, 149, 150, 151, 152, 154, 1
Enlightenment, 85, 110, 111, 127–64, 188–9, 190–1
entail (or tailzie), 92, 112, 149
entrepreneurs and businessmen, 74, 98, 100–1, 105, 106, 112–13
episcopalianism, 40–4, 47–8, 53, 56, 62, 63, 69, 167
Equivalent, 10, 13
Eriskay, 57
Erskine, Ebenezer, 26, 70, 72–4
Erskine, John, minister, 70, 71
Erskine, John, professor, 128
Erskine, Ralph, 72
Erskines of Mar, family, 26, 112, 182
Estonia, 166
evangelicalism, 64–5, 66, 67, 68–75, 79, 124, 183, 189
excise and customs, 24, 28, 116–17, 143
Excise Bill, 26

exploration and discovery, 171–2, 173, 179–80
exports, 9, 86, 97, 98, 99, 100–1, 102, 103, 106, 109, 176

fairs, 18, 87
Falkirk, 59, 93, 105, 171
Falkland, 17
famine, 7, 87, 97, 108–9, 167
farmers and farming, 74, 81, 87, 88–9, 90–2, 93–6, 103, 108, 110, 112, 114, 115, 116, 117, 180
Farquhar, John, 181, 183
Ferguson, Adam, 128, 129, 142, 143, 145–7, 148, 153
Fergusson, Robert, 155–6, 157
fermtouns, 90, 92
ferries, 19
Fife, 15, 17, 21, 25, 28, 34, 44, 46, 52, 79, 88, 89, 90, 98, 99, 110, 115, 120, 124, 153, 160, 162, 162, 163, 167, 174
Fife, James Duff, 2nd Earl of, 68
Fife, William Duff, 1st Earl of, 161
Finlay, James, 172
First Book of Discipline, 118
Fisher, Edward, 46
fishing and fishermen, 96, 98, 99, 102–3, 123, 181
Flanders, 58, 97, 111, 166, 171
flax, *see* linen
Fleming, Robert, 45
Fletcher, Andrew, of Saltoun, 7, 11, 87, 90
Fleury, André Hercule de, 56
Floors, 109
Florida, 167
Fochabers, 160
Fontenoy, 145, 171
food, *see* diet
Forbes, Duncan, of Culloden, 22, 26, 28, 94, 157
Forbin, Claude, Comte de, 52
forests and woodland, 89, 91, 93, 109
Forfar, 74
Fort Duquesne (Pittsburgh), 170
Fort George, 161
Fort William, 56
Forth, river and firth, 89, 98, 110
fossils, 136
France, 9, 30–4, 41, 45, 52–3, 54, 56–7, 59, 61, 62, 71–2, 75, 76, 88, 97, 98, 100, 101, 111, 113, 141, 145, 161, 165, 166, 167, 170, 173, 185, 187, 188
Frasers, clan, 62
Frederick the Great, King of Prussia, 56
freemasonry, 67, 131, 133, 135, 159
friendly societies, 123
Fullarton, William, 179, 181
fur trade, 171–2
furniture, 109, 113, 162

Gaelic society and language, 1, 36, 51, 56–61, 69, 77, 86, 93–4, 120, 145, 153–5, 167, 175, 177–9, 180
Galashiels, 107
Galloway, 116
gardens, *see* policies
Geddes, John, 75
geology, 133, 136, 146, 157
geometry, 121, 133
George I, King of Great Britain, 22, 51, 53
George II, King of Great Britain, 22, 61
George III, King of Great Britain, 22, 34, 101, 149, 171
Georgia, 173
Gerard, Alexander, 155
Germany, 4, 44, 55, 102, 141, 147, 154, 163, 165
Germiston, 170
Gibbon, Edward, 143
Gibson, John, 100
Gilchrist, John, 180
Gillespie, Thomas, 73–4
Gillies, John, 163
Girodet de Roucy, Anne-Louis, 154
Glas, John, 72
Glasgow,
  royal burgh, 13, 15, 28, 32, 47, 67, 69, 73, 74, 83, 84–5, 93, 97, 100–1, 106, 107, 112, 117, 118, 129, 131, 135, 143, 153, 160, 161, 168, 176, 187, 190
  University, 30, 31, 46, 65, 76, 122, 123, 134, 135, 137, 141, 143, 147, 152, 167, 179
Glasites, 72, 74, 172
Glassford, John, 100, 176
Glasslaw, 170
glassmaking, 107
Glen Shiel, 55
Glenaladale, 175
Glenelg, 95, 175
Glenfinnan, 57
Glengarry, county, 175
Goethe, Johann Wolfgang von, 154
Goldsmith's Hall Association, 31
Gordon, family, Earls and Dukes of Aberdeen, 109
  Alexander Gordon, 4th Duke, 160

Gordon, James, 75
Gosford House, 162
Gothic, 147, 154, 163–4, 188
grain, 88–9, 103, 109, 113, 117, 126
Grand Tour, 121
Grant, Andrew, 125
Grant, Archibald, of Monymusk, 91
Grant, James, 33
Grant, James, of Ballindalloch, 111
Greece, 163
Greek Revival, 162–4, 188–9
Green Thomas, 9
Greenock, 83, 100, 103, 121
Greenshields, James, 47
Gregory, David, 133, 134, 135, 141
Gregory, James, 133, 135, 141
Grenville, William, Lord, 181
Grotius, Hugo, 122
Guadeloupe, 34
guilds, 16, 17, 115–16
Gustavus Adolphus, King of Sweden, 166
Guthrie, William, 159

Haddington, 181
Haddington, Thomas Hamilton, 6th Earl of, 91, 92
haddock, 98
Haider Ali, Raja of Mysore, 179, 180
Hailes, David Dalrymple, Lord, 128
Haldane, James Alexander, 74, 183
Haldane, Robert, 74, 183
Halkett, Peter, of Pitfirrane, 26, 170, 182
Hamburg, 102
Hamilton, James Hamilton, 4th Duke of, 10
Hamilton, Robert, 123
Hamilton, Sir William, 186, 189
Harewood House, 162
Hargreaves, James, 104
Harris, 119, 181
Harrison, Thomas, 163
harvests, 7, 31, 87–8, 97, 108–9, 117
Hastings, Warren, 177, 180–1
Haughs of Cromdale, 43
Hawick, 107
Hawley, Henry, 59
Hay, George, 75
Hebrides, 57, 74, 86, 94, 96, 103, 119, 167, 174, 175, 181, 183
Henry, Alexander, 171
heresy, 46, 67, 75
Heriot's school, 119
heritors, 34, 115, 119
herring, 98, 103
Highlands and Highlanders, 1, 27, 36, 41, 43, 49–51, 54, 55–6, 57–64, 69, 75, 76, 82–3, 84, 87, 88, 89, 90, 91, 93–6, 100, 102, 108, 109, 115, 116, 117, 119, 120, 121, 122, 145, 153–5, 166, 170–1, 172, 173, 175, 176–7, 179, 185, 190
Hill, George, 64, 189
Himalayas, 180
hinds, 115
Hindustani, 179, 180
history and historians, 57, 128, 133, 142, 146–50, 158, 164, 171, 179, 188–9
Hobbes, Thomas, 137
Hogg, James, 46
Holland, 6, 7, 41, 42, 44, 87, 97, 100, 122, 166, 167, 179, 182, 184
Home, John, 60, 61, 64, 71, 145, 153, 189
Honourable Society for the Improvement of Agriculture, 91, 110
Hopes of Rankeillour, family, 110
Hopetoun House, 159, 161–2
Hopetoun, John Hope, 2nd Earl of, 161
Hopetoun, Charles Hope, 1st Earl of, 161
Horn, Janet, 79
hospitals, *see* infirmaries
Houghton Hall, 161
houses, *see* accommodation
Hudson's Bay Company, 171–2
Hume Campbell, Alexander, 132
Hume, David, jurist, 128
Hume, David, philosopher and historian, 38, 65, 67, 111, 121, 127–8, 138–42, 147–8, 149, 153, 154, 157, 158, 160, 162, 188, 191
Huntly, George Gordon, 4th Marquis of, 53
Hutcheson, Francis, 65, 137–8, 139, 140, 141, 142, 143, 144, 145, 157, 158
Hutton, James, 136, 143, 146, 157
Hyndford, John Carmichael, 1st Earl of, 19

identity, *see* patriotism
Ilay (or Islay), Earl of, *see* Argyll, 3rd Duke of,
illegitimacy, 124
imports, 97, 100–1, 102, 103, 106, 176
incomes, 84, 94, 95, 111, 114–15, 117, 118, 187
India, 6, 23, 24, 30, 53, 110, 112, 130, 146, 164, 165, 177–83, 185, 187
industrialisation, 15, 96, 98, 101–3, 103–8, 109, 115–16, 118, 144–5, 163, 176, 186, 187, 190
infirmaries, 84–5, 134
Innerleithen, 107

inoculation, 84, 134
insanity, 126
Inveraray, 15, 18, 153, 160, 161, 163
Inveresk, 37, 71
Invergarry, 93
Inverkeithing, 26, 65, 68, 73
Inverness, 55, 59, 102, 121, 125, 172, 181
Inverness-shire, 29, 30, 51, 75, 95, 153, 161, 175
Ireland, 4, 36–7, 38, 82, 83, 101–2, 117, 137, 166, 167, 173, 176, 177, 190
Irvine, 15
Islay, 174
Italy, 55, 57, 88, 150, 161, 165, 184

Jacobitism,
  origins and nature, 8, 35, 41, 43–4, 48, 49–53, 76, 140, 142, 151, 155, 174, 182, 184
  1708 adventure, 52–3
  1715 rebellion, 26, 53–4, 60, 76, 172
  1719 adventure, 55–6
  1745–6 rebellion, 18, 23, 26, 56–60, 76, 77, 112, 120, 135, 156, 171, 172, 173
  aftermath and demise, 60–3, 76, 93, 161, 171, 172, 176
Jamaica, 93, 182
James Bay, 172
James V, King of Scotland, 151
James VI and I, King of Scotland and England, 3, 4, 5, 8, 9, 151, 166, 167
James VII and II, King of Scotland and England, 4, 5, 8, 12, 35, 40–4, 45, 49, 51–2, 57, 147
Jamieson, John, 74
Jansenism, 75
Jedburgh, 17, 71
Jefferson, Thomas, 127
Jeffrey, Francis, 188
Jenner, Edward, 134
Jesuits, 76
Johnson, Samuel, 77, 88, 111, 154, 155
Johnson, Sir William, 173
Johnstone, John, 112
Jones, John Paul, 174
Josephine, Empress of France, 154
JPs, *see* commission of the peace
judicial system, *see* courts

Kames, Henry Home, Lord, 67, 91, 110, 128, 140, 143, 146, 154
Kant, Immanuel, 139
Kauffmann, Angelica, 162
Keith, George Keith Elphinstone, 1st Baron, 24
Kellie, Thomas Erskine, 6th Earl of, 150
kelp, 95–6
Kenmure, William Gordon, 6th Viscount, 54
Kenmore, 79
Kennoway, 88, 98
Kentucky, 173
Kettle, 44
Killiecrankie, 43
Killing Times, 40–1, 44, 63
Kilmarnock, 36, 110
Kilmarnock, Earldom of, 60
Kilsyth, 73
Kincardineshire, 16
King's birthdays, 31, 87
Kingskettle, 34
Kinnaird, 105
Kinross-shire, 74, 75, 125
kirk sessions, 13, 40, 47, 48, 64–5, 119, 120, 124–5
Kirk, Robert, 77, 78
Kirkcaldy, 102, 143, 161
Kirkcudbrightshire, 15, 18, 174
Kirkwall, 20
Knox, John, 149
Knoydart, 94

lairds and gentlemen, 20, 110, 111, 113, 119, 121, 132, 175
Lanarkshire, 15, 19, 21, 35, 86, 89, 90, 98, 103, 112, 116, 163, 174, 180
Lancashire, 59, 93, 106
Lancaster, 58, 59
landowners and landownership, 21, 29, 30, 48, 52, 54, 60, 61, 62, 63, 68, 71, 75, 85–96, 99, 107, 109–10, 111, 112, 116–17, 131, 152, 160–4, 167, 170
language,
  Scots, 38–9, 127, 151–6
  Gaelic, 1, 36, 69, 153–5, 167, 177–9, 180
  English, 38–9, 151–6, 180
  Ulster Scots, 167
Latin, 119, 122
law,
  Scots, 22–3, 110, 123–6, 128–9
  church, 40, 47–8, 64–5, 66, 124–5
  civil, 17, 18, 20, 23, 65, 66, 117, 125–6, 161
  company, 126
  criminal, 17, 18, 19, 22, 78–9, 116–17, 125
  family, 124–6
  franchise, 18, 26–7, 123, 125

Lawrie, John, 38
lawyers, 21–3, 26, 30, 37, 65, 91, 92, 110, 111, 128–9, 132, 153, 156, 161, 162, 163, 188
lazybeds, 95–6
lead 103
Leadhills, 151
Learmonth, John, 16–17
leather, 86
legal studies, 128, 146, 147
Leiden, 123
Leiper, Thomas, 174
Leith, 17, 98, 117, 166
Lennoxlove, 89
Levellers, 116
Leven, Earls of, 89
  Alexander Leslie, 1st Earl, 166
Lewis, 167
Liberton, 33
liberty, 25, 33, 35–6, 37–8, 47, 48, 147, 149–50, 160, 184
libraries, 110, 131, 149, 162
lime, 89, 107
Lindsays, Lords of the Byres, 17
linen, 9, 74, 86, 97, 98, 99, 101–2, 103, 104–6
Linlithgow, 21, 64–5
Linlithgow, Earls of, 17
literacy, 78–9, 118, 119–20, 121
literature, 7, 30, 31, 35, 36, 37–8, 46, 65, 66, 67, 69, 70, 71, 73, 111, 121, 130–56, 157, 158, 162, 182–3, 188
Liverpool, 172
living standards, 70, 81, 114–15, 117, 118, 187, 190
Livingston, 17
Loch, James, 187
Lochaber, 116
Lochbay, 103
Lochcarron, 69
Locke, John, 138, 139, 141, 158
Lockhart, George, of Carnwath, 11, 15, 35, 49
Lockhart, John Gibson, 186
Logan, John, 182–3
Logie, 44
Logierait, 145
London, 4, 5, 8, 9, 10, 11, 18, 27, 37, 38, 42, 47, 53, 56, 58, 87, 94, 103, 110, 127, 130, 133, 152, 154, 180
Lords Lieutenant, 19
Lorn Furnace Co., 93
Lothians, 89, 105
Loudoun, John Campbell, 4th Earl of, 170
Loughborough, Alexander Wedderburn, Lord, 37
Louis XIII, King of France, 116
Louis XIV, King of France, 6, 8, 52–3, 54, 166
Louis XV, King of France, 56
Louisbourg, 34
Louisiana, 170
Lovat, Simon Fraser, 11th Lord, 51, 55, 60, 170–1
Lovat, Simon Fraser, 12th Lord, 170–1
Low Countries, 165
Lowlands and Lowlanders, 1, 36, 41, 59, 74, 75, 76, 82, 83, 84, 88, 89, 90, 91, 94, 96, 98, 100, 103, 115, 119, 124, 152, 155, 167, 176, 187
Luncarty, 107
luxuries, 97, 109, 182–3

MacDonald of Clanranald, 51, 60
MacDonald of Sleat, 57, 94
MacDonald, Alexander (Alasdair Mac Mhaighstir Alasdair), 155
MacDonald, Allan, of Kingsburgh, 173, 174
MacDonald, Flora, 173
MacDonald, John, 175
MacDonell of Barrisdale, chieftain, 55
MacDonells of Glengarry, clan, 60, 61, 94, 175
MacDougall, Alexander, 174
Macfarlan, John, 70
MacGregor, Rob Roy, 93
Macintyre, Duncan Bàn (Donnchadh Bàn Mac an t-Saoir), 155
Maciver, Colin, 95
Mackay, Hugh, of Scourie, 43
Mackenzie, clan, 167
Mackenzie, Henry, 153, 154, 157
Mackenzie, Sir Alexander, 172
Mackenzie, Sir George, of Rosehaugh, 79
Mackintosh, clan, 173
Mackintosh, Sir James, 30
Mackintosh, William, of Borlum, 54, 93, 182
Maclaurin, Colin, 134–5, 136, 138, 140
Maclean of Duart, 51
MacLeod, Sir Alexander, 181
MacLeods of Lewis, clan, 167
MacLeods of MacLeod, chieftains, 57, 77
Macpherson, chieftain, 51; clan, 58, 59
Macpherson, James, 153–4, 180
Macpherson, John, 154, 180
Macpherson, Sir John, 180
MacRae, clan, 54
Madras, 177, 179, 180, 182

Makars, 151
Malcolm, Sir John, 180, 183
Malmaison, 154
malt tax, 27–8, 34, 99–100
management (political), 13, 20–5, 53, 176–7
Manchester, 58
Mandeville, Bernard, 137–43
Mangalore, 179
Mansfield, William Murray, 1st Earl of, 37
manufacturing, 81, 96, 97, 98, 101–2, 103–8, 116, 135, 144, 186
manure 89, 95–6
Mar, John Erskine, 11th Earl of, 35, 51, 53–4, 55, 57
Marchmont, Earls of, 25
Maria Theresa, Empress of Austria, 56
Marischal, George Keith, 10th Earl
markets, 17, 87, 88, 93, 100, 105
Marlborough, John Churchill, 1st Duke of, 52
Marrow controversy, 46, 72, 74
Martin, Martin, 77
Marxism, 144
Mary II, Queen of Scotland and England, *see* William II,
Mary, Queen of Scots, 149
Maryland, 101, 172
mathematics, 129, 132, 133
Mavisbank, 159, 161
Maxwells, family, 75
McCosh, James, 70
McGrugar, Thomas, 29
McIldoe, William, 78
McTavish, Simon, 172
Mealmaker, George, 32, 74, 113
Mearns, 88
medicine, 30, 78, 84–5, 122–3, 129, 133–4, 136, 152, 153
Melville Castle, 110
Melville, Andrew, 149
Mendelssohn, Felix, 154
Merchants' Maiden Hospital, school, 119
merchants, 17, 30, 74, 87, 98, 100–1, 105, 106, 112, 117, 132, 172, 174, 179, 180, 190
Merse, 88, 89
metal industries, 93, 101, 105, 107, 108, 113
Midlothian (or Edinburghshire), 23, 110, 115, 157, 163, 174
militia, 7, 32, 37–8, 59, 129
Mill, John, 68
Millar, John, 30, 147
Milton, Andrew Fletcher, Lord, 22, 28, 101, 145
Mocha, 182
Moderates and Moderatism, 63–8, 69, 70, 71, 75, 124, 137, 149, 186, 189, 190
Moffat, 93, 132, 183
Mohawk valley, 173
Moidart, 155, 175
monarchy,
  absentee, 4–7, 8
  Habsburg, 4
  Hanoverian, 8, 9, 35, 44, 51, 53, 55, 56, 58, 59, 62, 63, 93, 109, 120, 145, 149, 160, 172, 174, 184–5
  hereditary, 41–4, 49–51
  multiple, 3–4
  Stuart, 3–5, 40–4, 49–63, 151, 166, 167
Monboddo, James Burnett, Lord, 128
money, 97, 99, 112, 126
Monro, Alexander,
  primus, 128, 133
  secundus, 133
  tertius, 133
Montequieu, Charles Louis de Secondat, 25, 146, 148
Montreal, 172
Montrose, James Graham, 1st Duke of, 54
Montrose, 54
Monymusk, 91
Moray (or Elginshire), 29, 83, 120, 160
Moray Firth, 88
Moray, Sir Robert, 133, 166
Morison, James, 74
Morton, James Douglas, 14th Earl of, 135
Motherwell, 15
Mudie, Robert, 163
Muir, James, 69
Muir, Thomas, of Huntershill, 31–2, 62, 113
Mull, 103
Munro, Sir Hector, of Novar, 116, 177–8, 181
Munro, Sir Thomas, 179, 180
Murray, Alexander, 61
Murray, George, Lord, 57–9
Murray, James, of Elibank, 171
music, 150
Mylne, Robert, 162

nabobs, 112, 181–2
Nairn, 20
Nairnshire, 15, 75
Napoleon, Bonaparte, Emperor of France, 154, 181
National Debt, 10
natural philosophy (or science), 45, 64, 65, 67, 76, 78, 127, 128, 129, 132, 133–6, 146, 150

Nelson, Horatio, 105
neo-Palladianism, 161
New Brunswick, 175, 185
New Galloway, 167
New Inverness, 173
New Jersey, 65, 167
New Lanark, 106, 108
New Light, 73, 74
New Town, Edinburgh, 159–60, 182
New York, 170, 171, 173, 174, 175
Newark, David Leslie, 1st Lord, 166
Newburgh, 17
Newbyth, 179
Newcastle, 54
Newcastle, Dukes of, 109
  Thomas Pelham-Holles, 1st Duke, 26
Newcastleton, 91–2, 160
Newhailes, 110
newspapers, 25, 126
Newton, Sir Isaac, 76, 122, 133, 134–5, 138, 158
Newtonianism, 45, 122, 129, 134–5
Nithsdale, Earldom of, 54
nobility, 14–15, 19, 52, 62, 86, 109–10, 127, 132, 149, 162
non-jurors, 43, 44–5, 49
North, Frederick, Lord, 23, 27
North Uist, 96
North-West Company, 172
Nova Scotia (or Acadia), 167, 175
novels, 121, 152–3, 156, 157
numeracy, 119

oats, 88, 89, 91, 114
Ochiltree, James Stewart, 4th Lord, 167
Ogilvie, William, 30
Old Light, 73, 74
Oldmixon, Sir John, 165
Orkney, 15, 20, 74, 75, 112, 172
Orléans, Philippe, Duc de, 54
Orwell, 74
Osnaburgs, 102
Ossian, 153–4, 156, 162, 180
Oxenfoord Castle, 110, 163
oysters, 98

painting, 71, 128, 154, 156–8
Paisley, 83, 102, 108, 117, 118, 121
Palmer, Thomas Fysshe, 32, 37
Panmure, Earldom of, 54
Papacy, 75
Paris, 75
parishes, 34, 37, 44, 48, 66, 72, 73, 74–5, 111, 119, 120, 121, 123, 124–5
Parliament,
  Scots, 1, 4, 5, 6, 7, 8, 8, 10, 11, 12, 14, 42–4, 46, 86, 87, 98, 99, 127, 128–9, 167
  English, 1, 4, 5, 8, 9, 10, 11, 41, 42
  British, 14–16, 24–5, 29, 35, 47, 79, 126, 135, 177, 181, 184
parties,
  system, 20, 24
  Country, 10, 12, 20
  Court, 12, 20
  Squadrone Volante, 12, 20, 22, 26
  Tories, 20, 29, 41, 47, 48, 53, 62, 147, 171, 188
  Whigs, 20, 26, 27, 29, 30, 31, 35, 41, 49, 53, 56, 57, 135, 138, 147, 161, 170, 181, 188
Paterson, George, 112
patriotism,
  British, 34–9, 71, 91, 145, 149–50, 160, 184–5, 189–90
  Scottish, 1–2, 34–9, 91, 149–50, 184–5
peas, 89
Peebles-shire, 75, 83, 107
peerages, 14–15, 54, 60, 111
Penicuik, 106, 110, 154, 161
Pennant, Thomas, 64, 186
Pennsylvania, 173, 174
Penrith, 59
Pepys, Samuel, 87
Pericles, 163
Persian, 179
Perth, 32, 54, 70, 72, 74, 83, 93, 106, 107, 108, 110, 121, 125, 129, 160, 183, 188
Perthshire, 15, 21, 60, 75, 77, 79, 86, 88, 93, 94, 98, 110, 114, 131, 145
Peterhead, 54
Philip II, King of Spain, 184
Philip V, King of Spain, 55
philosophy, 65–6, 70, 127, 128, 129, 130, 132, 137–42, 143–4, 146, 150, 153–6, 187–8, 191
  common sense, 140–2, 158
  empiricism, 137–42, 134–7
  moral sense, 137–8, 143–4, 157
  scepticism, 138–42
physiology, 131, 134
Picts, 154, 155
Pike Plot, 33, 185
Pinkerton, John, 151, 154, 163
Pitcairn, Archibald, 145
Pitlessie, 17
Pitlour House, 162
Pitt, William, the younger, 23, 27, 76, 187

Pittenweem, 15, 28, 79, 99
Plassey, 177, 183
ploughs, 89
poetry, 49, 130, 140–1, 146, 150, 151–2, 161, 191
Poland, 166
policies, 89–90
politeness, 64, 70, 130–3, 144–5, 147, 152, 153, 158, 159, 160, 162, 182, 199
political economy, 128, 142–5, 190
Pollilur, 177
poor relief, 123, 189
Popular Party, 68–72
popular politics, 25–34, 36–7, 113–14
popular protest, 13, 27–9, 116–17
population,
  birth-rates, 83, 84
  death-rates, 83, 84–5, 87, 109, 115, 187
  expansion, 15, 81–5, 109, 121, 122, 123, 132, 176
  illegitimacy, 124
  infant mortality, 85, 109
  life expectancy, 84–5, 109
  marriage, 84
  migration, 83, 94–5, 100–1, 121, 123, 124, 125, 165–76, 185, 187, 190
  urbanisation, 15, 66, 82, 83, 85, 102, 104, 108, 118, 120–1, 124–5, 176, 190
porcelain, 109, 182
Port Glasgow, 103
Porteous, John, 28
Porteous, William, 69
Porteous riot, 28–9
Portland, Dukes of, 109
Portmoak, 125
potato, 91, 95–6
preaching and sermons, 63, 66, 69, 70, 145
presbyterianism, 40–8, 54, 56, 59, 60, 61, 63–8, 69–75, 77, 79, 111, 118–25, 128, 145, 149, 161, 166, 167, 173, 175, 186, 189, 190
Preston, 54, 58, 172
Prestonpans, 57, 105, 107
prices, 17, 19, 114, 117, 118, 126
prime ministers,
  Bute, James Stuart, 3rd Earl of, 22, 24, 146
  Newcastle, Thomas Pelham-Holles, 1st Duke of, 26
  North, Frederick, Lord, 23, 27
  Pelham, Henry, 26, 27
  Pitt, William, the younger, 23, 27, 76, 187
  Walpole, Sir Robert, 27, 28, 29, 99–100, 161
Prince Edward Island, 175
Privy Council, 22, 47
professions, 110–11, 112, 113, 114, 121, 128–9, 132, 165–6, 175
Propaganda Fide, 75
property and proprietors, 16, 19–20, 26, 34, 62, 66, 86–7, 90, 91, 92, 93, 94, 95, 96, 100, 108, 109–10, 111, 112, 114, 116–17, 118, 125, 144, 146, 160–4, 171
Protestant Association, 68
proto-industrialisation, 104–5
publishing and publishers, 35, 49, 111, 113, 114, 142, 148, 151–2
Pufendorf, Samuel, 122
Pulteneytown, 103

Quakerism, 45, 167
Quarterly Review, 188
Quebec, 170–1, 174
Queensberry, Charles Douglas, 1st Duke of, 161
Queensberry, James Douglas, 2nd Duke of, 12
Queensferry, 93

Raasay, 86
radicalism and reformism, 20, 30–4, 36–7, 43, 70, 71–2, 113–14, 187–8
Raeburn, Henry, 71, 156, 157, 158
Raith, 89
Ramillies, 52
Ramsay, Allan, the elder, 49, 131, 151–2, 157, 182
Ramsay, Allan, the younger, 128, 156, 157, 158, 162, 184
Ramsay, John, of Ochtertyre, 131, 182
Rankeillour, 110
reading, 64, 119, 121, 130–3
Red Sea, 179, 182
Redshanks, 166
Reformation, 1, 40, 43, 69, 118, 125, 140, 149, 165
regenting, 122
regiments,
  1st Foot (Royal Scots), 59, 166
  9th Foot (East Norfolks), 111
  19th Foot (The Green Howards), 111
  Earl of Mar's (21st Foot, Royal Scots Fusiliers), 59, 166
  Earl of Leven's (25th Foot, King's Own Scottish Borderers), 166
  Cameronians (26th Foot), 166
  43rd [later 42nd] Highlanders (Black Watch), 145, 170

74th Highlanders, 182
77th (Montgomery's) Highlanders, 173
78th (Fraser) Highlanders, 170–1
Scots Guards (3rd Foot Guards), 166
Royal Scots Greys, 166
84th Royal Highland Emigrants, 175
North Carolina Highlanders, 174
Argyll militia, 59
Reid, Thomas, 140–2, 143, 157, 158
Relief Church, 73–5
religion,
Arminianism, 46
Calvinism, 40, 45–7, 63, 66, 67, 68, 72, 97, 122
Cameronians, 72
Catholicism, 8, 9, 41–3, 45, 49, 56, 58, 67–8, 69, 74, 75–6, 77, 149, 167, 175, 190
Covenanters, 40, 43, 44, 72, 73, 118, 140, 166, 167
Deism, 45, 136, 140
episcopalianism, 40–4, 47–8, 53, 56, 62, 63, 69, 167
evangelicalism, 64–5, 66, 67, 68–75, 79, 124, 183, 189
Glasites, 72, 74, 172
Old Scotch Independents, 72
presbyterianism, 40–8, 54, 56, 59, 60, 61, 63–8, 69–75, 77, 79, 111, 118–25, 128, 145, 149, 161, 166, 167, 173, 175, 186, 189, 190
Quakers, 45, 167
Relief Church, 73–5
revivalism, 69, 73
Sandemanians, 72, 172
Secession Church, 72–4
Renfrew, 98, 112
Revolution (1689–90), 41, 44, 45, 48, 49, 118–19, 122, 128, 147, 166
Reynolds, Sir Joshua, 140
rhetoric and criticism, 143, 154, 155
Rhode Island, 167
rice, 103
Richmond and Lennox, Dukes of, 89–90
Ridpath, George, 64, 111, 135, 182
rioting, 13, 27–9, 87, 99–100, 117, 161, 185
roads, 19, 54, 88, 93
Robertson, Alexander, of Struan, 55
Robertson, George, 28
Robertson, James, 114
Robertson, William, 38, 64, 65, 67, 128, 142, 148–9, 150, 153, 163, 183, 189
Robertsons, clan, 58
Romanticism, 152, 153, 154, 156, 188–9
Rome, 57, 76, 146, 148, 161, 182, 183, 184
Rose, Alexander, 44
Rosebery, Archibald Philip Primrose, 5th Earl of, 181
Roses of Kilravock, 20
Ross, Arthur, 44
Ross-shire, 15, 20, 33
Rothes, Earls of, 89
Rothesay, 15, 106
Roxburghe, Earls and Dukes of, 109
John Kerr, 5th Earl and 1st Duke, 12, 13, 28
Roxburghshire, 75, 89, 91–2, 152
Royal Bank of Scotland, 99, 106
Royal Navy, 23, 24, 34, 52, 59, 91, 110, 152, 180, 187
Ruddiman, Thomas, 35, 49
rum, 103
Runciman, Alexander, 154, 156, 157
runrig, 90
Ruthven, 59, 153

Sage, Aeneas, 69
St Abb's Head, 136
St Andrews,
royal burgh, 60
University, 64, 91, 122, 133, 145, 149, 155, 179, 184
St Clair, Arthur, 174
St Kilda, 26
St Ninians, 68
salmon, 103
salt, 89, 107–8
Sandeman, Robert, 72, 172
Sandemanians, 72, 172
sanitation, 85, 118
Sanskrit, 180
Saskatchewan, 172
Scandinavia, 100, 166
scepticism, 138–42
scholars and scholarship, 35, 38–9, 46, 49, 70, 74, 97, 110, 111–12, 121, 127, 128, 137–50, 162–3
schools and schooling, 60, 118–22
Academies, 121–2
adventure, 120–1
burgh, 119–20, 156
finishing, 121
parish, 34, 119–20
private tutors, 121, 146
spinning, 121
Sunday, 120
schoolteachers, 38, 113, 119, 120
Scots Colleges, 75

Scots Magazine, 159
Scott, David, 24
Scott, Sir Walter, 19, 28, 77, 81, 111, 153, 155, 156, 157, 162, 163, 171, 180, 186, 188
Scottish Association of the Friends of the People, 31–2, 36–7
Seaforth, William Mackenzie, 5th Earl of, 54, 55
seaweed, 89, 95–6
Secession Church, 72–4
Secretaryship of State, 19, 28, 51
Selkirk, 21
Selkirk, Thomas Douglas, 5th Earl, 172
Selkirkshire, 19, 156
Sellar, Patrick, 187
Seringapatam, 179
Seton, Sir William, of Pitmedden, 12
sexual offences, 124–5
Shaftesbury, Anthony Ashley Cooper, 3rd Earl of, 138, 145, 157, 161
Shawfield riots, 27–8, 99–100
sheep, 9, 95, 96, 102, 109, 115, 116
Sheridan, Thomas, 38
Sheriffmuir, 54
sheriffs and sheriff courts, 18–19, 79, 117, 125, 126, 156
Shetland, 15, 25, 68, 74, 112
ships and shipping, 91, 98, 100, 101, 112, 113, 172, 176
shires, *see* counties
shops and shopkeeping, 31, 74, 108, 112, 113, 176
Sibbald, Sir Robert, 133
Siccar Point, 136
silks, 97, 102, 182
Simprin, 46
Simson, John, 46
Sinclair, George, 76
Sinclair, Sir John, 82
Skene, Philip, 162
Skye, 57, 77, 103, 154, 174, 180
slaves and slavery, 71, 103
Sleat, 154, 180
Small Isles, 183
Smeaton, John, 93
Smellie, William, 142
Smith, Adam, 24, 121, 128, 142–5, 146, 148, 153, 160, 162, 180, 188, 190
Smith, James, 161
Smith, William, 174
Smollett, Tobias, 24, 61, 127, 152–3, 157, 186
smuggling, 100, 116
social life and recreation, 64, 67, 70–1, 109–10, 111, 128, 129–33, 160, 188
societies and clubs, 128, 129–32, 188
  Aberdeen Philosophical (Wise Club), 129, 132
  Academical, 129
  Cape Club, 129, 132, 157
  Easy Club, 131, 152
  Literary, 129, 143
  Newtonian, 129, 142
  Perth Literary and Antiquarian, 129, 183, 188
  Philosophical (later Royal Society of Edinburgh), 134, 136, 150
  Poker Club, 129, 145
  Political Economy, 129, 143
  Royal Society (London), 133, 134, 135
  Select, 128, 129
  Speculative, 129, 156
  Society of Antiquaries of Scotland, 163
Society for Propagating the Gospel at Home, 74, 183
Society in Scotland for the Propagation of Christian Knowledge (SSPCK), 61, 69, 120, 121
sociology and social science 128, 142–3, 145–6, 150, 183
Somerville, Thomas, 71
songs and ballads, 155, 156, 162
Sophia, Electoress of Hanover, 8
South Uist, 175
Southesk, Earls of, 54
Spain, 6, 55, 167, 184
spas, 132
Spectator, 130, 153, 188
spices, 97, 182
Speirs, Alexander, 112, 176
Spinningdale, 106
spuilzie, 18
Squadrone Volante party, 12, 20, 22, 26
Stamitz, Johann, 160
steam engines, 107, 108, 135, 187, 191
Steele, Sir Richard, 130
Steuart, Sir James, 142
Stewart, Dugald, 142, 146, 148, 151, 156, 157, 158
Stewart, James, of Appin, 18
stewartries, 18
Stirling, 68, 70, 93, 182
Stirling, William Alexander, 1st Earl of, 151, 167
Stirlingshire, 24, 25, 64–5, 73, 78, 105, 112, 177
Stitchill, 64

Stonehaven, 16, 18
Strathblane, 78
Strathmiglo, 44
Strathmore, Earls of, 112
Stuart's Town, 167
Stuart, Charles Edward, 55–63, 94, 172, 173
Stuart, Gilbert, 147, 163
Stuart, James Edward, 35, 52–5, 61
succession, 8–9, 14, 49
sugar, 103, 176
Sulivan, Laurence, 177
superstitions, 76–80
supply, *see* taxation
surveying, 92, 121
Sutherland, 20, 21, 75, 79, 96, 111, 175, 187
Sutherland, Earls and Dukes of, 21, 109
  Elizabeth Leveson-Gower, Countess and 1st Duchess, 21, 126
Swann, James, 174
Sweden, 55, 166
Switzerland, 166, 179

tacksmen, 94, 115, 173
Tain, 20
taxation, 9, 17, 19, 27–9, 34, 92, 99–100, 116–17, 119, 123, 179
Tay, river and firth, 44, 49, 93, 103, 107
Taynuilt, 93
tea, 64, 97, 182
Tealing, 72
teinds, 111
telescopes, 64, 135
tenants and tenancy, 90, 92, 94–6, 114–15, 160, 175
Tennessee, 173
Teshu Lama, 180
Thomson, James, 152, 155, 157, 159
Thurso, 174
Tibet, 180
Ticonderoga, 77, 170
Tipu Sahib, 179
Tiree, 74, 94
tobacco, 97, 100–1, 103, 106, 112, 174, 176, 179, 180
Tobermory, 103
Tolbooth Kirk school, 125
toleration, 47, 48, 62, 63–8, 131, 149, 190
Tories and Toryism, 20, 29, 41, 47, 48, 53, 62, 147, 171, 188
Torphichen, 64–5, 68
Torridon, 94
towns, *see* burghs
trade societies and unions, 117, 187
Trades' Maiden Hospital school, 119
Tranent, 32
Treason laws, 34
Tucker, Josiah, 95
Tullibardine, William Murray, Marquis of, 55
Turnbull, George, 157–8
turnips, 91
Twain, Mark, 163
tweed, 107
Tweed, river, 93
Tweeddale, Marquises of, 89
  John Hay, 2nd Marquis, 12, 13
  John Hay, 4th Marquis, 23
Tyninghame, 92, 160

Ullapool, 103
Ulster Scots, 135, 137, 166, 167, 173
unemployment, 7, 116, 123, 125
Union of the Crowns, 3–5, 127
Union, Treaty of, 1–14, 15, 16, 17, 18, 19, 20, 21, 22, 23, 24, 25, 26, 28, 29, 33, 34, 35, 36, 37, 38, 39, 47, 51, 62, 63, 86, 91, 92, 96, 99, 100, 101, 110, 117, 127–9, 132, 146, 149, 150, 151, 156, 161, 163, 165, 166, 167, 177, 182, 183, 184, 185, 188
United Irishmen, 32
United Scotsmen, 32, 188
universities, 44, 45, 48, 118, 122–3, 129, 133–6, 141–2, 175
  Aberdeen,
    King's College, 30, 49, 122, 155
    Marischal College, 49, 122, 134, 155, 157
  Edinburgh, 43, 46, 64, 122, 123, 133, 134, 135, 136, 141, 142, 146, 150, 153, 162, 174, 186
  Glasgow, 30, 31, 46, 65, 76, 122, 123, 134, 135, 137, 141, 143, 147, 152, 167, 179
  St Andrews, 64, 91, 122, 133, 145, 149, 155, 179, 184
  American, 65, 70, 174–5
  English, 133, 143
  Indian, 180
urbanisation, 15, 66, 82, 83, 85, 102, 104, 108, 118, 120–1, 124–5, 132, 176, 186, 187
Urie, 18
Urr, 69

vaccination, 134
Vale of Leven, 152
Venice, 7
villages, planned, 91–2, 160
Virginia, 101, 167, 170, 171, 174, 175

Voltaire, Francois-Marie Arouet de, 25, 127
Volunteers, 32–3
voters, *see* elections

Wade, George, 28, 55–6, 58, 59, 93
Wales, 58, 64
Walker, Robert, minister of Cramond, 71
Walker, Robert, minister of St Giles', 71
Wallace, Robert, 64
Wallace, William, 36, 149
Walpole, Horace, 112
Walpole, Sir Robert, 27, 28, 29, 99–100, 161
Wardhouse, 180
wars,
  American Revolutionary, 24, 69–70, 101, 111, 170, 173–5, 184–5
  Austrian Succession, 24, 53, 56–7, 101
  Bishops', 4
  French Revolutionary and Napoleonic, 29–34, 76, 96, 111, 114–15, 150, 179
  Seven Years' (or French and Indian), 24, 34, 53, 101, 111, 112, 170–1
  Spanish Succession, 6–7, 9, 12, 52–3, 97
Washington, George, 170
Water of Leven, 107
Watson, James, 151–2
Watson, Robert, 149, 155, 184
Watt, James, 135, 191
Watt, Robert, 32, 33
weavers and weaving, 31, 32, 74, 98, 101–2, 107, 112, 115–16, 117, 123
Webster, Alexander, 70–1, 75, 82, 83, 84
Wellington, Arthur Wellesley, 1st Duke of, 105, 180
Wemyss, Francis Wemyss, 7th Earl of, 162
West Indies, 93, 106, 114, 115, 117, 120, 172, 176, 177
West Lothian (or Linlithgowshire), 32, 75
Wester Ross, 94, 95, 103, 105, 175
Whigs and Whiggism, 20, 26, 27, 29, 30, 31, 35, 41, 49, 53, 56, 57, 135, 138, 147, 161, 170, 181, 188
whisky, 99
Whittinghame, 138
Whytt, Robert, 134
Wick, 20, 103
Wightman, Joseph, 55
Wilkie, William, 153, 155
William II, King of Scotland and England, 5, 6, 7, 8, 11, 41–4, 47, 53, 166
Williamson, John, 183
Wilson, Andrew, 28
Wilson, James, 174
witchcraft, 78–9
Witherspoon, John, 65–6, 69, 70, 137, 138, 174
Wodrow, Robert, 47
Wolfe, James, 170–1
women, 102, 106, 114, 115, 117, 120, 121, 126, 147
wool and woollens, 9, 86, 95, 98, 102, 106–7, 113
Worcester incident, 9
workhouses, 123
Wright, William, 36
Writers to the Signet, 110

Yester, 89
York Buildings Co., 54, 91, 93
Yorktown, 170